Global Justice and Finance

Can global justice be promoted by distributing money more equitably? Could even relatively small financial sacrifices by the affluent work, through benign leverage, to achieve that goal? *Global Justice and Finance* casts new light on such questions by considering what is presupposed about finance. Redistributive proposals assume money to be a reliable measure, store of value, and medium of exchange. Yet maintaining stable interest, inflation, and exchange rates in a dynamic capitalist economy is a considerable achievement involving a complex financial system. Such global coordination could, if so directed, contribute immensely to humanity's betterment, yet under the direction of a profit seeking elite it leaves a majority disempowered, impoverished, and indebted. To pay debts, ever more desperate measures to wrest value from the world's natural resources increase ecological pressures to harmful extremes, and those pressures do not stop short of driving wars. The profit seeking economy is held in place by the complex legal arrangements that constitute finance. Globally, there has developed, unannounced and unaccountably, what amounts to a *privatised* constitution—binding agreements that transcend sovereign jurisdictions. Hopes of redirecting the financial assets created within this system, by means of modest reforms, towards objectives of social justice and ecological sustainability may prove illusory. To achieve such objectives arguably requires the constitution of a global normative order guided by public and political decision making. The achievement of a publicly accountable constitutional order that is superordinate to the financial system might be regarded as a revolutionary transformation.

Praise for *Global Justice and Finance*

'*Global Justice and Finance*... is particularly strong in its criticisms of approaches to global justice that simply take the transfer of money and finance to be adequate responses to the problems of global justice without examining the background nature of the institutions of global finance... The questions Hayward's book raises are central to thinking about what an alternative requires.'

Professor John O'Neill, *Contemporary Political Theory*

'Hayward argues that scholars have been amiss in assuming that monetary transfers can adequately address global poverty. Insofar as their solution leaves our financialized economic paradigm unquestioned, it may even reinforce an unjust institutional order. Hayward exposes the normative commitments underlying this paradigm and, in the process, successfully recenters the global justice debate around finance.'

Aatif Abbas, *Business Ethics Quarterly*

'*Global Justice & Finance* seldom invokes Marx... Yet its questioning of what money might achieve, and the real conditions of doing so, assembles in meticulous detail as damning an indictment of capitalism in an imperialised world as ever was made in more overtly Marxist critiques.'

Philip Roddis, *OffGuardian*

Global Justice and Finance

TIM HAYWARD

OXFORD
UNIVERSITY PRESS

OXFORD
UNIVERSITY PRESS

Great Clarendon Street, Oxford, OX2 6DP,
United Kingdom

Oxford University Press is a department of the University of Oxford.
It furthers the University's objective of excellence in research, scholarship,
and education by publishing worldwide. Oxford is a registered trade mark of
Oxford University Press in the UK and in certain other countries

First published 2019
First published in paperback 2022

Published in the United States of America by Oxford University Press
198 Madison Avenue, New York, NY 10016, United States of America

British Library Cataloguing in Publication Data

Data available

Library of Congress Cataloging in Publication Data

Data available

ISBN 978-0-19-884276-7 (Hbk.)
ISBN 978-0-19-286275-4 (Pbk.)

Acknowledgements

This book developed from a single chapter originally planned for another book, on ecological debt. It was some incisive questioning by my colleague Kieran Oberman that led to the scaling up of the undertaking. Another Edinburgh colleague, Iain Hardie provided indispensible advice on how to transform some initially inchoate ideas into a core thesis firm enough to be presented in the form of this book. For much of the inspiration for the book I am grateful to Brett Scott. Early versions of several chapters benefited from discussions in the Political Theory Research Group at the University of Edinburgh, and I should like to thank particularly Philip Cook, Elizabeth Cripps, Christina Dineen, Lynn Dobson, Andrew Drever, Louis Fletcher, Vinit Haksar, Yukinori Iwaki, Russell Keat, Mihaela Mihai, Mihal Rozynek, Lukas Slothuus, Mathias Thaler, Chiming Zhong, and all those who have participated in our seminars. Students and tutors at Edinburgh who have also given helpful feedback on draft chapters include Abrahim Assaily, Samuel Phillips, and Rick Sendelbeck. While apologizing to friends and colleagues whose contribution or influence I fail to record here, I should like to thank for their advice or comment at various stages Ashok Acharya, Elizabeth Ashford, Zenon Bankowski, Richard Bellamy, Gillian Brock, Daniel Butt, Luis Cabrera, Simon Caney, Monique Deveaux, Iason Gabriel, Carol Gould, Pia Halme, Mai Hamed, Yukinori Iwaki, Teea Kortetmäki, Carl Knight, Avery Kolers, Sulian Lizé, David Miller (Warwick), Darrel Moellendorf, Margaret Moore, Ingrid Robeyns, Miriam Ronzoni, Mitu Sengupta, Henry Shue, Sigrid Sterckx, Leif Wenar, and Heather Widdows. Thanks as well to participants at the *Global Justice and the Global South* conference (University of Delhi 2014), the Workshop on *Duties to Create and Support Just Institutions* (Nuffield College Oxford 2014), the symposium on *Global Justice: New directions in research and advocacy* (Ghent 2015), the *Intersections of Finance and Society* conference (City University London 2016), and the *Médecins Sans Frontières Operational Research Day* (Brussels 2017).

On completion of its first draft I had the honour of discussing the manuscript in a symposium of the 2018 Oxford Political Thought Conference. I am deeply grateful to Iseult Honohan for organizing it, as well as to Sabrina Martin and Anahí Wiedenbrüg for their incisive commentaries. John O'Neill also contributed a commentary, thereby further adding to an already long list of reasons for my gratitude to him. Other readers of early versions of the full manuscript were the anonymous readers for Oxford University Press, whose comments were immensely valuable, especially those of the reviewer who additionally commented on a second draft, and I am most appreciative of the responsive and encouraging support provided throughout by commissioning editor Dominic Byatt. Thanks go also to Kim Allen for such thoughtful and sensitive copy-editing.

In writing the book it has been fascinating to glimpse a field of inquiry in which I have no expertise, and for helping me understand a little how finance works I have been glad of the chance to learn something from Randall Germain, Paul Gilbert, John Kay, Donald Mackenzie, and Anastasia Nesvetailova. A special word of appreciation goes to Nathan Coombs, who not only provided valuable advice on critical studies of finance but also stood firm for academic freedom—a value we are fortunate that our university still treats as non-negotiable. Because respect for this value is not something everyone everywhere can take for granted, I would like to thank our colleague Charlie Jeffrey for his principled leadership over the years. Also standing for the value of rigorous academic research in the face of challenges to it are those associated with the *Working Group on Syria, Propaganda and Media,* including friends Louis Allday, Tara MacCormack, Paul McKeigue, David Miller (Bristol), Piers Robinson, Simone Rudolphi, and Florian Zollmann. A personal word of appreciation goes to Vanessa Beeley, Jonathan Cook, Sheila Coombes, Davids Cromwell and Edwards, Patrick Henningsen, Caitlin Johnstone, Craig Murray, John Pilger, Sami Ramadani, Sonia Mansour Robaey, and Mike Robinson. The number of good people beyond academia to whom I'm grateful for keeping alive hopes of greater justice in the world has grown almost exponentially in the last two years—not least thanks to social media—and it would be impossible to thank by name everyone. But the greatest impossibility for me would be to find words to convey what I owe to my beloved wife, Karolina. Were there words, and with love being indivisible, they would touch the rest of my wonderful family too.

Contents

1
Introduction

Finance can be used to serve the ends of justice, or it can work to thwart them. Philosophers concerned about what global justice requires often think in terms of transferring funds as a means to achieving its ends. Yet we are aware that how the global financial system operates today is problematic in some major respects. Manifest tensions are evident between the good that finance can in principle do and the harms its mismanagement has, in practice, proved capable of causing. In thinking about the aims of global justice, therefore, it is certainly appropriate to consider the role of finance in achieving them, but this must be undertaken with awareness, I shall emphasize in this book, of the nature of the attendant difficulties.

1.1 Opening New Lines of Inquiry

A quite common assumption in the philosophical literature on global justice is that a central challenge is to raise sufficient financial resources, from those able to provide them, for deployment in meeting pressing goals such as eliminating severe poverty. Finding secure ways to effect the requisite transfers is generally regarded as a relatively minor, and essentially technical, matter. Certainly, there is abundant awareness in the literature of the problem that even when financial flows reach their destination they can be misappropriated and, more insidiously, offset—or even exceeded—by flows outwards, through various illicit and exploitative arrangements. It is of course also recognized that not every problem of global justice is necessarily best thought of as having money as its solution. A central line of inquiry pursued in this book, however, is distinct from those oft-discussed concerns. It addresses the basic assumption that provided financial flows are directed aright, they can then make a beneficial contribution to the achievement of any goals that can, in principle, be achieved with money. For the inquiry turns on the difference between what in principle money might be thought capable of achieving and what in practice are the real conditions of its actually achieving such purposes. This involves considering not only the benefits of using money but also the costs of seeking to do so.

The Costs of Money

The problem of money, as it is to be discussed in this book, is not directly or irreducibly the same as the sort of money problems that everyone is familiar with in day-to-day experiences of trying to make ends meet or help others to do so. In those contexts, it is generally the case that lack of money is a problem, and provision of it is a solution. We do understand the cautionary wisdom of familiar sayings about money not being everything and the love of it being the root of all evil, even as we recognize why people also say that money makes the world go round. But as we think both of the value money has for us and of the vices it can tempt us into, we tend not to think so much about what money actually *is*. We are aware of its powers but most of us do not generally reflect on how it comes to have them.

Without realizing it, we tend rather to fetishize money. Even when being very practical, or prudent, or calmly calculating, we seldom reflect on the occult nature of the powers seemingly possessed by the paper in our pocket or by the position of electrons in our digital wallet. Yet we know that the misplacement of a dot within a row of zeros in an account can spell the difference between great wealth and destitution. How can an electronic twitch, or an inky gesture on a piece of paper, have such power? More tangibly, do we understand how it is, for instance, that some young financial market trader can quickly become a millionaire just through buying and selling other people's contracts, or that a group of venture capitalists can access billions of dollars worth of assets, without apparently bringing any new material goods or inherently worthwhile venture into the world? Perhaps we find it less puzzling that people might amass monetary wealth through theft and piracy, and yet even in such cases of tangible expropriation, do we fully understand what is being taken when what is taken is not directly useful stuff but only money? Do we understand how certain individuals' holdings of money can be augmented to such an extent that they can lay claims of ownership to far more resources than they could ever possibly take physical possession of? To pose the same general question in starker and more specific terms: do we really understand how it is possible for eight particular human beings in the world today to have as much money as some 3,500,000,000 other human beings who are struggling to stay alive?[1] This is an important question to consider given that, from a variety of standpoints, such circumstances can be regarded as problematic and even deeply troubling. Something we need to understand is whether money is merely a medium through which the underlying problem is communicated, or whether there is, as well, something about money itself that is a problem. We are

[1] The numerical estimate here from Oxfam (2017) is cited to illustrate how the scale of the problem is qualitatively significant.

accustomed to think about the benefits of money—as achieved in its presence and forgone in its absence—and the justice of their distribution. But what about its *costs*?

This question is central to the inquiry: what does it mean to speak of the *costs* of money? There are innumerable ways in which putting pecuniary goals ahead of other kinds of desirable end can be accounted costs in moral senses. But while the concept of a cost can encompass more than monetary price, it importantly includes that.

There are the three kinds of 'price' of money to be particularly aware of, since a token of money can be exchanged in three distinct kinds of market. First, there are the ordinary markets of consumption and trade where money is exchanged for goods and services: we tend to think of the latter as having a price, but we can as well, by inverting the terms of the equation, think of the things as the price to be paid for having some of the money. Hence, with inflation, as its spending power decreases, money becomes cheaper in price, for you can 'buy' more of it for the same outlay of goods or services. A second kind of market is one on which money is borrowed, and here the price of money is like a rent on its use, and this price is usually called the *interest rate*. The third kind of market is where money in one currency is exchanged for money in another: on foreign exchange markets the price of money in one currency is expressed in terms of the value of another. In a world where credit arrangements are possible and where there is international trade across different currencies, the value of any given token of money at any given time and place will be contingent on material factors in those different markets. This makes for a degree of fluidity and uncertainty about the value of money once it starts being used and moved around. In fact, uncertainty can be very acute in some markets: with the speed of trades now possible on international exchanges, the value of money can actually change faster than a human brain can register.[2]

Viewing the matter in this light, we should be conscious of the possibility that stability in the value of money is something that needs to be achieved and assured rather than simply assumed. What actually makes for monetary stability is a matter on which economists do not have a fully agreed view. Some of the orthodox economists' most central models rely on heuristic assumptions about money that are known to be empirically suspect but are allowed for the purposes of their calculations because none of the available theories offer reliably true assumptions. So when crises occur in the real world manifesting severe problems of instability, most orthodox economists look for what they call 'external shocks' to explain how the otherwise normally stable system has been knocked out of kilter. A minority of economists, however, take a 'heterodox' view and seek to understand how elements of instability are inherent in the market economy and give rise to 'endogenous

[2] Fascinating studies of the lengths now gone to in order to accelerate high frequency trading are found, for instance, in Donald MacKenzie et al. (2012).

shocks' from within the monetary system itself. What we do know, regardless of whose explanation is more correct, is that crises of instability can occur, because they do. So if economics falters when it tries to use methods akin to those used more successfully in the natural sciences, there are nevertheless questions here that social scientists need to try to grapple with by using appropriate methods. Patterns of behaviour and the conditions for these that institutions supply are matters over which we can and must try to form sensible views. For some view of how money works is implicit in any proposition involving the use of money in attempts to make the world more just; so to assess any such proposition sensibly, we need to understand what is assumed about money and under what conditions the assumptions will be warranted.

Tasks for Political Philosophers

Political philosophers have the task of thinking about the best possible way to organize a society within the constraints of what is known and understood about the enabling and restricting conditions that exist in the kind of society they are thinking about. In a society that is particularly stable, socially and economically, with international relations of relative stability too, it may be quite reasonable to assume that money has a fairly stable value, and to think about prudent policy-making on the basis that these conditions will persist into the foreseeable future. This, I would suggest, has been the situation assumed to hold for liberal political theory in what might now be defined as the *Era of Rawls*. The postwar reconstruction of Western economies proceeded apace in the period between 1945 and 1971, the year *A Theory of Justice* finally appeared, after a long gestation. The postwar reconstruction was the backdrop to some quite steady assumptions for the next quarter century. So steady did they appear to some, in fact, that by the 1990s Francis Fukuyama (1992) could pronounce liberal democracies to have reached *The End of History*. Fukuyama's claim would soon prove to be as ironic as it was hubristic, however.

With the benefit of hindsight, it is poignant to reflect on the fact that in the same year *A Theory of Justice* was eventually published, the price of the US dollar as a currency was detached from the price of gold. If Rawls had at last fully articulated the understanding of justice that had been consolidated for liberal thinking in the period of postwar reconstruction, the departure from the gold standard marked the beginning of the end of the international institutional framework, as agreed at Bretton Woods, that underpinned the specific circumstances of justice to which his account applied. The period between the publication of books by Rawls and Fukuyama saw the ascendancy of neoliberalism around the world and the deregulation of financial markets. By the 1990s the world had changed beyond recognition in key respects, with the Bretton Woods agreement being displaced by the Washington Consensus. Particularly ironic about Fukuyama's *End of History* is that it presents liberal democracy as the final form of human government at just the historical moment when, thanks in large measure to the practical implementation of the neoliberal philosophy the book celebrates, that form of government is being undermined. Upon its publication at the end of the twentieth century there was serious, if critical, discussion of the proposition that the world could be witnessing 'the end of history': this would be 'the end point of mankind's ideological evolution' and the 'universalization of Western liberal democracy as the final form of human government'. The mere existence of such discussion was evidence of a sort for its author's claim of a 'total exhaustion of viable systematic alternatives to Western liberalism'. Whether there was any other evidence than this exhaustion of constructive political thought, I leave to historians to judge. It is all too apparent that they don't find themselves out of a job just yet.

An interest animating the present work is to understand whether it is necessary or possible to conceive of a systematic alternative to a belief in liberal democracy as 'the final form of human government'. There are prima facie reasons to think it might be necessary: one is that liberal democracy is a form of government that has worked for certain nation-states in a context where they stand in a relatively advantageous position vis-à-vis other peoples in the world that Rawls (1999) grouped into the categories of 'decent hierarchies', 'burdened peoples', or 'outlaw peoples'. To universalize it would mean eliminating relationships of advantage, and that might not be something liberal democrats want to undertake when faced with the full consequences of doing so. In fact, the actual record of history—before and after 1999—shows how the liberal economy is deeply bound up with the prosecution of expensive and highly destructive *warfare*. Certainly, taken as a whole, the wider world order dominated by the liberal democracies appears to be far from stable and peaceful. At present it may seem quite well ordered and prosperous in places, but in others, and for the majority of humankind, it is not. Furthermore, the trajectory towards the future does not bode well. For on top of the existing effects of economic inequality, the ecological effects of the current global order's rampant material destructiveness are now beginning to register. At the heart of this vortex of upheaval is the concentration of financial assets into the hands of a tiny minority of the planet's population; a concentration that appears to thrive on the promotion of wars, more than peace or stability, and to become more extreme and more ineluctable with each passing day. What is thus perhaps more evident from Western perspectives today than it was in 1999 is that there is a case for thinking about revolutionary change, and on an international basis. The liberal democratic states have overseen the development of an international order whose financial architecture rests on authority that largely escapes political control. Under an unaccountable and fundamentally irresponsible global elite, it would appear, the global financial order today is driving calamitous harms on a global scale.

A central task of this book, then, is to understand the role of finance in this general global crisis. The starting point for the inquiry is the concern that the global financial order appears to be both dysfunctional and unjust. While the purpose of finance—viewed in terms of substantive aims of human social cooperation—is to facilitate projects that build the economic basis upon which people may pursue a good life, the ways finance works today tend to incentivize short-term profit taking over longer-term wealth creation, and, in the process, they make life worse for many people. As the global financial order continues to generate debts for the greater mass of human beings, a grotesquely disproportionate holding of credits among a tiny elite is enabling them to gain effective control over the world's real assets. As a further consequence, our treatment of the nonhuman world is being pushed to harmful extremes. People are driven to ever more desperate measures in their attempts to wrest value from the world's natural resources. In short, we seem to be headed towards a 'perfect storm' of economic unproductivity, gross social inequality, and ecological catastrophe.

The Challenge

The first part of the book introduces the intellectual challenge of grasping the role of finance and its relation to those great problems of our time. Chapter 2 examines how ideas about finance have figured in political philosophers' recent proposed strategies for achieving global justice. In making explicit some of the assumptions about money that are operative in those proposals, the chapter highlights questions that are not always noticed or therefore addressed by theorists of global justice. For instance, the literature offers various proposals that would raise funds by means of taxes for the purpose of achieving global justice. These assume that, provided finance can be raised, directing it to the goals of alleviating poverty, or, in some cases, remedying ecological harm, is in principle an unproblematic matter. Yet such proposals tacitly depend on the existence of monetary and fiscal arrangements that are absent in the global context. While this need not matter for philosophical discussions at a certain level of abstraction, it is a relevant factor for any proposal that is intended as a potential contribution to achieving global justice in practice. We should not assume that just *any* principles can be applied via the existing institutions of the world so as to deliver money that will solve the problems of global injustice.

Finance does in principle have a valuable social function to fulfil, as Chapter 3 starts by emphasizing, because it can facilitate the investment of resources that enable humans to engage collectively in worthwhile enterprises. However, the way the financial system works today it does not necessarily fulfil its social function very well and can even do more harm than good. A critical concern is that an open-ended system of money and credit creation appears to have broken free of political control to become socially, economically, and ecologically irresponsible. With the perpetuation of debt as both its outcome and its *modus operandi*, the system tends to syphon money away from productive outlets and thus does not contribute positively to social purpose. The imperatives of the financial system have increasingly come to influence other aspects of associational life, including other economic sectors, where the problem is sometimes referred to as *financialization*. Processes of financialization can significantly exacerbate the exploitative tendencies of a capitalist economy.

It is possible to distinguish three bases upon in which a critique of financialization can be advanced, each with its distinctive understanding of the potential good of finance that is in jeopardy. These can be categorized under broad headings: social justice, economic productivity, and ecological sustainability. The most directly ethical criticism is of the social irresponsibility of financialization in that it leads to considerable social injustice, as is particularly conspicuous globally in the form of radical inequality.[3] At present the global elite leverage value from the rest of the world's population to an extreme—and still increasing—degree. It bears repeating that, at the time of writing, estimates indicate that eight super-rich individuals have financial assets that weigh in the balance with those of half of the other human beings on this planet; and 1 per cent of the world's population owns half of its total.

In addition to this criticism from the perspective of social justice are criticisms from both economic and ecological perspectives. From a mainstream economic standpoint,[4] the dominance today of finance over other sectors of political and economic life can be criticized for its tendency to divert assets away from productive uses: the growth of finance comes at the expense of the 'real economy' of material productivity. This can exacerbate the problem of injustice by constraining the amount of goods available even in principle for the benefit of the worse off. The ecological criticism is that the perpetual regeneration of indebtedness characteristic of financialization drives, in turn, the problem of ecological overshoot,[5] since people trying to redeem their debts are driven ever more desperately to seek ways of wresting profitable activity from engagement with the world, regardless of the harm it might do to habitats, other creatures, or even the human environment.

[3] The idea of radical inequality was first set out by Thomas Nagel (1977): it refers to a situation in which the worst off are poor in absolute terms and relative to others, and where the poverty is impervious to whatever efforts they make to try to alleviate it; their poverty is also pervasive, affecting every aspect of their life. It is a matter of normatively unacceptable inequality rather than misfortune in that a redistribution of relevant assets and opportunities could in principle remedy the severe harms suffered by the worst off.

[4] For a discussion of such categorizations as 'mainstream' and 'orthodox' in relation to economics see David Dequech (2007).

[5] The idea of ecological overshoot can be explicated, for instance, by reference to the idea of the 'planetary boundaries' as discussed, for instance, by Rockström et al. (2009).

However, while both the economic and the ecological critiques, separately, are consistent in their own way with the critique of social injustice, it might be supposed that they are in tension with each other: for complaints about lack of economic productivity suggest financialization inhibits the economy from producing enough, whereas ecological criticism suggests that financialization is driving economic agents to try to produce too much. That leaves us with a question of whether finance is an inhibiting or a driving factor in relation to the 'real economy'. To answer this one must first address a more basic question, namely, what should the term 'real economy' be taken to refer to?

Chapter 4 addresses that question by highlighting two quite distinct senses in which one might speak of a 'real economy'. In one, its reality resides in the materiality of relationships among human beings, including as they interact with the natural world: this is the reality as studied by ecological economics, for instance. In the other sense, economic reality is represented by market price, which, rather than material transactions, is the subject matter of more mainstream economics: thus transactions of all material kinds are regarded as equivalent insofar as they can be measured in terms of monetary movements. The problem with the mainstream economic critique of financialization, I argue, is that it has an equivocal understanding of the 'real economy': the complaint about financialization draws on material ideas about productivity, but the analysis of the problem utilizes the immaterial—monetary—framing of it. The underlying difficulty, in fact, is that the very notion of a 'real economy' understood in terms of generating monetized values cannot be clearly distinguished from that of a 'financial economy'.

In appreciating this point we are brought to question what one should assume about the nature of money itself. In fact, as we shall see, an adequate appreciation of the nature of money is crucial not only for understanding the problem of financialization, but also for formulating possible solutions to it.

1.2 Justice and the Problem of Money

How money figures in relation to questions of social justice might seem in principle quite straightforward to understand. Justice can reasonably be thought to require that, if there is inequality of income or wealth such that some people have insufficient amounts to serve their basic needs, interests, rights, opportunities, or capabilities, while other people have considerably more than would be required for a happily flourishing life, then there should be some steps taken to redress the imbalance, and these would, one way or another, involve some redistribution of money. Debates in global justice to date have tended to accept this general view and have focused on questions of whether and how to extend principles of just distribution, as established within contexts of national societies, to the world as a whole. On this basis, political philosophers have put forward various proposals for how justly to raise and distribute funds that would serve to redress radical global inequalities of income and wealth. These proposals have mostly focused on questions of principle, and, to the extent that they include practical considerations, these tend to be concerned with how funds might justly be raised. As for how the money might be *transferred*, this seems generally to be assumed a straightforward technical matter of implementation rather than a matter of any particular or inherent philosophical interest.

What I aim to show is that questions of principle are very much affected by the practical difficulties that arise not only from the presumptively unjust distribution of monetary assets in the world but also from the conditions of their production, which in turn bear on the conditions of their transfer too. Money in its various forms as created by banks and other financial institutions today involves a considerable amount of *leverage*: the amount of tangible assets held by the issuers represents a tiny fraction of the sums created as credit. The power to affect the supply of money is inescapably a power to affect its value too. If one understands the value of money to be determined at least as much by decisions of those with command of the financial system as by the material value to human beings of products it can be exchanged for, one has reason to be cautious about thinking that money can necessarily be regarded as a reliable substitute for the material things humans value.

However, some influential political philosophers assume money to be a stable store of value, a neutral measure and a reliable medium of exchange. This assumption is implied by the various proposals to use financial means in the pursuit of morally just ends. The proposal of Peter Singer and 'effective altruists', as examined in Chapter 5, for instance, is that by earning as much as they can, people in affluent parts of the world can then donate a portion of their income to effective charities, and thereby the problems of severe global poverty can be eliminated. Acknowledging, however, that the effectiveness of charities is not always assured, a noteworthy recommendation they make involves the deployment of 'direct unconditional cash transfers' from the more affluent to the world's poorest. Among the concerns I highlight, however, is the paradoxical finding that the advocated transfers turn out in fact to be entirely *cashless*, with their receipt being *conditional* on joining a digital money system—involving global banks, mobile phone companies, and the third party aggregators who provide the 'last mile' interface for which the cash transfer charities line up customers—and thus *not exactly direct*. This is not to say such schemes cannot be beneficial at all, but to question whether, given how global corporate finance is implicated in driving inequality, there could be any unnoticed downside in relying on it for a key instrument in the struggle against inequality. I suggest that those who believe the technology is neutral with respect to the ends it might serve ought to do due diligence in this matter rather than offer an unqualified endorsement of it.

Even supposing that substantial sums of cashless cash could be unproblematically transferred, there is another, more basic, assumption to examine. It is the assumption that, with a relatively small amount of money, measured in terms of what people in affluent countries can afford to donate, a great deal of good can be done for a great number of the poorest people in the world. This is an assumption of Singer and the effective altruists which is also shared by those political philosophers of global justice who think that the obligation to make such transfers should be regarded not only as a matter of charity but as a more stringent demand of *justice*. Thomas Pogge, for instance, advocates a global redistribution such as might be implemented by means of a tax that he refers to as the Global Resources Dividend. Others have offered different suggestions aimed at achieving a similar goal. Common to these 'tax and fund' proposals is the view that the redistribution required is relatively modest, quantitatively speaking, and that the only significant impediment to its implementation is lack of political will.

Chapter 6 considers what is presupposed by the belief that a relatively small sacrifice of spending power by the better off can yield a large material benefit for worse off people. This is what I refer to as the assumption of *benign leverage:* by doing relatively little, the affluent of the world—individually and collectively—can achieve a great deal of good for the mass of the worst off people in the world. When we seek to understand how benign leverage is possible, we encounter something of a paradox. For in order that only a little effort by the affluent might suffice to lift a great many people out of poverty, it has to be the case that the affluent are well off and the poor are very badly off, but as soon as that imbalance starts to be redressed, the ratio of effort to outcome also starts to shift. An implication is that on making clear progress towards achievement of the goal, the goal becomes harder to achieve. This is not necessarily a fatal flaw, since the amount of effort that it is feasible to make could conceivably be sufficient to alleviate *severe* poverty. However, in order for what is conceivable to become a reality, there are two further potential problems that need to be taken into account. One has to do with generating the income to help the poor without counterproductive attrition occurring to the incomes of the affluent. The other is a concern about whether it can be assumed that the value of income transferred will be preserved. This second question is reserved for treatment in Chapter 9.

Chapter 7 meanwhile discusses the first of those questions, which arises in connection with the observation that if the poorest are to be lifted out of severe poverty without the effort required from the affluent becoming more than merely modest, it must be the case that aggregate economic productivity continues to grow.[6] Yet there are ecological constraints on the extent to which the material basis of the economy can grow, and, arguably, even an ecological imperative to

[6] I am assuming that population growth in the foreseeable future follows the curve researchers plot for it. Were there to be a dramatic decline in population, this in principle could alter the equation, but whatever was the cause of a dramatic decline, I also assume, would itself be a major problem that would likely require us all (who survive and are capable of doing so) to review all our theories.

contract the extent of that material interaction. Furthermore, having noted in Chapter 4 that the processes of financialization tend to drive ecological wantonness, we now identify the problem that ecological harm can in turn also drive financial instability. This compounds radical uncertainties about both the consequences of ecological transformations and the future of money prices. In view of this, I suggest that philosophers of global justice should be cautious about embracing some of the sorts of solution proposed within the framework of understanding I call liberal environmentalism in depicting a much more gradualist approach as a 'solution'. This can include endorsement of strategies of ecomodernization and the countenancing of a role for carbon markets, but it can also just mean acquiescing in policy recommendations that involve postponing or shifting the burdens of material responsibility in exchange for some form of monetary compensation. The creation of various sorts of offset, substitution, and compensation envisaged by sophisticated growth-friendly strategies as encouraged, for instance, by the Stern Review, involves a similar leveraging of promises as is tacitly relied on when thinking that transfers of monetary sums necessarily equate to a transfer of determinate quanta of economic goods.

The bottom line reality is that material questions of justice and sustainability relate to the real services and goods that human beings are able to render each other and on the available ecological capacity to support their economic activities. Economic reasoning can 'create' value on the basis of futurity, just as it does by 'leveraging' debt, but these creations of credit are but promises, and promises are sometimes simply not fulfilled. One should therefore be very cautious in assessing the prospects of strategies based on profit seeking leading to outcomes that enhance social justice or ecological sustainability.

Given the tacit assumptions of arguments involving compensation or discounting that money can represent the goods we aim to achieve, Chapter 8 offers some clarification of what can and should be assumed about the nature of money and the kind of good that it can serve as. We are accustomed to thinking about money in terms of the goods and services that sums of it can be used to acquire, but we also need to reflect on how money itself, as a social phenomenon, does service as a public good. Money is not like a natural phenomenon that exists in the world in determinate quantities awaiting decisions different people may choose to make about how to use it. For its very existence depends on decisions people make, as does the particular form that money assumes in a given system. Because money has several functions, it can serve as a public good in several general ways, and it can also come in different forms, each of which is more optimally suited to fulfilling some functions rather than others. Consequently, different ways of administering a system will have different socio-economic effects, including effects with distributive implications. So a lot of practical decisions, political as well as economic, are involved in managing a monetary system. Determining who has the power to make crucial decisions relating to the creation and operation of the monetary system, and with what aims uppermost in mind, is a matter of great significance. With an awareness of the importance and contingency of powers relating to the monetary system, one may then think about how the workings of the financial system might have effects that are systematically problematic from the point of view of concerns about global justice. In particular, there is the second of the problems alluded to earlier.

The problem picked up in Chapter 9 can be described by reference to a hypothesis. This, in its general version, is as follows. Even if there were the political will and technical means to transfer income or wealth in the order of the 1–2 per cent deemed necessary to alleviate severe poverty globally,[7] the real economic effects of so many people undergoing such a significant change in circumstances would be great enough to register in the calculations entered into market decisions affecting the prices of money. The more specific hypothesis is that a global redistribution of an order of magnitude of 1–2 per cent could prompt reactions in the financial system that would cause counter-distributive effects—potentially offsetting any gain to the worst off, possibly even to the extent of exacerbating the initial injustice.

Some political philosophers have addressed related concerns about the *illicit financial flows* that carry funds away from poorer countries, notwithstanding inward aid and foreign investment, as companies exploit tax competition and tax havens, as well as sometimes engaging in various kinds of illicit transaction and filtering their proceeds via Offshore Financial Centres (OFCs). Although this focus on the problem of illicit finance brings important considerations to light, a deeper problem can be discerned when we consider the very reason that those flows are referred to as *illicit* rather than clearly and unequivocally illegal. For they often involve the 'creative' use of law and its loopholes or of discrepancies between different legal jurisdictions. This means that attempts to regulate them are hampered by lack of clear legal authority. In fact, part of the problem is that the so-called 'shadow banking' system itself has become integrated into systems of international finance that are recognized as legitimate. Licit and illicit flows thus intermingle in global finance. The problem then is not only about how and where money illicitly flows but about adulteration of the quality of the money itself. Here we come to problems attendant on the fact that various innovative securities and derivatives contracts are treated as money equivalents in financial flows in today's system. These instruments introduce deceptive forms of liquidity that make the financial system more vulnerable to instability, while, in the process, making possible the extraction of considerable profit by market players who know how to exploit market turbulence. The system thus makes it possible for a few to become very rich, even while allowing considerable harm to productive economies

[7] This indicative figure is taken from Thomas Pogge (2002: 7).

and ordinary people's livelihoods. So while the hypothesis under consideration remains to be confirmed or refuted in practice, we can see good reason to be alert to the problem it depicts. In fact, what the considerations of Chapter 9 suggest is that this problem could be a real one with or without attempts to achieve global redistribution.

In light of this, we see good reason to urge investigation of how global transfers could be undermined by counter-reactions of actors in financial markets. For as long as the system functions as described, inequalities look set to continue increasing. Global finance appears to be overrun by 'mad money'—money backed by little real collateral but having a very real capacity to increase indebtedness around the world. This is something that would need to be brought under political control and accountability in order for anything approaching justice to be possible in relation to global finance. The issue is about who controls the monetary system. Money is a crucial public good, and yet it is not under public, political, control. This critical problem is the focus of Chapter 10.

Control of the monetary system ought to be under public and political control, I claim, because all the considerations set out in this book suggest that allowing it to be controlled by private interests is unlikely, even in principle, to place it at the service of the greater public good. In practice, it demonstrably tends to do the opposite. Yet the problem today is that globally there is developing, unannounced and to a large extent unnoticed, what is in effect a privatized global order of a quasi-constitutional kind. On review of the evidence for this, I argue that we need to think of the production and governance of money as a fundamental social process requiring normative guidance in much the same way as we consider the judicial system to be guided. The general idea that monetary governance should be one of the major provisions of a state constitution is not new, but it has been relatively neglected in political philosophy, particularly considering the material importance of our monetary arrangements to all social institutions and practices. With an increasingly globalized financial system that is expanding in scale and power relative to institutions of politics, economics, and law, the need for some kind of constitutional constraints and direction becomes a pressing normative imperative of our time. There is good reason for concern at the absence of overarching agreement on how finance could and should be constituted as an international public good. Indeed, in the absence of a widespread perception of the need for such an agreement, there has developed, largely unannounced and entirely unaccountably as far as the global public is concerned, what amounts to a *privatized* global constitution. A set of binding legal arrangements that bypass and transcend sovereign jurisdictions and even other aspects of international law has been building up in support of the global financial system. The legal system within which finance operates has become increasingly autonomous of the control of states or international law. Part of the problem is that the private ownership of even central banks is strongly encouraged by the coordinators of the banking system itself. Yet, while there are certain good reasons for a central bank to be independent of government, there is no necessity for it to be privately owned or controlled. The administration of money might be compared, I argue, to the administration of justice. The judiciary can be constitutionally immunized against political interference from the government without being privatized. Nonetheless, those good reasons presuppose that the organs themselves have a clear constitutional mandate in the first place, and that is what the global banking system does not have. On the contrary, we find, it is run by a small group of private owners and controllers whose locus of coordination is the Bank for International Settlements. Effectively the central bankers' central bank, this inconspicuous organization sits at the apex of the international financial system. Its effective power not only transcends legal and tax jurisdictions of states, severally and jointly, it also exercises material power over states by maintaining a system of privately controlled central banks. Its transnational character is so strong that even at times of war between states, the close cooperation of its members is maintained.

The fact that financial relationships can be maintained even during times of war demonstrates that human beings have collaborative concerns that rise above the conflicts that can occur. It also serves to point up a bitter irony. Of the billions of human beings on this planet I doubt that very many actually desire ever to have a war, but few have any opportunity to 'rise above' a conflict if it is generated in their vicinity or in their name. The further a person is from the apex of the financial system, the less chance they have of escaping the effects of war when it comes. They are also the people with the least power to decide whether or when there should be a war in the first place.

This thought prompts the question, why are there so many wars? One perspective on this question explored in Chapter 11 links it to consideration of how banks appear able to rise above the actual hostilities of wars. Further questions follow when we reflect on just how important finance is to the prosecution of war. The next thought is that since the provision of finance is a business, a profitable one, and controlled by private actors who seek profits, there are structural incentives within the financial sector to view warfare as a business opportunity. Given how antithetical war is to the aims of global justice and ecological sustainability, it is important to try to understand how the financial system may operate quite differently than it would if guided by human and ecological desiderata. A brief consideration of circumstantial evidence relating to some of the countries that have been the site of the most recent wars—overt, covert, and proxy—suggests worrying correlations with factors such as resistance to dollar hegemony or privatized central banking or thoroughgoing integration into the system of globalized financial capitalism. Another perspective on the question prompts puzzlement as to why, despite the obvious harms that wars cause for ordinary people, populations can nevertheless be brought to acquiesce in their inevitability, and even their moral necessity. Looking particularly at wars where foreign powers intervene against another state with the declared purpose of bringing freedom and democracy to its people, there is a weighty burden of proof to discharge regarding the justice both of ends sought and means deployed. The idea of delivering freedom and democracy to people by means of bombs ought to be sufficiently disturbing to warrant very careful analysis of the arguments offered in justification for it. What I show by reference to some recent indicative cases, however, is that philosophers who comment on justification in particular cases may not always exercise sufficiently thorough due diligence on empirical claims, but may take rather too much on trust the summaries of information that are disseminated in the media. For the media are almost entirely owned by the same corporate interests that benefit from the preservation of global capitalism.

The book's fundamental argument is that the financial system has to change, and what is effectively a set of privatized quasi-constitutional global arrangements needs to be brought under public control. The questions broached in the book indicate areas in which future research, both theoretical and practical, could fruitfully be pursued. One point, particularly emphasized for the development of a forward-looking political philosophy, is that in thinking about the relevance of money to global justice we need to attend to how money functions in reality. Certainly, due diligence should be done regarding proposals for apparent ethical bargains involving money and easy 'win–win' scenarios—whether in relation to eradicating poverty or achieving ecological sustainability. We need to be as clear sighted as possible about the nature and magnitude of the institutional transformation required to achieve those goals. This means being open to recognizing that any real prospect of global justice may depend on a radical transformation of the global financial system. As flagged more than forty years ago by the economist James Tobin (1978), a fundamental problem is that the profit-driven global financial system has been organized more quickly and completely as a normative framework for global order than any political arrangements aimed at promoting public interests in justice and sustainability. There is real reason to doubt whether mere reform, or modest regulation, or simple correction of 'imperfections', will bring that system to yield justice, prosperity, a healthy environment, or peace for the people of the world. Because the financial system has developed something akin to a privatized global constitution, to secure conditions of social justice for the people of the world and ecological sustainability for the planet may require the constitution of a global normative order guided by public and political decision-making. The achievement of a publicly accountable and responsive constitutional order that is superordinate to the organizations of finance might be regarded as a revolutionary transformation.

2
Money for Justice?

The central concern of this book is to understand the role that money can play, or is expected to play, in efforts to make the world more just. In view of the great prevalence of extreme poverty in the world, the unequal distribution of money would appear to be a considerable part of the problem. Accordingly, contributors to recent philosophical debates about global justice have proposed various ways to make the world more just by means of transferring money, and the general idea of raising taxes for this purpose has been proposed by a number of them (e.g. Steiner 1999, 2011; Pogge 2002; Brock 2008, 2015; Casal 2011; Armstrong 2012, 2015; Mawe and Bufachi 2015). These proposals reflect a belief that the goals of global justice can be achieved by directing funds in appropriate ways. This belief, in turn, rests on certain assumptions about the nature, or functions, of money. The objective in this chapter is to make these assumptions explicit and to indicate why they are significant.

In normative discussions of principles of global justice, the nature of money itself is not usually a focus of conceptual analysis, and its fitness to serve as a means for implementing recommended principles is quite routinely assumed. In one respect, this assumption is not particularly remarkable or unduly controversial: insofar as principles of justice are concerned in a general way with the distribution of the benefits and burdens of social cooperation, whatever those might be, there is scope for referring to the abstract quanta of social goods that people may share according to one distributive principle or another.[1] This is to posit, at least for heuristic purposes, a unit of account. Since providing a unit of account is one of the generally recognized functions of money, contributors to the debate fall quite naturally to talking about just distributions in terms of money. This discursive practice, I clarify in Section 2.1, may be accepted as unproblematic as long as one keeps in mind that these references to money are purely heuristic and cannot be assumed to stand for any facts about actual monetary systems in the real world. This caveat is important, I suggest, in relation to proposals for using money to achieve the ends of global justice when these

[1] I have said *largely* unproblematic, not entirely unproblematic, because there are issues of incommensurability and value pluralism that may stand in the way of 'reducing' all benefits and burdens to a single measure (see e.g. John O'Neill 2002); and some political philosophers have quite systematically argued for distributive justice to be sensitive to the different sorts of distribuenda (notably Walzer 1983). Tobin (1970) had made a related point regarding 'specific egalitarianism'.

involve recommendations of *policy* measures of the kind advocated on the tax and fund approach to global justice. For one assumption of this approach is that the purposes of global justice may be achieved by applying, in a global context, the kind of redistributive fiscal policy that has proven capable of supporting social justice in the domestic context of a welfare state. Thus the focus of attention in debates about these proposals tends to be on the normative justifications offered for various alternative bases upon which taxes might be levied. In such discussions, it is generally assumed that, provided funds can be raised somehow, directing them to the goals of alleviating poverty, or, in some cases, remedying ecological harm, can be achieved by means that need not attract the particular interest of philosophers. It is assumed empirically unproblematic to suppose that the funds raised will achieve the ends intended, provided only that they *get through*—that is, they are not lost through inefficiency, corruption, or crime. As I argue in Section 2.2, however, while this assumption—of the stable transferable value of money—may be a reasonable one in the domestic context of a well-ordered state, where monetary and fiscal arrangements have been developed to serve and mesh with productive economic activity, it stands to be warranted in global or international contexts. For although the function of being a store of value is—like that of being a unit of account—a generally recognized function of money, this does not mean that all forms of money in all material circumstances fulfil that function equally well.

Prior to working out what policy instruments might most appropriately implement ideal distributive principles, the pursuit of global justice requires some clarity about the institutional circumstances that need to be in place for the successful implementation of any such policies at all. One should not automatically assume that heuristically developed distributive principles can simply be plugged into the existing institutions of the world so as to deliver money that will solve the problems of global justice. The possibility of success for such measures depends on both fiscal and financial institutions being under the political control of those who would aim to implement them. A politically unaccountable global financial system is not the most promising basis upon which to implement elements of a fledgling global welfare system. In this circumstance, I point out, not only are the prospects of effectively raising and disbursing tax revenues attenuated in various significant ways, but we also have to reckon with the problem that the *value*—even of the taxes successfully raised and transmitted—is subject to volatilities in financial markets. Although the former problem is generally acknowledged in the literature, the second tends not to be. This, I note, is somewhat ironic, given that the problem was sharply diagnosed more than forty years ago by James Tobin. Today, Tobin is cited by political philosophers as an early proponent of a tax and fund approach. However, the so-called 'Tobin Tax' on currency exchange transactions was not primarily proposed as a means of revenue-raising but as an attempt to *prevent* the kind of currency speculation that has since become endemic in a deregulated global financial system so inimical to welfarist strategies. My argument is that we need to focus more clearly on the problem. In the absence of global political institutions and a single global currency, it would be premature for a political philosopher to make policy commendations whose effectiveness would presuppose their existence. I suggest that our attention should be directed to thinking about the institutional conditions required for the purposes of global taxation as well as for the governance of global finance being more generally in the public interest.

2.1 The Heuristics of Monetary Reasoning

Money typically features in philosophical discussions of distributive justice as a general-purpose unit of account. When, in such discussions, it is assumed that certain limited resources should be subject to some non-arbitrary delimitation of entitlements, the argument developed is not typically taken to depend critically on what particular resources might be at stake. Discussions of distributive principles often proceed by representing people's interests in resources as a general one that can be expressed—for convenience—in terms of shares of income and wealth (e.g. Rawls 1971). This is not necessarily simply to assume that income and wealth are goods in themselves; it merely reflects the assumption that since the goods in question will *de facto* fall under some distribution or other, then in the name of justice we should strive to commensurate them as best we can for the purpose of ensuring their distribution *de jure* is not morally arbitrary. The heuristic role of money in this thinking is as a pure unit of account.

Such thinking is epitomized in Ronald Dworkin's method of arriving at a just distribution of goods. In a thought experiment, set on a desert island, with the aim of fairly distributing whatever is found, each member of a shipwrecked community is initially allocated an equal amount of clamshells (Dworkin 1981: 285–7). These are not a store of any value but function simply as a unit of account by means of which to allow quantitative expressions of preference strength. The clamshells are, 'in themselves valued by no one' but are simply there 'to use as counters' (Dworkin 1981: 286). In the course of a reiterated series of auctions, the participants bid with their clamshells for whatever of the island's natural assets they choose until each and every one gets the best bundle of goods for themselves that they can under the given choice constraints. That is to say, a point in the process is reached at which no participant would prefer to have any of the other participants' bundles instead of the bundle they have negotiated.

What Dworkin has done with his thought experiment is to foreground an important part of the logic of thinking about justice with respect to the distribution of resources. Resources do not have any determinate value in virtue purely of their natural qualities; value is an attribute arising in virtue of people's valuations and the social practices that mediate these. The use of money allows the convenient expression of value comparisons. As a pure unit of account, the form of money used is indifferent: it could be represented in pretty much any form, including such things as tally sticks, a ledger, a collective memory, a bank account, a blockchain, cigarettes, or, as here, clamshells. A unit of account is, ontologically speaking, a pure mental representation; it does not have or correspond to any inherent value. Hence different currencies and different forms of money can come in and out of acceptance and, even when accepted, can fluctuate wildly in the value attributed them. Some forms of money may, of course, be attributed something closer to inherent value than others: gold coins, for instance, can be valued for the gold they contain as well as for the currency they may serve to denominate, and this value can therefore transcend the vagaries of more purely symbolic currencies; some other forms of money may *represent* inherent substantive value of that kind, as, for instance, can promissory notes issued against a treasure of gold. In this regard, one might think in terms of a 'hierarchy of money', as helpfully explicated by Perry Mehrling (2013). The point I am emphasizing here, meanwhile, is that we can think of money, as Dworkin's experiment has us do with his inherently unvalued clamshells, *heuristically*. We can compare perceptions of the relative justness of different scenarios by means of such heuristics.

In doing so, however, we should be clear that we are precisely not talking about financial realities. These are deliberately abstracted from in Dworkin's thought experiment: it takes place on a desert island, with no pre-existing economy, and with each individual simply being given an equal initial allocation of inherently unvalued counters; it is possible thereupon for an unlimited number of bidding rounds to take place before a corresponding substantive distribution is settled upon; furthermore, acceptance of the outcome by all concerned is simply assumed. In all those defining respects it is quite unlike the real world where we all start with different amounts of money, in different places—and, in a global context, in quite different currencies—with imperfect information, limited opportunities, and manifold issues of compliance, not to mention inefficiency, corruption, and crime. Furthermore, money in the real world is not just magicked into existence as Dworkin has us imagine the clamshells are: its production, as we shall in due course reflect on more carefully, is an intensely complex matter of political economic processes unfolding in real history.

My point, then, is that when we refer to money heuristically, we need to be careful not to confuse such references with propositions about the nature of money in reality. In the context of a critical investigation into the adequacy for the ends of justice of the system of global finance, it is important to be able to distinguish heuristic ideas that are expressed for convenience in the language of abstract general money, from propositions about the actual workings of money in the real economy.

When thinking about principles of just distribution, we can for some purposes think about *what* has to be distributed—the *distribuendum*—in quite abstract and non-specific terms, which can then be treated as units of account. Money being the most familiar phenomenon to serve as an all-purpose unit of account, we can often discuss principles of distributive justice as if what they apply to is the distribution of money. But we need to be very wary of then assuming that redistributing money is tantamount to redistributing whatever social goods or services may substantively be required to achieve the ends of justice. We may think heuristically in monetized terms, for the purpose of deciding between different principles of distribution, but we should not assume that those principles can be applied in policy-making without careful critical analysis of how money does in fact relate to actual goods and services under determinate economic conditions. We need, furthermore, to recognize that being a unit of account is only one of the functions that money needs to fulfil when serving fiscal purposes. It has also to function as a medium of exchange and a store of value.

2.2 The Challenge of Money for Proposals of a Tax for Global Justice

In recent years, a number of ways have been proposed through which global taxes might be levied and deployed as a means to solving problems of global injustice. Influential in the development of these proposals were early suggestions by Brian Barry (1982) and Charles Beitz (1979). Barry took the conceptually and normatively straightforward view that it would be just for rich people to be taxed wherever they live for the benefit of the poor wherever they live (Barry 1982: 242). The taxes would be set at the global level (according to cosmopolitan principles of global justice)—and at globally harmonized rates among states—but collected by states (according to principles deemed to be socially just within each state). As Gillian Brock has more recently observed, 'the way global taxes could gain legal standing is through agreements between nation states in an "internationally-harmonized tax regime"' (Brock 2008: 174). It is not difficult to see the ethical attractions of such proposals, and the economist Thomas Piketty (2014) has also affirmed their theoretical feasibility. His own view is that a solution to the worrying rise in inequality in our time would be a progressive annual tax on global wealth. His focus on wealth is itself a modification of earlier ideas for a global tax on income—a principle he broadly accepts, but which he believes would be much easier to avoid or evade. Piketty is nevertheless clear that the proposal is, under the current circumstances, not a realistic proposition but 'a utopian idea', due to the near impossibility of envisaging any international agreement being reached to establish such an arrangement.

Does it matter that we are dealing here with a utopian idea? The cosmopolitan approach has been criticized by some for commending a moral ideal that is detached from considerations of political realism. Some influential realists—notably Amartya Sen (2006, 2009)—even question the usefulness of theorizing a moral ideal of a just world at all. The argument I shall present here, however, does not involve denying the importance of thinking about the ideal goals of global justice, and of doing so uninhibited by recognition of the inherent constraints of the institutional status quo.[2] For I grant the view that unless we have some definite conception of the ideal goals of justice, even if we know these may not be immediately or fully attainable, we risk lacking a normative frame of reference within which to investigate whether 'achieving a certain improvement in justice now would prevent us from achieving greater justice in the future' (Valentini 2012: 661). What I shall in fact argue is that this consideration in favour of a certain kind of ideal theory obliges us to appreciate the force of a particular kind of realist critique against proposals of taxes for global justice. Our thinking about how the world could be more just should not be constrained by proscriptions on ideal theorizing, for we do need to think about how a more just world would differ from what we find in present reality. What I would also emphasize, however, is that doing this meaningfully requires us to be clear about what would need to be changed in the world for the ideal to become more real. On this score, I shall argue, some of the cosmopolitan proposals are not so much 'too demanding' as insufficiently clear about the demands actually entailed by them. Specifically, this has to do with what is assumed about the institutional preconditions for the effectiveness of a tax and fund scheme.

An evident problem is that, in the absence of a world state, or its functional equivalent, there is nothing to bind the multitude of competing political and economic interests in the world into a scheme of cooperation of a kind that has the scope to support universal welfare provision. The actual tax-raising powers at present still rest with states rather than transnational bodies, and there is a formidable practical challenge in getting states to develop the political will needed to fulfil cosmopolitan moral obligations. But if that challenge is no light one, the advocates of taxes for global distributive justice nonetheless believe it is clear that, in principle, the requirement is to enact a fiscal scheme designed to achieve that goal.

However, there is a further problem. Something Piketty emphasizes is that 'a tax is always more than just a tax: it is also a way of defining norms and categories and imposing a legal framework on economic activity' (Piketty 2014: 520). In other words, if we are concerned about how to institute a redistributive scheme, we cannot simply think in terms of distributive principles in isolation from the wider frameworks of activity into which such a scheme would be inserted. It is in

[2] These issues have been much discussed in the literature, helpful contributions to which include Ingrid Robeyns (2008), Adam Swift (2008) and Laura Valentini (2012).

this respect that the various tax and fund proposals put forward by political philosophers could be more problematic than might at first be supposed. The issue here has to do with certain pre-requisites for the effective operation of any fiscal scheme at all.

One thing we know about the real world of fiscal policy is that its operation can never be unaffected by the operations of *monetary* policy. These two are the primary instruments of macroeconomic governance in a modern state, and understanding their interaction is indispensible for thinking about how any arrangements for taxing and spending may work out in practice. Within a state, governments can adopt a chosen macroeconomic strategy and attempt to pursue integrated fiscal and monetary policies with the aim of balancing inflation and interest rates. This will be more challenging to manage at some times than at others, given the business cycle and events, but it is meaningfully within the state's power to attempt. Even the impacts of foreign exchange rate changes can be managed to an extent by domestic policy, so that if they at times move unhelpfully, the internal fiscal arrangements of the state are not necessarily seriously affected. At least, this is not immediate or direct with respect to the value of the money that is spent for example on welfare, since revenues raised and funds spent are all denominated in the same currency.

The problem for transposing a tax and fund theory from the domestic context to the global is that those powers to control and insulate the value of money against shocks will not be available to any reformed international order short of one with significant features of a world state, including a single currency and unified fiscal and monetary policies. In the absence of those conditions, there is no good reason to assume the value of money raised in one economy will be preserved in the process of seeking to achieve redistributive justice for another. There are quite powerful reasons, as we shall see in later chapters, to assume the contrary. This means there could be more problems with money than the philosophers of global justice to date have tended to appreciate.

The assumptions brought to discussions of global distributive justice in the contemporary literature are for the most part those that were settled upon in the context of thinking about justice within a modern nation-state. We have also noted the quite prevalent assumption that tax and fund proposals need only involve some specific international agreements rather than full world-state-like cooperation on a global scale. Yet even if we suppose that such arrangements might be put in place, one question to address is this: if there is no world state or its functional equivalent to ensure a fully integrated fiscal regime and a single monetary regime, can we assume that the transfer of value globally would be as straightforward as it is within a state? In order for transfers of money to be able to serve the ends of global justice in reality, the value of money raised, as taxes, must actually be transmitted. This means that the money used has to fulfil the functions of both medium of exchange (since the value transmitted has to be accepted into the destination economy) and a store of value (since what is accepted must be worth something). Within the domestic context of a modern nation-state, money typically tends to fulfil these functions unproblematically. However, similarly smooth functioning cannot simply be taken for granted in an international or global context.

So my argument is that ideal theory is not necessarily 'naïve and ineffective' in seeking 'to hold existing societies to account on the basis of such demanding moral standards', an objection addressed for instance by Valentini (2012: 659), but that cosmopolitans ought to be more steadfast in thinking through the demands of those moral standards. For where there is a risk of being naïve and ineffective is in supposing that the existing global financial system can be bent to the service of justice if only there is the political will to do so. Before we can consider whether a theory is too demanding, we need to be reasonably clear what the demands actually consist in. The abstract specifications of a purely moral cosmopolitanism need to have some definite point of purchase in socio-economic realities. For this reason, some questions have to be asked about proposals of tax and fund for global justice that philosophers have rather neglected up to now.

2.3 Global Finance as Help or Hindrance for Just Redistribution?

The questions to be asked arise out of reflection on the differences between the circumstances of global justice and those of justice within a nation-state. In the domestic context, the raising of funds through taxation, and their disbursement through state spending, are staple activities of public policy. And yet, in the global context, there exists no single authority with the power to levy taxes and disburse funds. It is perhaps reasonable to allow that this fact might be bracketed when debating the general justificatory principles according to which taxes ideally should be raised. A different question, though, assuming funds can be raised as required, is whether *disbursement* of those funds could be meaningfully discussed in similarly abstract terms. One obvious complication is that recipients or beneficiaries of funds may live in different jurisdictions from those where the relevant taxes are raised. A general circumstance that cannot simply be bracketed from consideration of tax and fund proposals, then, is that the two processes fall within quite separate fiscal locations.

Within a state there is a single fiscal regime subject to political governance—this is part of what I take it to *mean* when we refer to a particular assemblage of institutions as a state. Revenues and expenditures are balanced according to principles politically decided as optimal for that state. Justifications for the incidence of taxes, on the one hand, and for the disbursement of them, on the other, may involve quite separate normative considerations. However, some reconciliation or trade-off between and among them has to be made, given the state's distinctive further normative imperative to maintain an equilibrium between revenues and expenditures. In administering taxation and spending, then, a state has political control over its own fiscal policy. This is not merely a contingent or technical necessity, since it is the responsibility of the state—insofar as this lies within its power—to protect and maintain the very substance of revenues, that is, the value of the money transferred. The state acts as a broker between various earners and drawers—past, present, and future—mediating people's various claims on each other to various social and economic services and underwriting the due performance of undertakings by putting the full weight of state power into its legal system. A state also has some authority over macroeconomic aspects of monetary policy—even if nowadays that authority may be severely constrained in practice by global financial markets and institutions. Within the institutional framework of a state, then, taxation and expenditure are maintained in a politically decided equilibrium maintained by means of a currency over which the state has significant, if less than complete, control.

Something taken for granted in this context is that the value of money raised as taxes is essentially equivalent to the value of the money that thereby becomes available to spend. That is to say, while the marginal utility of a given sum levied may be greater for its recipient than for its payer, the goods that the recipient can buy with it are the same as the payer could have bought, if desired. So within the context of a state, it can be reasonable to assume that the value of taxes raised is broadly equivalent to the value of the funds disbursed.

A critical question for tax and fund schemes advocated in a world of separate states and globalized finance is whether a comparable assumption is warranted. If it is not, then there is a real possibility that tax and fund schemes—even if the significant hurdles to agreeing, implementing, and effectively enforcing them could be surmounted—would anyway be undermined or even potentially defeated through the normal play of financial forces. For in the absence of a world state, and as globalization is increasingly financialized, the possibility of supporting a sustainable tax and fund regime, even domestically, becomes an increasing challenge for states. National economic strategies, and the social policy goals that depend on them, are susceptible to powerful influences from global financial markets over which they have very little reciprocal influence. In a globalized context, the relative value of different currencies responds *inter alia* to fiscal policies in different countries; and, reciprocally, fiscal decisions are taken in the light of monetary considerations. This means *both* that the prospects of effective taxation are constrained in various significant ways *and* that the value of taxes raised is subject to volatilities in financial markets.

Regarding the prospects of effective taxation, a central matter is that some factors in value creation can be taxed more readily than others. Factor *mobility* is a critical variable. A government's ability to tax depends on its ability to maintain its tax jurisdiction, and factor mobility erodes this.[3] Howard M. Wachtel (2000) has pointed out some evident problems in the financialized world order that tend to erode the tax base in both developed and developing countries, affecting in particular their ability to tax the proceeds and profits from corporate investment and finance:

> In developed countries (DCs), financial and tangible forms of capital roam the globe, rendering it difficult both to define profits for tax purposes and to decide in which country the taxable profit is earned. Less developed countries (LDCs) find themselves under such pressure to grant tax holidays, tax abatements and generous land giveaways that they cede their tax base in an obsessive competition for foreign investment. Corporations have then used these concessions from LDCs to leverage tax reductions in their home countries in what is by now a well-tuned orchestration of political pressure. (Wachtel 2000: 335)

So a practical problem for tax and fund proposals is that even if they could get political support, they could only collect revenues on condition either that the mobility of factors is somehow counteracted or that taxes are levied on the least mobile. Given that capital—especially when uncommitted to any productive enterprise—can more easily flee tax jurisdictions, this means that labour and land, including natural resources, tend to bear the burden, thereby adding to the pressures on social and ecological well-being. The problem can also be something of a vicious circle, intensifying debt-based inequalities, as we shall see in Chapter 3.

Regarding the value of revenues raised for purposes of international disbursement, a central matter is that of converting the currency of donors into that of recipients. A reason why we cannot necessarily expect value to be preserved through international transfers is that exchange rates—that is, the various relative prices of money—are vulnerable to market volatilities. The underlying problem was described, some forty years, ago by James Tobin: 'private financial markets have become internationalized much more rapidly and completely than other economic and political institutions. That is why we are in trouble' (Tobin 1978: 5–6). Tobin presented the basic problem of international monetary instability as lying in 'the excessive international—or, better, intercurrency—mobility of private financial capital' (Tobin 1978: 153). That instability is a problem because 'national economies and national governments are not capable of adjusting to massive movements of funds across the foreign exchanges, without real hardship and without significant sacrifice of the objectives of national economic policy with respect to employment, output, and inflation' (Tobin 1978: 154). The problem is

[3] 'Of the three factors of production, capital is the most mobile and land is the least mobile. Labor is somewhere in between but definitely at the immobile end of the spectrum, except for some very high-profile, extremely wealthy individuals. Globalization, therefore, has forced a fourth criterion on governments: *taxing the factor of production that is less mobile.*' (Wachtel 2000: 336–7).

exacerbated by how 'speculation on exchange rates, whether its consequences are vast shifts of official assets and debts or large movements of exchange rates themselves, [has] serious and frequently painful real internal economic consequences. Domestic policies are relatively powerless to escape them or offset them' (Tobin 1978: 154).

On the basis of Tobin's diagnosis of the problem, two sorts of prescription are possible: one would involve a 'common currency, common monetary and fiscal policy, and economic integration'; the other would involve 'greater financial segmentation between nations or currency areas, permitting their central banks and governments greater autonomy in policies tailored to their specific economic institutions and objectives' (Tobin 1978: 154). Given that the first is 'clearly not a viable option in the foreseeable future', Tobin concludes, 'I therefore regretfully recommend the second'. His financial transactions tax is thus put forward as a proposal 'to throw some sand in the wheels of our excessively efficient international money markets' (Tobin 1978: 154).

The best remedy for volatile money markets—his 'One World' solution—Tobin believed to be politically unviable, so he proposed a more modest pragmatic alternative, his now-famous tax on currency transactions. The *Tobin Tax* was originally put forward with the specific objective of counteracting exchange-rate volatility in international financial markets. The purpose was not to raise revenues but to support national economies in meeting the imperative of sustaining monetary stability. Regarding use of the funds, Tobin said little more than to suggest their possible administration by the World Bank or International Monetary Fund (IMF).

Some philosophers of global justice have nevertheless suggested that the Tobin tax could be used in a tax and fund strategy, since the funds that are raised could be disbursed to support equitable and sustainable development goals.[4] With regard to this general suggestion, however, I think we should remember that Tobin's proposal—expressly a second best solution from his point of view—is premised on the political impossibility, according to his assessment, of achieving the state-like circumstances globally that would coordinate tax and fund programmes aimed at global social policy objectives. It is therefore not obvious that his proposal could be taken to provide an example of how a strategy centred on such programmes might succeed.

This represents a challenge for a political philosophy of tax and fund, in a global context, that appears to have been insufficiently heeded in the literature to date. In fact, the Tobin tax proposal itself is taken by several philosophers to be a

[4] 'A number of people', according to Simon Caney, have argued that the Tobin Tax 'would be a useful policy instrument for furthering global justice', and 'many have seized on his proposal and argued that the proceeds of such a tax should be employed to assist the weak, destitute, ill and starving' (Caney 2006: 126).

promising illustration of global tax and fund in action. To be sure, most are aware that fund-raising is not its primary purpose, and that the better it serves that primary purpose—of constraining exchange transactions—the less funds it would have to offer for disbursal to other ends. Yet we nevertheless encounter suggestions that the proposal offers some reassurance about the prospects of raising taxes for the purposes of global justice. For instance, Chris Armstrong writes: 'Although it has not been achieved in practice, the Tobin Tax performs well in terms of feasibility, in at least one respect: it seems the reform most likely to attract popular and elite support' (Armstrong 2015: 300). Yet even allowing this rather undemanding notion of feasibility, understood as a potential for attracting support, rather than proven practicability, the basis of the claim seems questionable. The reason Armstrong offers as motivating support for it is 'that the Tobin Tax is directed at an activity that is widely seen as having "little social value"' (Armstrong 2015: 300), but since the proposition has not in fact garnered the elite support needed to implement it over the past forty years, this suggests that the consideration does not particularly move the relevant elite. For similar reasons I also find it unclear why Simon Caney believes that the Tobin tax serves 'to illustrate the ways in which cooperation to achieve a cosmopolitan goal can be reached' (Caney 2005: 138–9). Caney claims this in responding to the sceptically realist view that 'states cannot act in the way required to bring about cosmopolitan justice' (Caney 2005: 137). He does not expand, though, on how the positing of an as yet non-existent tax illustrates how actual cooperation to institute such a thing might be achieved. One only needs to secure agreement of key states to make the Tobin tax effective, Caney suggests. Yet apart from arguably making light of the difficulties of getting such an agreement, this claim also assumes that states would have a capacity to assert effective control over global financial markets, which is in fact uncertain, as later chapters will discuss. In short, I think we need to be clear on the difference between a proposal being easily argued for, by reasonable people, and it being feasible to implement in the real institutional circumstances of the world.

Meanwhile we have to record a concern that, with global finance having disproportionate power in relation to other actors and institutions, and with a lack of overarching political authority, there is an absence at the global level of the conditions that facilitate cogent tax and spend policy-making within nation-states. Furthermore, an important power that a state normally has—namely, to determine the value of money within its jurisdiction (albeit within limits set by international finance and trade arrangements)—rests globally not with the decisions of any political body but with the spontaneous market reactions of the financial sector. This means it is possible for the value of funds to be lost in the process of their translation.

We thus reach a position where we can appreciate not only that the question of raising funds, on the one hand, and disbursing funds, on the other, can involve different distributive principles, but also that there are questions to be asked about the nature of the *distribuendum* itself. For tax and fund proposals, the *distribuendum* is money. In order to fulfil its intended role throughout the process of taxing and funding, money needs to have the form of a reliable medium of exchange and a reasonably stable store of value. These are requirements, however, that may not be met as straightforwardly as proponents of tax and fund approaches to global justice assume.

2.4 Conclusion

This chapter has shown that certain assumptions implicit in the tax and fund approach to global justice are potentially more problematic than proponents of the approach typically acknowledge. To allow an assumption that money can serve as a unit of account when thinking about distributive principles is reasonable, provided that its heuristic limitations are understood. However, in thinking about the potential role of money in achieving practical ends of justice, one needs to recognize that more is involved than enters the reckoning when it is simply thought of as fulfilling the role of a notional unit of account. For the implementation of any actual tax and fund proposal in practice will also require the money transferred to fulfil more substantive functions.

To be the vehicle of an actual transfer of spending power, money has to come in such a form that it can function as a real store of value and medium of exchange—that is to say, in a form that people are actually willing to surrender goods and services for. In order to hold the real trust of real people, a money form has to be embedded in a system of norms that command general recognition and respect. The creation and maintenance of such a system depends on a high degree of social cooperation and coordination. These are conditions that can be challenging to secure, so their existence should not simply be assumed when suggesting practical proposals for achieving greater global justice.

If there were a world state or its functional equivalent, and a single global currency, then the problems identified might not be critical ones; but it would be a mistake for a political philosopher to make policy commendations whose effectiveness is premised on the existence of a condition that does not (yet) pertain. The particular argument of Tobin has been shown to be salutary in this regard. He affirmed the desirability of a common currency, with common monetary and fiscal policy in a globally integrated economy, but precisely because of its absence he proposed a tax on currency speculation as a secondbest measure to offset the worst effects of currency exchange volatility. While that measure can be expected to have some redistributive effects, at a systemic level, its rationale is not to raise funds for redistribution, and, in fact, the more successfully it deters speculative transactions, the less revenue it will raise. Quite generally, it is as well to be cautious about thinking of any tax aimed at impeding a practice as a potential source of revenue.

More fundamentally, the absence of monetary and fiscal integration globally stands as a reminder of the distance to be travelled before tax and fund proposals for global justice can safely be assumed to have any very robust basis. What is missing—a basic precondition—has still to be brought into being. Accordingly, our attention would appropriately be directed to thinking about principles for the institutional underpinnings for a possible system of just global finance.

3

The Good of Finance and the Critique of Financialization

In this chapter, a brief account is offered of the general function that some form of finance has to play in a society, and of how a banking system can in principle be expected to fulfil it. Given the concern of this book with how things can go wrong with finance in practice, attention is also paid to some of the key features of the global banking system as it has actually developed. We then go on to consider how the valuable social purpose that finance can in principle serve—the coordination of advance commitments to engage in worthwhile undertakings—is not necessarily achieved if finance is organized in inappropriate ways. Especially when new financial arrangements are created for no other purpose than to make a profit from financial arrangements that already exist, the primary social purpose of the practice can even be undermined. It is this general idea that is captured by the term 'financialization'. While that term is subject to numerous more particular definitions, it can be taken to refer quite generally to the kind of problematic situation that arises when the practices internal to finance are allowed to develop according to the logic of internal profit-seeking rather than as a response to the substantive social purposes that activities in the rest of the economy and society more widely are intended to achieve. The processes referred to as financialization, in short, can be said to undermine the good functioning of finance.

The financial system operating globally today can be criticized in three major respects: for hampering economic productivity, undermining distributive justice, and driving ecological irresponsibility.

The main focus of this chapter is on the first of these criticisms. After briefly characterizing the good of finance in Section 3.1, Section 3.2 examines the basic economic objection. One issue noted is that while the terms of that objection are compatible with those of the justice objection—in that restoring productivity and ensuring distributive equity can be mutually reinforcing goals—the pursuit of increased economic productivity can conceivably militate against the need for restraint implied by the ecological critique. At this stage in the inquiry, however, this suspected problem for an integrated critique of financialization is merely noted. Before dealing with it, we need to examine more carefully the basis of the economic critique itself. For, as will be shown in Section 3.3, there is actually disagreement among economics scholars as to how, and even *whether*, financialization is a problem for the 'real economy'. Recognizing that there is something to be said for each of two competing perspectives on monetary economics—the Keynesian and the monetarist—we can appreciate that insights of both have to be accorded some credibility in an appropriately dialectical account of what would be involved in the collectively rational governance of finance in the service of the public good as consistent with the demands of social justice. What the dialectical perspective allows us to see, in Section 3.4, is that just as it may be true to say that economic productivity is compromised by financialization, financialization can as well be seen as an effect of problems within the economic system. In light of this, Section 3.5 makes explicit that a solution to the problems associated with financialization cannot satisfactorily be tackled through steps to improve governance of the monetary system without addressing the problematic tendencies in the productive economy itself. In formulating the requirement of collective rationality in the governance of monetary economics, we find reason to challenge the irrationality of the proposition that any activity that stimulates economic 'growth' is as good as any other, including even when the activity itself may be regarded as useless or even deleterious from perspectives of more substantive social—or ecological—values. We therefore arrive, in the end, at a question of whether the anomaly within the three-part critique of financialization may lie not in the ecological perspective, as provisionally had been suspected, but in a certain version of the economic perspective. That question will then be picked up in Chapter 4.

3.1 The Good of Finance

Finance has an important social function to fulfil. Any constructive activity in life will typically involve forward planning and require some organization prior to fruits or rewards of the activity coming forth. This is as true of the planting of seeds in anticipation of a harvest as it is of setting up a new factory or providing training for the staff of a hospital. In the initiation of practically any economic activity, as also of many social and cultural ones, various material resources need to be in place; if an advance of such resources were unavailable, the activities could not occur. Advances can be made in various forms. Finance is most usually thought of in monetary terms, due to an assumption that money can serve as an all-purpose resource, being exchangeable for any of the actual things required in order for an enterprise to generate mutual benefit for lender and borrower.

When we speak of money in this context, in an ordinary everyday way, we tend to assume a fairly straightforward notion. If some people have more of it than others, this is because they have been party to, or beneficiary of, some prior successful venture from which rewards have already been reaped; these are now 'ploughed back' into a new generation of undertakings. In our everyday thinking, money has value for us because it is part of a system of trust at the basis of which is the general idea that just as someone has previously worked to produce something of value that is now represented by a price, so the money received for its sale will in turn be usable to purchase something else that embodies equivalent value. We thus have a fairly straightforward association of ideas about money being earned and debts standing to be repaid that is a weighty moral anchor of our normative thinking.

In the framing imparted by this mindset, a bank would appear to be a paradigmatically upstanding institution, its dignified solidity residing in the accumulation of monetary representations of the fruits of hard work and industry on the part of the depositors that have entrusted it to safeguard and facilitate their business. This association of ideas is also invoked in our everyday assumption that, in lending money, what one transfers represents some real asset in the world. Repayment of the money will represent the result of the lender having produced something of value.

As history shows, however, and events continually remind us, this everyday understanding does not capture the whole story about banking, let alone about the various more arcane 'financial services' that have evolved in association with it. While finance can fulfil a valuable social function, the institutions that govern it can also allow its deployment in anti-social ways. The socially desirable functions that financial institutions can in principle perform, and what financial institutions actually do in practice, are not necessarily the same. Just a glance at the history of modern banking reveals a certain logic that has unfolded whereby the interests of the protagonists rather than those of the general public have more decisively shaped the practices. The logic of the development can be summarized quite concisely. In the early days of modern banking, the practice of issuing notes of receipt for specific amounts of treasure deposited for safeguard developed into a practice of issuing notes backed more generally by the holding of treasure from numerous sources; thence banks increasingly exploited the possibility of issuing more notes than they had treasure to back, on the confident assumption that the inconvenience and risk to its owners of physically removing the treasure would mean there was never likely to be a call on more than a fraction of their reserves. The practice of fractional reserve banking became the norm, with the fraction actually held in reserve tending to diminish as the scale of the operation increased. Of course, with so many uncollateralized notes circulating, it was important that they be universally accepted in exchange. Hence banks formed mutual associations for clearing funds—that is, netting off each other's credits to one another. In this way, the associations of private banks operating within a jurisdiction would work together with a central clearing bank. With the globalization of the financial system, the central banks of developed countries came to coordinate their own respective activities under the auspices of the Bank for International Settlements (BIS), which, amongst other things, serves, in effect, as the clearers' clearer. This global hierarchy of financial institutions, as will be discussed in Chapter 10, has come to stand aside from, and, in many material ways, above, the law and politics of even the most powerful states.

Meanwhile, the practices of banks have departed much further from maintaining any direct connection with material collateral. The practice of fractional reserve banking might be regarded as a defensible means of keeping the wheels of industry and commerce oiled by ensuring that funds can circulate and be invested, which they cannot do if they sit in bank vaults. The greater are the loans made in proportion to the reserves, the greater are the potential economic benefits. At the same time, though, the smaller the fraction reserved, the greater will be the potential risk to all concerned: for in the event of concerns about a bank's solvency, it would take only a small run on its assets to initiate a crisis. Fractional reserve lending can be regarded as a form of a more general practice of leveraging—by which we understand attributing more value to an asset than it would be directly attributed at current market rates. In certain situations and within certain limits, it is rational to 'overvalue' an asset in this way. For instance, when a farmer grows crops or raises livestock she may need some money early in the year in order to be able to bring her produce to market later. At time t her crops or livestock are not currently worth much, but a prospective buyer knows that at time t_2 they will be worth a substantial sum, so it is rational at time t for the buyer to enter a futures contract for them at a price that takes into account their anticipated final market value. Furthermore, as other prospective buyers and producers adjust their estimates of needs and offerings, those options themselves may come to be treated as independent 'items' to be traded. However, as we were made particularly aware with the collapse of the system of mortgage-backed securities that precipitated the financial crash of 2008, leveraged valuations are ultimately only as reliable as the assets that underlie them. A farmer committed to work hard at bringing produce to market is—barring unforeseen diseases or adverse weather events—a fairly good bet; the sort of Ponzi scheme represented by the American mortgage business in the early years of this century—where poor quality debts were repackaged in derivative instruments as apparently sound assets—was a great bet for those who knew the score, but a disaster for others. Leveraging practices of the former kind tend to work in favour of the social rationale of finance described at the outset; those of the latter kind tend to undermine it. Accordingly, a principle of responsible banking is to determine a ratio of lending to reserves that is optimal with regard to risk and return.[1] This

[1] Exactly which risks and returns to weigh, and how much, are substantive questions, of course, involving considerations that go beyond the technical financial expertise that might determine optimal quantitative ratios once answers to those questions are fed into deliberations. In other words, technical experts may be able to determine what is an optimal ratio, but they cannot determine what risks anyone should be willing or permitted to run for what kind of reward. So banking needs technical regulation but also political regulation; yet a paradox is that it also needs political independence. These broader themes relating to the dialectics of banking arguably merit more attention by political philosophers than they have hitherto received (and see Chapter 10 for more on this).

need to strike an optimal ratio illustrates just one aspect of the multiple tensions inherent in any financial system.

Banking is, in fact, a thoroughly dialectical business, for it involves the negotiation of several tensions that are constitutive of its social role. A need to balance the opposed tendencies of risk and reward associated with any investment in future ventures is only one particularly obvious potential dilemma-producing tension. We might refer to it as the soundness dilemma. Associated tensions give rise to what we might call the security dilemma: while it is in the interests of everyone for a bank to appear responsible and trustworthy, in order to be trusted it has functional needs to maintain secrecy with regard to the affairs of those who trust it, as well as being materially impregnable against raids. In response to this dilemma, banks have built reputations of trustworthiness by ensuring as little as possible is publicly known about how they operate.

Responsible banking could be said to involve maintaining a sense of balance in negotiating such dilemmas: in balancing risks against rewards, it engages in proper assessment and due hedging; in maintaining security, it maintains the trust not only of clients and shareholders but also of the wider public by allowing its processes and governance to be appropriately transparent to auditors and regulators. Arguably, the very sustainability of a financial system ultimately depends on the observance of basic principles of responsibility: if excessively secretive security works to conceal unsoundness in lending practices, for instance, or if a problem is allowed to develop unchecked within one corporation or institution, then due to its inter-linkages with others, this will potentially be contagious for the wider system. In short, it may be said that responsible finance requires sound governance of the banking and finance sector.

Within mainstream monetary economics, there are contrasting views about what sound governance implies in practice. There are disagreements of both economic and political kinds about the necessary conditions for a well-functioning economy and even about what it means for an economy to be functioning well. On one view, responsible banking is *well-regulated* banking, where this means the sector is politically regulated in the public interest. But while this view is a staple of Keynesian schools of economic thinking, it is not uncontroversial for everyone. In particular, those schools of monetary thought that have been more influenced by thinkers like Milton Friedman, and Friedrich Hayek before him, advance the view that governments and politics should be kept out of financial matters and not allowed to interfere with the spontaneous workings of financial markets. A question at issue between the Keynesians and the Hayekians, then, is how much, if at all, the financial sector should be subjugated to directives from the political arena. A dialectical perspective on this question would acknowledge a truth highlighted by each: the financial system, in order to have the requisite stability and trustworthiness, needs to be independent of the vicissitudes of everyday political calculation; on the other hand, what a *democratic* society requires of its financial system should be decided on the basis of properly social decision-making processes and not left to the play of market forces where principles of plutocratic oligarchy can trump and trounce those of democracy.

The situation of the financial order in these respects is analogous to that of the judicial:[2] the ultimate substantive goals of a country's monetary policy, like a country's laws, are appropriately set by the elected branches of a democratic government. Responsibility for implementing the means to achieve those goals should be delegated to properly competent institutions. Exactly how the powers should be divided and separated, whilst also articulating with each other, is another of the dialectical questions about finance and its governance in the public interest. From a philosophical perspective on political economy, a number of questions might be gathered under the rubric '*who regulates the regulator?*' When fundamental disagreements affect matters of important public concern, there are questions not only of how they should be dealt with, but also of who decides how, and even of what principles should govern decisions about who gets to determine that. In fact, such questions—about what procedures there should be and who should get to decide—could, in principle, be pressed without end and are of the kind that might be appropriately settled in the manner that constitutional matters are. For the very idea of constituting a people as a people is—from an abstract conceptual perspective—similarly aporetic, since, arguably, there cannot be a people prior to its already having been constituted as a people (cf Olson 2007). In practice, where a constitution is always already presupposed, questions about fundamental social institutions that are subject to significant political disagreements are sensibly lifted above the political fray and dealt with by an authoritative body that is capable of representing the general and longer-term public interest.

It may thus be argued that taking a dialectical perspective on these matters is essentially akin to taking a *constitutional* perspective. For it involves reflecting at a high level of abstraction on a society's most basic institutions in terms of their crucial functions in supporting a stable, peaceful, and prosperous society. The institutions underpinning and governing the monetary system are clearly no less important than those of the judicial system. If they do not normally figure so prominently in debates about the nature of a legitimate or democratic or just constitution it is perhaps because they are not so obviously or directly concerned with the enforcement of specific socially endorsed norms that can in principle be chosen on the basis of deliberations of public reason. Yet it is worth heeding the analogies between the goals of a dependable monetary system and of a trustworthy judicial system. If we think that leaving justice in the hands of unaccountable organizations with considerable power over the conditions of people's lives would be unacceptable and undemocratic, we should be similarly concerned about the

[2] For an interesting discussion of comparisons between central banks and supreme courts see Goodhart and Meade (2004).

organization of a largely unaccountable monetary system. Just as there can be legitimate public concerns about the organization of a judiciary on the part of people who are not legal experts, so there can be legitimate public concerns about the organization of financial institutions on the part of people who are not experts in monetary economics. These concerns, that we may share as citizens and analyse as philosophers, are what I aim to highlight in this chapter and in the book as a whole. They relate to questions of fundamental principle about how a society organizes its material relationships and its normative relationships of debt and obligation.

3.2 Criticisms of Financialization

Finance can fulfil a valuable purpose when applied appropriately, even if it can also function so as to thwart or undermine such a purpose when applied less appropriately. When things go right with finance, it serves valuable social goals by enabling useful enterprises to be undertaken with success. To get any enterprise going initially involves some 'heavy lifting', in terms of mustering resources, and finance arrangements enable those undertaking it to 'leverage' the future commitments of others on the basis of a promise of good returns for all. The promise of sharing in a return is what normally motivates people to invest themselves in this leveraging process. The return itself might be the satisfaction of achieving the social goal served by the enterprise (because that goal is valued in its own right), or it might be the individuated reward of a 'share of the action' (with relative indifference as to the substantive nature of the achievement generating the pecuniary reward). The two kinds of motivation need not be mutually exclusive in practice, but we can draw a conceptual distinction between investing in an economic activity undertaken for specific substantive purposes and an investment made, indifferently, in anticipation purely of a pecuniary return. We can then further distinguish between investments made in productive economic activities, even if with the aforementioned indifference, and investments placed in purely derivative financial instruments where the expectation of a return is based on market movements per se, rather than substantive productive outcomes. As an economic order becomes increasingly dominated by purely financial transactions, the situation that arises is sometimes referred to as financialization.

Financialization can be criticized from an economic perspective. Contemporary Keynesians and post-Keynesians, in particular, use the term in a critical way to refer to the crowding out of investment in productive activity in the 'real economy' by increasing investment in financial assets (Orghangazi 2007). Their concern is with *disproportionate* growth in the financial sector. Gautum Mukunda, for instance, cites an IMF study showing that 'once the [financial] sector becomes too large—when private-sector credit reaches 80 percent to 100 percent of GDP—it actually inhibits growth and increases volatility' (Mukunda 2014). The financial services industry is criticized for its rent seeking behaviour, which tends to reduce productivity, and for trying to make further profits by manipulating government policy, thereby aggravating the problem. Particularly since the significant financial deregulation of the early 1980s, the complaint is that the services provided by finance have increasingly been services primarily *for* the financial sector. The dazzling array of financial instruments that slice, dice, repackage, and reconfigure relationships of indebtedness, using algorithms that only highly qualified specialists can understand, mainly serve the interests of the players in the financial sector. Much of this activity does not even purport to be meaningfully connected with productivity,[3] consisting as it does of essentially nothing more than placing bets on market movements—movements around the world at the speed of electrons, that can create or wipe out value in an instant. The situation today, according to John Kay (2013), is one where capital markets are no longer mechanisms for putting money into companies, but mechanisms for getting money out. Thus the criticism of financialization is that it can operate to undermine the 'real economy' where actual goods and practically useful services are produced. In recent years, according to Magdoff and Foster, corporations have been sitting on trillions of dollars of unutilized cash and cash equivalents. When they do use this money, it is seldom for productive purposes but, more often, 'to pay dividends to stockholders, buy up other companies, or else to buy company stock in the hope of driving share prices up: a pure speculative endeavor' (Magdoff and Foster 2014).

Consistent with that economic criticism are concerns from the perspective of social justice. If economic activity is diverted from maintaining supplies of goods and services, then access to the basic means of subsistence for the poorest people can also become less secure and more difficult. Thus while the respective interests of business owners and their workers can in some ways be antagonistic, both can be adversely affected by financialization, as, too, can those of other members of the community who depend on resources for infrastructure or welfare. Processes of financialization can significantly exacerbate the exploitative tendencies of a capitalist economy. Owners of productive businesses, we may suppose, even when their primary aim is to make profits, have at least some pragmatic interest in maintaining a healthy and able workforce; and their managers may also regard aspects of the human relationships in a firm as important. Financial enterprises, however, tend to be further removed from the realities of human relationships and even from the impacts of their own activities. If the financial sector is allowed untrammelled freedom, accordingly, this tends to be used in favour of the richer and more powerful, but to the detriment of the disadvantaged.

[3] Nor does it necessarily even make for efficiency within the financial sector itself, for, as Donald MacKenzie (2016) has shown, the cost of financial intermediation hasn't fallen over the long term, despite all the technological advances made, since it appears that any benefits of these have been captured by finance's senior employees in the form of higher pay.

Financialization can thus also have unfavourable effects in relation to concerns of social justice. We need not assume that members of the financial elite want, in some psychological sense, to exploit everyone else. Yet there is clearly a problem with the incentive structure instituted in market arrangements when this objectively favours the extraction of short-term 'shareholder value' over longer-term and socially wider interests (Stout 2012; Mazzucato 2013). So if those arrangements can be criticized from the standpoint of economic efficiency they can also be criticized from the perspective of a concern with distributive justice.

Concerns about the effects of financialization processes on social justice are not confined to purely domestic contexts. The political economic linkages between the advanced capitalist economies being deep and extensive, developments tend to affect them in comparable ways, even if, within limits, they can be managed differently. The process has distinctive and amplified effects in the globalized economy more widely. If the period after 1980 in world financial markets was, in the words of George Soros (2008), a 'superbubble', with economic growth becoming dependent on unstable financial relations, then the evidence further shows, according to James K. Galbraith, that 'the superbubble was also a supercrisis for the world's poorer people—a prolonged period of worsening pay gaps in most countries around the world' (Galbraith 2012: 73). Both lower-income countries and lower-income people lost out, while their debts also started to mount at the personal and international levels. The economic elite in the advanced capitalist countries, observes David Harvey (2005), have been drawing heavily on surpluses extracted from the rest of the world through international flows and structural adjustment practices. The elite benefit from the increased financialization of the global economy that they also drive. From the perspectives of concern with both economic productivity and social justice, the global financial system appears to be problematically structured with perverse incentives. As Richard Westra vividly puts it, 'financialization operates with a centrifugal force leeching wealth from material goods production centered activities toward an opaque world existing in the interstices of the globe' (Westra 2010: 98).

Evidently, then, the economic critique of financialization as an unproductive mode of extracting profits and rents from a declining basis of 'real' economic activity is quite consistent with a critique of financialization from the standpoint of a concern with justice, both social and global. For not only is the aggregate 'pie', as produced by 'real economic' activity, diminished in size, but shares of it become increasingly unequal, and in a radically polarized way, involving great hardship and harm to a great many people. Criticisms of those two kinds of problem are mutually consistent in the sense that they imply a solution to the one that could also be a solution to the other: an increase in equality will favour an increase in productivity, while an increase in productivity will support better returns for those on the disadvantaged side of inequalities.

However, this potential solution to the problems of social justice and economic productivity could appear to be at odds with the possibility of dealing effectively with the ecological challenge. From an ecological perspective, there are limits to the extent to which we can continue to increase the use of natural resources and ecosystems, and since we are already transgressing safe planetary boundaries (Rockström et al. 2009) we should not hope to rely on economic growth to deal with distributive injustice; rather, we need to tackle it more directly by way of constraints on ecological overusers and redistribution to the ecologically marginalized.

Before examining the ecological perspective, though, we need to look more carefully at the terms on which the economic and social justice critiques of financialization are compatible. For although it is possible to find a solution that meets the requirements of both economic productivity and social justice, there are also possible solutions to one that would fail to satisfy the requirements of the other. So even before entering the ecological considerations, we need to be clear on the more exact terms of compatibility between the economic and social justice critiques of financialization. This task is complicated, however, by the fact that economists do not agree amongst themselves about exactly how, or even whether, financialization is a problem.

3.3 How Can the Problem of Financialization be Explained?

The criticisms of financialization that we have noted come mainly from economists who could loosely be described as Keynesian. Their understanding is that as financial practices become increasingly unconstrained by the requirements of the productive economy, they can have the kinds of counterproductive effect indicated. Their answer to this problem is to regulate financial markets more firmly while using fiscal measures to regenerate the 'real' economy. On this view, the economy needs to be protected by the state from untrammelled markets and provided with some political management. An opposing school of economic thought, however, takes the view that markets need to be protected from interference by states and that the less the state is involved in the economy the better. From this perspective, the phenomenon of financialization would be perceived, while painful to many in society, as the manifestation of a rational response to a deeper problem. Accordingly, one has to appreciate that to understand the phenomenon may require considering how to reconcile apparently conflicting insights from at least two quite distinct perspectives.

The Keynesian view of macroeconomic prudence came to prevail for certain periods of history in the developed world. Notably, in the decades following World War II, the developed countries adopted broadly Keynesian fiscal and monetary policies to dampen business cycles and to ensure reasonably full employment.

David Harvey speaks of this as a period of 'class compromise' between capital and labour in which domestic stability was assured through a form of political-economic organization—'embedded liberalism' (Ruggie 1982)—in which 'market processes and entrepreneurial and corporate activities were surrounded by a web of social and political constraints and a regulatory environment that sometimes restrained but in other instances led the way in economic and industrial strategy' (Harvey 2005: 11). This, we may also note, is the setting clearly reflected in the period's defining work of political philosophy produced by John Rawls (1971). His theory of justice rigorously focused on questions of normative logic that arise under such material circumstances as pertained in the postwar conditions of the developed countries of North America and Europe. At that time, Western political theorists did not treat international relations as integral to their studies. Insofar as they considered the problem that for poorer or developing countries, including former colonies, the achievement of embedded liberalism was not really possible, they tended to assume that it would in due course become possible thanks to the continued advance of liberal economics and political institutions.

However, before such hoped-for progress could occur in the poorer countries, embedded liberalism began to break down even where it had been successful. The context in which it had arisen was that of the postwar political economic world order constructed within the framework of the Bretton Woods institutions. With the United Nations, the World Bank, the IMF, and the BIS in Basel aiming to help stabilize international relations, free trade in goods 'was encouraged under a system of fixed exchange rates anchored by the US dollar's convertibility into gold at a fixed price' (Harvey 2005: 10). However, the Bretton Woods system was eventually to prove unsustainable, especially as US trade deficits and spending increased to the point that its economic stability appeared to be under real threat. In response, the United States, in 1971, floated the dollar free of gold on the foreign exchanges, but the crucial move was to establish an alternative basis for confidence in the dollar. This came with the deal struck in 1973 with Saudi Arabia, and subsequently with other oil extracting and exporting countries, too, that ushered in the era of the petrodollar.[4]

The agreement of Saudi Arabia to price its oil exports in US dollars meant that international demand for the dollar was assured: for oil importers needed to buy dollars in order to buy oil. The deal made the value of oil revenues to exporters dependent on the health of the US economy, but it also contributed significantly to

[4] Petrodollars may be defined simply as oil revenues denominated in US dollars. The point is they bind in the value of subsoil resources to the United States' economic and monetary systems (Oweiss 1974). The security and military dimension is also central. Oil producers place themselves in a position of dependence vis-à-vis the United States by allowing the value of their export to be contingent on the US maintaining the value of the dollar; in return they also get development assistance, and, especially, a commitment to their security. This is met in significant measure by the provision of armaments that help absorb the petrodollar surplus while also militarily securing allied interests in the region.

the latter. A key benefit for Saudi Arabia and other Western-aligned countries in the Middle East, on the other hand, was that the agreement also involved a commitment to their security. The fact that providing technological modernization and military provision secured US economic interests while also ensuring security for friendly regimes made this a workable deal for both sides, regardless of how equal or otherwise were its terms or how enthusiastic were the different parties to it.[5] This development clearly increased the extent to which the value of money internationally is bound up in complex ways with geopolitical issues.

The upshot of the introduction of the petrodollar system was that where demand for the dollar had been faltering, because it was overpriced against gold, it now soared, as demand for it began to be generated in tandem with the global demand for oil. With oil being used to burn, the increase in dollars circulating resulted in more noticeable inflation than productivity. The 1970s saw a global period of 'stagflation' in which fiscal crises hit some of the most developed countries, and even Britain, for example, had to be bailed out by the IMF. It became apparent, as tax revenues diminished and social expenditures rose, that Keynesian policies were no longer working as they had. So as well as dealing with the dysfunctionality of fixed exchange rates by allowing them to float on markets, it became necessary to critically review the idea that had reigned for some time about how, with an ever-growing economic pie to be shared, the worst off could become ever better off even as the wealthiest became ever richer.[6] By the end of that eventful decade, a dramatic change in political economic policy was looming. The incoming regimes of Thatcher in the UK and Reagan in the United States heralded the abandonment of Keynesianism in favour of the monetarism

[5] Interesting insights into the making of the deal are reported by self-confessed 'Economic Hit Man' John Perkins in his first-hand reflections: 'It was a deal the House of Saud could hardly refuse, given its geographic location, lack of military might, and general vulnerability to neighbors like Iran, Syria, Iraq, and Israel. Naturally, therefore, Washington used its advantage to impose one other critical condition, a condition that redefined the role of ['economic hit men'] in the world and served as a model we would later attempt to apply in other countries, most notably in Iraq. In retrospect, I sometimes find it difficult to understand how Saudi Arabia could have accepted this condition. Certainly, most of the rest of the Arab world, OPEC, and other Islamic countries were appalled when they discovered the terms of the deal.... The condition was that Saudi Arabia would use its petrodollars to purchase U.S. government securities; in turn, the interest earned by these securities would be spent by the U.S. Department of the Treasury in ways that enabled Saudi Arabia to emerge from a medieval society into the modern, industrialized world. In other words, the interest compounding on billions of dollars of the kingdom's oil income would be used to pay U.S. companies to fulfill the vision I (and presumably some of my competitors) had come up with, to convert Saudi Arabia into a modern industrial power. Our own U.S. Department of the Treasury would hire us, at Saudi expense, to build infrastructure projects and even entire cities throughout the Arabian Peninsula' (Perkins 2004: 90). (The significance of these interconnections between financial, geopolitical, and military-industrial interests is further discussed in Chapter 11.)

[6] 'Even before the Arab-Israeli War and the OPEC oil embargo of 1973, the Bretton Woods system of fixed exchange rates backed by gold reserves had fallen into disarray. The porosity of state boundaries with respect to capital flows put stress on the system of fixed exchange rates. US dollars had flooded the world and escaped US controls by being deposited in European banks. Fixed exchange rates were therefore abandoned in 1971. Gold could no longer function as the metallic base of international money; exchange rates were allowed to float, and attempts to control the float were soon abandoned' (Harvey 2005: 12).

promoted by Milton Friedman. This spelled the end of 'embedded liberalism' and the dawn of the era of 'neoliberalism'.

The neoliberal embrace of monetarism marked the ascendancy of a competing political vision to that of social democracy concerning what economic efficiency and social justice consist in. This free market ideology went with the grain of financialization rather than against it. Supporters of liberalizing financial markets believed that this could bring great benefits. They claimed it stimulated competition and innovation while reducing the costs of trading and allowing markets to operate more efficiently. Credit for loans and mortgages would increase and capital could flow more freely across borders; and with enhanced foreign investment, transfer of technology and management skills would follow too—all of which, they would emphasize, are functional for increased growth. With inflation coming to be brought under control in the leading economies, and with buoyant markets, the problem of stagflation seemed to them to have been resolved. Nevertheless, as the final two decades of the millennium saw the unleashing of this counter-Keynesianism on a global scale, a consequence was that asset bubbles became both more frequent and more sizeable.

The downside of this strategy became most publicly apparent by the time of the 2008 financial crash, at which point even Alan Greenspan—the individual who had been in charge of US monetary policy for the previous eighteen years—admitted before a congressional hearing in October 2008 that he had 'made a mistake in presuming that the self-interests of organisations, specifically banks and others, were such that they were best capable of protecting their own shareholders and their equity in the firms'. Setting a new benchmark for bathos, he confessed: 'I discovered a flaw in the model that I perceived is the critical functioning structure that defines how the world works. I had been going for 40 years with considerable evidence that it was working exceptionally well.'[7]

So while Keynesianism and monetarism both seem to have credible points to make in their reciprocal criticisms of each other, the policies of neither camp had been able to head off the crisis tendencies that came to a particular head in 2008, and nor had proponents of either publicly predicted such events. In the decades of ascendant monetarism, most economists seem to have been satisfied that business was working much as usual in the developed economies—indeed, notwithstanding various regional crises, global business was thought by and large to be booming.[8] It seems reasonable to suggest that neither school of thought had a

[7] Greenspan's words were reported in the press at the time, including in the *New York Times* 23 October 2008: https://www.nytimes.com/2008/10/23/business/worldbusiness/23iht-gspan.4.17206624.html [accessed July 2018]

[8] Exceptions, however, were thinkers in certain minority strands of economic thought who had diagnosed a fundamental problem and predicted its outcomes. Post-Keynesians like Hyman P. Minsky and James Tobin, for instance, had identified some of the fundamental issues—including particularly the destabilizing effects of financialization on the rest of the economy. For more on this see Chapter 9.

sufficient understanding of the nature of the problem. Although a proximate cause was quite evidently deregulation of the financial sector, that policy had itself been introduced as a *solution* to problems antecedently perceived. Hence, while Keynesians may not approve of financial deregulation, monetarists had reasons to see it as functional for the capitalist system. Nor does one have to be an apologist for their view to acknowledge this particular point, as we find in the appraisal offered by Magdoff and Foster:

> Financial deregulation in this period was not mainly the product of mere greed and corruption, as is sometimes supposed, nor was it based simply on faulty economic principles; rather it had as its object the further expansion of existing financial bubbles. (Magdoff and Foster 2014: 18)

No financial regulators wanted a major financial bubble to burst on their watch, he points out, so they generally acceded 'when the financial institutions demanded deregulation which would give them more slack and allow them to expand into new, previously restricted markets' (Magdoff and Foster 2014: 19). Financialization, then, can be viewed as a rational response from the perspective of the capitalist economic system to stagnation in the sphere of productivity.

Thus a basic question can be identified, at the level of underlying causation, concerning whether financialization is the problem causing stagnation in productivity or whether heightened activity in the financial sector is a rational market response to the problem of stagnation (Toll 2010). We may stylize this explanatory question in terms of a 'financialization thesis' versus a 'stagnation thesis'.

3.4 Financialization and its Relation to Stagnation: Cause or Effect?

The financialization thesis, as advanced by Thomas Palley, for instance, holds that the problematic changes in macroeconomic patterns and income distribution 'are significantly attributable to financial sector developments' (Palley 2007: 4).[9] The way to deal with the problem, on his account, includes instituting greater policy control over financial markets, making corporations responsive to wider interests than just financial markets, and reasserting political control to counteract the influence of corporations and wealthy elites. This sort of prescription, though,

[9] On Palley's understanding of financialization it is 'a process whereby financial markets, financial institutions, and financial elites gain greater influence over economic policy and economic outcomes. . . . Its principal impacts are to (1) elevate the significance of the financial sector relative to the real sector, (2) transfer income from the real sector to the financial sector, and (3) increase income inequality and contribute to wage stagnation. Additionally, there are reasons to believe that financialization may put the economy at risk of debt deflation and prolonged recession. Financialization operates through three different conduits: changes in the structure and operation of financial markets, changes in the behavior of nonfinancial corporations, and changes in economic policy' (Palley 2007: 2).

could be regarded as somewhat optimistic in its presuppositions, and in two in particular. First, it would require that political processes and policy-making are more amenable to rational control in the public interest, so as to counteract the powerful vested interests of corporations and wealthy elites, than they have seemed to be in recent years. Second, it is optimistic in the more profound matter of whether the underlying problem is still in fact not one of stagnation. Certainly, without calling into dispute any of the ill effects caused by financialization, one can raise critically probing questions about the underlying causes of financialization itself. We need to recognize that ameliorating some of the worst excesses of a problem does not necessarily do anything to resolve the underlying problem of which they are symptoms. In fact, as Palley himself recognizes, ameliorating some symptoms can sometimes exacerbate the problem. He refers to the *paradox of financial reform*: 'reform that stabilizes the system also stands to deepen the tendency to stagnation ... by limiting the possibilities for [financial] exuberance' (Palley 2012: 78).

An alternative thesis, then, is that stagnation is the underlying problem to which financialization has proved to be an unsatisfactory solution. The problem of 'secular stagnation' briefly figured in mainstream economic thinking in the late 1930s, when the American Keynesian economist Alvin H. Hansen[10] coined the term to refer to what he saw as an endemic condition of mature industrialized economies. This condition arises because, as capital investments become more efficient and profitable, the returns are not needed for further capital investment. Thus the modern developed capitalist economy has an enormous capacity to save. If profitable investment opportunities are lacking, then savings translate 'not into real capital formation and sustained growth but into lowered income, mass unemployment, and chronic depression, a condition summed up in the term stagnation' (Sweezy (1982) reproduced in Magdoff and Sweezy 1987: 30). Hansen's proposition became the subject of a high-profile debate in the late 1930s, with Joseph Schumpeter prominently disputing it,[11] but that debate was truncated and rendered moot by World War II. The military-industrial stimulus of the war itself and the reconstructive tasks of the postwar era provided ample scope for investment. To the problem of stagnation there was thus supplied a solution that lasted until the onset of the 1970s. By then, with a great deal of the work of reconstruction done in the most advanced national economies, the productive capacity that had been developed to support it began to fall idle. Not only was

[10] Hansen, a former student of John R. Commons (whose work we will be considering in Chapter 3), and, in turn, a teacher of James Tobin, was influential in imparting a Keynesian framing to economic thinking in the United States.

[11] 'Schumpeter labelled Hansen's theory the "theory of vanishing investment opportunities," and it is an apt characterization' (Sweezy (1982) reproduced in Magdoff and Sweezy 1987: 29–30). Schumpeter challenged Hansen's account of how the weakening of demand for investment comes about.

there a return of stagnation, it was accompanied by inflation. The monetarist policies that underpinned financial reforms, both domestic and global, in response to the perceived failure of Keynesian solutions, had achieved the goal of reducing inflation but sent the economy of the United States and elsewhere into recession.

It is in this context that Marxist economists Sweezy and Magdoff, with colleagues associated with the *Monthly Review*, were to argue that the discussion of stagnation needed to be resumed, and with some urgency. In the early 1980s, while Keynesians and post-Keynesians such as Tobin were concerned that the monetarists' liberalization of finance was having detrimental effects on the 'real economy', Magdoff and Sweezy were clear that financialization was functional for capitalism in the context of a tendency to stagnation. It was not that they were oblivious to the ills of financialization but they sought to probe deeper into their underlying causes.

> Does the casino society in fact channel far too much talent and energy into financial shell games? Yes, of course. No sensible person could deny it. Does it do so at the expense of producing real goods and services? Absolutely not. There is no reason whatever to assume that if you could deflate the financial structure, the talent and energy now employed there would move into productive pursuits. They would simply become unemployed and add to the country's already huge reservoir of idle human and material resources. Is the casino society a significant drag on economic growth? Again, absolutely not. What growth the economy has experienced in recent years, apart from that attributable to an unprecedented peacetime military build-up, has been almost entirely due to the financial explosion. (Magdoff and Sweezy 1987: 149)[12]

Under conditions of oligopolistic capitalism, the polarized distribution of income and wealth reduces the effective spending power of the many, so this wider suppression of income levels suppresses demand, and therefore the underlying growth dynamic of the capitalist system is set to a condition of stagnation. Financialization is a means to overcome stagnation, but it can temporarily achieve this only by further exacerbating the underlying problem that real productive activity is stagnant. The boom in sales of various kinds of financial product does not represent any actual increase in any real wealth in the system. Thus Sweezy warned that the ballooning of the financial sector would not be a sustainable solution to the problem and that it harboured crisis-inducing tendencies. Accordingly, his recommendation at the time was:

> rather than wait around for a miracle (or an irretrievable disaster), it is high time to dedicate our thoughts and energies to replacing the present economic system with one which operates to satisfy human needs and not as a mere by-product of

[12] As will be noted in Chapter 4, the standard rankings of jurisdictions according to their GDP sees tax havens among those at the top of the list.

> the presence or absence of investment opportunities attractive to a relative handful of socially irresponsible capitalists.
>
> (Sweezy (1982) in Magdoff and Sweezy 1987: 36–7)

This was not a mainstream view, however, and for many years, until around 2008, it was almost exclusively those Marxist scholars—notably Magdoff and Sweezy—who focused on the problem of chronic stagnation as a critical feature of the advanced stages of the socially irresponsible system of the global capitalist economy. Keynesians meanwhile appear to have believed that the problem of stagnation was being avoided.[13]

Since the financial crash of 2008, however, the agenda of mainstream economic discussion has changed again, with economists such as Lawrence Summers and Paul Krugman recently making public pronouncements on how to deal with the rediscovered problem of secular stagnation. Summers, not being a Marxist, and far from finding the crash to be a predictable effect of a fundamentally irresponsible system of economic organization, has reflected on how not only the financial crisis itself, but also the subsequent response of markets to it, took economists by surprise. The very low official interest rates that have since the crash prevailed in developed countries—being close to zero in the United States and even dipping into the negative in parts of Europe[14]—would have been expected to fuel inflation, according to standard economic assumptions, yet low inflation has remained the predominant concern of most leading central banks. Finding this to be an unprecedented situation, both Summers and Krugman think it is best understood as a manifestation of secular stagnation, and thus as an implicit challenge to the consensus view on macroeconomic policy objectives inherited from the 1980s. This was the view that inflation should be kept low and stable, with independent central banks setting targets in order to control expectations. The danger in monetary policy is now thought to lie 'not in politicians eager to inflate away problems but in bankers refusing to generate enough demand to bring inflation up to target levels and permit reductions in real interest rates' (Summers 2016: 6). Meanwhile, fiscal policy is attributed renewed significance as a tool in economic

[13] At any rate, this is what N. Gregory Mankiw writes in 1992: 'some early Keynesians feared that the economy might suffer from "secular stagnation" if the propensity to save were too great. By contrast, few economists today believe that excessive saving threatens the economy. Instead, almost all economists now believe that additional saving will, in the long run, lead to additional investment rather than inadequate aggregate demand. Indeed, rather than being concerned with excessive saving, most American economists fear that the U.S. saving rate is inadequate to maintain America's high standard of living' (Mankiw 1992: 562). Mankiw even speaks of Friedman 'winning the hearts and minds' of his generation (1992: 563): 'In many ways, the Keynesian economics of the 1990s does not look like the Keynesian economics of the 1930s, or even that of the 1960s.... Indeed, new Keynesian economics may appear more similar to the classical economics of David Hume, or even to the monetarist economics of Milton Friedman' (Mankiw 1992: 560).

[14] Government bond yields were negative in Europe and the United States; short-term official interest rates were negative only in a small number of places (most notably Sweden). I am grateful to Iain Hardie for this clarification (personal correspondence).

stabilization: 'An expansionary fiscal policy can reduce national savings, raise neutral real interest rates, and stimulate growth' (Summers 2016: 7). Summers notes that 'Keynes, writing in a similar situation during the late 1930s, rightly emphasized the need for policy approaches that both promoted business confidence—the cheapest form of stimulus—and increased labor compensation' (Summers 2016: 7). Summers sees the prospects of fiscal expansion raising demand on a global basis. So although he presents secular stagnation as a 'potentially permanent' condition, Summers nevertheless appears to think it can quite readily be transformed by implementing appropriate—and quite standard Keynesian—policy. He invokes Keynes' own metaphor to depict the situation:

> A car with a broken alternator won't move at all—yet it takes only a simple repair to get it going. In much the same way, secular stagnation does not reveal a profound or inherent flaw in capitalism. Raising demand is actually not that difficult, and it is much easier than raising the capacity to produce. The crucial thing is for policymakers to diagnose the problem correctly and make the appropriate repairs. (Summers 2016: 9)

Krugman, broadly endorsing that view, argues that the secular stagnation hypothesis has some radical implications. It means recognizing that the financial crisis itself is not over and that most of what would be done with the aim of preventing a future crash would be counterproductive: 'even improved financial regulation is not necessarily a good thing', he suggests, because 'it may discourage irresponsible lending and borrowing at a time when more spending of any kind is good for the economy' (Krugman 2013). Of course, he thinks, *responsible* lending would be preferable—and lending for the pursuit of worthy goals, like green technology, for instance, would be best—but irresponsible lending is, from his point of view, better than nothing. His Keynesian point is to get things moving; and, like Keynes, he shows a notable indifference in this to the substantive purposes of human beings having an economy in the first place. Conditions of stagnation are those 'in which Keynes's hypothetical policy of burying currency in coalmines and letting the private sector dig it up—or my version, which involves faking a threat from nonexistent space aliens—becomes a good thing' (Krugman 2013).[15] Spending is good, no matter what on, because

[15] The passage from Keynes that Krugman has in mind is this: 'If the Treasury were to fill old bottles with banknotes, bury them at suitable depths in disused coalmines which are then filled up to the surface with town rubbish, and leave it to private enterprise on well-tried principles of laissez-faire to dig the notes up again (the right to do so being obtained, of course, by tendering for leases of the note-bearing territory), there need be no more unemployment and, with the help of the repercussions, the real income of the community, and its capital wealth also, would probably become a good deal greater than it actually is. It would, indeed, be more sensible to build houses and the like; but if there are political and practical difficulties in the way of this, the above would be better than nothing' (Keynes 2008: 116).

> the resulting investment boom would have given us several years of much higher employment, with no real waste, since the resources employed would otherwise have been idle. OK, this is still mostly standard, although a lot of people hate, just hate, this kind of logic—they want economics to be a morality play, and they don't care how many people have to suffer in the process. (Krugman 2013)

We do not need to think of economics as a morality play, however, to pose reasonable questions about just how far from reality Krugman's profession has moved that it can seriously equate pointless activity with productive activity. It seems fair to ask about the longer-term prospects beyond a boom that gives 'several years' of higher employment, particularly in a context where 'real waste' in resources would not be the idling of labour but the dissipation of the earth's ecological capacities. In the absence of serious consideration of such questions, I suggest, there is, in the position he announces, manifest irresponsibility of both material and moral kinds.

If the cure for the ills of financialization entails a commitment to material and moral irresponsibility, then one's understanding of the initial problem is somewhat called into question. Financialization was initially characterized as an undermining of the social purpose of economic activity; but the Keynesian response to financialization seems to have little direct connection with any social purpose of economic activity. Snapshots of unemployment statistics are treated as proxies for how well people's lives and livelihoods are going, and monetary indices like GDP are treated as proxies for social wealth and welfare. If economic life were really guided by social purpose, the whole question of how financialization bears on the 'real economy' might appear differently than it does to mainstream economists. A feature of the 'real economy', on mainstream assumptions, is that it must continually grow. It is true that this imperative is immanent within a capitalist economic system, for this is an inherently dynamic mode of production that is indeed likely to collapse if it does not continue to grow, and it is indeed likely to cause disproportionate social upheaval when production is stagnant. But if stagnation is peculiarly a problem for a specific kind of economy, the question arises whether the real problem might lie with the kind of economy that is prone to suffer when growth falters. The question is scarcely an idle one, given not only the apparent facts of secular stagnation but also reasonable and prudent speculation about the ultimate 'external' imperative for a dynamic economy, in a finite environment, to achieve a 'steady state'.

So the problem of financialization can be explained as a cause of stagnation, or as an effect of it, or as both. That leads to questions about what kind of a problem stagnation is that we should care so much about it as to shape entire strategies of monetary policy or fiscal policy, or both, to deal with it. In thinking a little more carefully exactly how stagnation is a problem, we may find it appropriate to reintroduce to the picture both morality and materiality. Insofar as these are methodologically abstracted from by the mainstream economic critique of financialization, that critique itself can be criticized immanently. This would proceed from the basis that, for all that Krugman and Summers may proclaim they are laying down a 'radical manifesto', their inquiry allows certain problematic assumptions to stand unchallenged. For them, no underlying explanation for the problem of stagnation is offered or needed—it is likened to the breaking of a relatively simple component of a car engine that just needs fixing or replacing. It is the failure of a component, in other words, not a failure of the system. The idea that capitalism itself might be called into question is implicitly cast as such an inappropriate overreaction to the problem as not to warrant considered attention. But to be *radical*, as Marx famously reminded us, means to get at the *root*. It is far from evident that the new Keynesians get to the root of the problem.

3.5 Why Is Stagnation a Problem?

Financialization is explained as a problem by reference to the stagnation that it causes, according to Keynesians, whereas, for monetarists, it is not so much a cause of as a response to the problem of stagnation. They could both be right, since stagnation and financialization could reciprocally cause each other. The central point is that stagnation is a fundamental issue of concern for mainstream economists.

From those mainstream perspectives, it is inconceivable that stagnation could be regarded as anything other than a bad thing. Stagnation refers to conditions under which economic growth, according to certain indicators, particularly GDP, is sluggish, static, or negative. With these conditions, interest rates, profits, and employment rates will all tend to fall, markets will become unstable, and these processes will tend to exacerbate each other. While there can always be hope that the low point in a business cycle will be succeeded, in due course, by renewed expansion, there is no inherent systemic guarantee this will happen. The idea of *secular* stagnation is used to refer to circumstances where there is no clear path back towards sustained growth. The effects of weak growth become more persistent and harder to weather as the gains inherited from more buoyant times become exhausted. Difficulties for businesses arise from the contraction of their activities and the diminution of their profits; difficulties for ordinary people are experienced as increased unemployment and lower incomes relative to prices.

If stagnation is a problem, then, this is because growth is a functional necessity for the dynamic system that is the capitalist mode of production. If we think outside the particular constraints of that system, though, the need for constant growth appears less clear-cut. There can be a need for growth in an economy when it does not produce the goods and services that the society needs; but once it is able to deliver those on a sustainable basis there is no inherent reason for it to continue growing. What I am suggesting, then, is that stagnation is only clearly a problem for an economic system that has an internal imperative to maintain its growth dynamic in order to function.

To appreciate the specificity of that perspective, let us consider the matter from the contrasting perspective of a concern to achieve an overarching social goal such as ensuring that nobody lacks sufficient access to goods and services for at least a minimally decent life. I shall refer to this, for short, as *the social perspective.*

Seen from the social perspective, the significance of economic growth has three aspects: quantitative, qualitative, and distributive. Quantitatively measured, the volume of productive activity has to be great enough in aggregate to supply the whole social requirement; qualitatively assessed, what is supplied has to be of an appropriate material nature to meet the requirement; the distributive concern is that what is supplied has to reach everybody in due proportion. Failure to achieve the social imperative can, correspondingly, arise in any or all of three ways: aggregate social product may be quantitatively insufficient; the particular goods produced may not be qualitatively appropriate to meet all the particular needs that have a claim to be met, or their production may entail by-products that are detrimental to the meeting of needs; the total goods produced, even if in aggregate they may be sufficient in quantity and quality, are not distributed in such a manner that all adequately benefit. The first failure is remedied by increasing the aggregate volume of production; the second by better regulating the quality and substantive goals of production (including with attention to environmental by-product effects); the third by adopting appropriate fiscal or other distributive measures. Thus, the quality and distribution of growth, and not simply its volume, matter from this perspective.

From the social perspective, there is no reason for a blanket presumption that 'growth is good'. Growth is good to the extent that it serves to meet the social imperative; growth is harmful if its pursuit militates against that service. Correspondingly, the faltering of growth, should it occur in an economy, is not necessarily or unconditionally a bad thing. For instance, if and when the pursuit of growth involves harmful or destructive activities, then the social imperative would be to curtail it; or if the quality of growth is not socially beneficial, then there is no imperative to pursue it or to think it 'good'. Such qualitative considerations set the social perspective off from the Keynesian view that pointless activities can be worthwhile if they get people employed and incomes rising. From the social perspective, it is not the volume of market transactions per se that matters, and if levels of unemployment or income matter it is because of what these mean in terms of human fulfilment, social esteem, and access to the means of life, livelihood, and welfare. After all, a life of leisure is not necessarily an unattractive prospect if one has the wherewithal—material and cultural—to enjoy it, and so whether unemployment is a good or bad thing for a person may depend on the social and economic circumstances they find themselves in. Likewise, a lack of income is not a problem if one has free access to all one needs without having to pay money, and so, again, it is a problem that only arises under determinate types of socio-economic circumstance: by contrast, a society with socialized health, education, and transport systems combined with cooperative production units, for instance, needs to rely a lot less on incomes than a society in which everything comes with a monetary price attached.

So perpetual growth, where development has reached a point of material sufficiency, is not a *necessary* condition of basic social and economic well-being. It is no wonder, therefore, that critics of the mainstream consensus in economics and policy-making question the tenability of GDP as an indicator of substantive well-being (e.g. Layard 2011; Philipsen 2015). An economy is defined as growing, on the consensus view, when key indicators, particularly GDP, show a clear positive rate of increase, but one can question whether a rise in GDP is a necessary condition for addressing the ills associated with unemployment and low incomes. Doubtful, too, of course, is whether it could be a sufficient condition, given that an economy can grow under circumstances of social inequality whereby high profits may be taken by the owners of capital while workers are paid low wages and a large reserve of unemployed people serves to make the low-paid workers feel glad of the little they have.

On the question of if and why stagnation is a problem viewed from a social perspective, then, an answer would be nuanced. Certainly, there are problems if its effects compromise people's livelihoods. But if the effects arise due to maldistribution rather than insufficient aggregate production levels, then the root of the problem would not seem necessarily to be lack of quantitative growth. Hence a social perspective differs from the mainstream economic perspective. It also challenges any political theory premised on the idea that quantitative growth is also necessary for dealing with challenges of distributive justice—whether that would be by means of 'trickle down', as monetarists (and libertarians) imagine, or by more conscious social democratic policy-making, as Keynesians (and political liberals) believe.

So although there seems to be congruence between mainstream Keynesian economics and concern with social justice and social democracy, its basis is shallow, conditional, and transient. If as much attention is paid to distributive matters as to quantitative ones, the case for growth is not so unconditional, viewed from a social perspective, as it is assumed to be on mainstream economic assumptions.

A further critical question that follows, if growth is not necessarily good, is whether it may not actually, under certain circumstances, be *bad*. Such a thought is anathema to mainstream economics. Considering this possibility means broadening the conceptual frame.

3.6 Conclusion

This chapter has considered the kind of good that finance is when it is fulfilling a valuable function in the pursuit of worthwhile social purposes, and it has sought to offer a correspondingly broad framing account of what goes wrong—in relation to its valuable function—under circumstances that can be described as financialization.

At the outset we noted three principal perspectives on what is socially valuable and can be vitiated by financialization, each of which centres on a fundamental desideratum: economic productivity, social justice, and ecological sustainability. From each perspective, we can consider in terms both descriptive and normative how finance can function *as it should* and also about how it *can go wrong*. When functioning as it should, from the point of view of economic productivity, valuable goods and services are produced in the necessary abundance and quality. From a social justice perspective, the goods and services are not only produced in aggregate sufficiency but they are also allocated and distributed according to principles of social justice. From a perspective of ecological sustainability, productive activities should be organized in such a way as to preserve the ecological preconditions of their own continuation.

The main focus for this chapter was on the economic criteria. The key criticism of financialization from this perspective is that the financial sector pursues profits by means of purely financial activity that is not productively harnessed to the 'real economy' in which tangible goods and services are produced and exchanged. This tends to exacerbate economic inequalities by drawing command of resources away from widely distributed economic activities into a few hands at the apex of financial system. Different views on how to respond to the circumstances of financialization depend on different understandings of how, if at all, they are problematic. The broadly Keynesian view of financialization as a problem arising from excessive deregulation of the financial sector is contested by monetarists who see deregulation as a rational response to problems caused by political interference with the operation of markets. Interestingly, while Marxian political economists are in normative agreement with Keynesians that the financial system does not serve the desired socio-economic ends of finance, they are also in accord with the monetarists in seeing as self-contradictory the idea that in an economic system that determines value by market prices there can be some basis of economic values other than what market prices determine. The Marxian position is that we should just not assume that a financial system constrained to serve a capitalist economy is capable of delivering the valuable functions sought from finance. Even the goal of productivity founders when owners of capital accumulate more claims to resources and labour than ecology and humanity can deliver; the goal of social justice is scarcely promoted thereby; and nor is that of ecological sustainability.

So it is possible to see the three kinds of critique of financialization as mutually consistent, but only if one takes a view of economic productivity that is at odds with that assumed by orthodox economists. The question now to consider, accordingly, is whether there is good reason to take a more ecological view of the 'real economy'.

4
Financialization and the 'Real Economy': an Ecological Perspective

Chapter 3 introduced the claim made by some economists that the processes referred to as financialization tend to undermine productivity in the 'real economy'. This chapter examines that claim from an ecological perspective, viewing the economy not only as a set of institutionalized practices that people engage in, but also as material interaction with the natural world. By taking this view, one can appreciate how the economists' claim can be true without this entailing that financialization, in virtue of reducing productivity, will tend to ease pressures on ecological systems. It is important to establish this point because increased economic productivity is generally associated with increased ecological pressure, and this might mistakenly be taken to imply as a corollary an ecological case for welcoming the adverse effects of financialization on the 'real economy'. The argument of this chapter is, rather, that the ecological critique entails a more careful examination of the terms of the contrast between financial activity and economic productivity.

Section 4.1 establishes that it is possible to accept the economists' claim that financialization is problematic in that it undermines productivity while nonetheless also maintaining that productivity does need to be constrained. For it can be the case both that processes of financialization inhibit productivity and that those processes do not necessarily inhibit ecological destructiveness. The possibility of ecological destruction without growth does not imply the possibility of economic growth without ecological destruction. The latter possibility, however, cannot be ruled out without further investigation. In fact, a counter-criticism sometimes made of the appeal to ecological limits is that it naïvely conflates the realm of economic valuation with that of material natural processes. However, if the economic perspective is more sophisticated than the ecological, it is also more puzzling, in relation to the claim that is the focus of our attention here. The economists who argue that purely financial activity can and should be distinguished from real economic productivity appear, in their response to the ecological challenge, to elide that very distinction. So the question then is, if the realm of economic valuation is distinct from that of materiality, in what sense is it 'real' while the financial system is not?

Section 4.2 considers how the financial system is 'less real' by reference to the difference between money and tangible assets. Money does not have any use apart from the value it has in exchange for things that are useful. In fact, with the highly leveraged forms of money in the financial system today, any connection between money and real assets is loosened still further. A fundamental problem, though, is that while money may not represent actually existing assets, it does represent forward-looking claims on those who have been credited with it as debt. In order to meet their obligations they are driven to try and earn more money. Across the economy this process is manifest as a drive for quantitative growth. This drive has little regard to the actual benefits or harms it may yield for human society or the natural world. The critique of financialization from a social justice perspective is thus shown to align with an ecological critique.

By contrast, conventional economic accounting of productivity does not deliver the clear contrast with finance that the critique appealing to it might have us expect. As Section 4.3 discusses, the distinction between the financial and the economically productive spheres is not very clear in practice, and some critical economists argue that it is illusory. A key observation is that both economics and finance are centrally about *business*. People engage in business for profit, and what happens under conditions of financialization can be seen as an intensification of the domination of the profit motive. Profits have no necessary correlation with productivity, and can sometimes even be achieved by liquidating or exhausting productive capacities. Profits taken under a capitalist system of ownership accrue to private actors whose allegiances and time horizon are far more restricted than those of wider societies.

So the argument of this chapter is that in order to understand what kind of problem the concept of financialization refers to, it is necessary first to clarify what, by contrast, the idea of a 'real economy' refers to.

4.1 The Critique of Financialization from an Ecological Perspective

The argument of this section is that if it is true, as some economists argue, that the processes they refer to as financialization undermine economic productivity, it does not necessarily follow that those processes ought to be welcomed by those who, from an ecological perspective, are concerned to restrict economic growth.

To start with, we should register the point that, on standard assumptions of mainstream economics, according to which economic growth is always desirable, any suggestion that it should be reduced would seem perverse. In Chapter 3, however, we distinguished quantitative, qualitative, and distributive aspects of growth, showing that the economic concern is restricted to the first of these, and is largely indifferent to the others. Concern from an ecological perspective is not 'anti-growth' in some totalizing or dogmatic way, even in the quantitative sense, and it can be consistent with being pro-growth on the qualitative and distributive dimensions. What is problematized is an *unconditional* attachment to quantitative growth. For it is necessary to heed the nature-given constraints of ecological systems. In saying this, I should emphasize that to *heed* constraints found in the natural world is not to assume they operate as a deterministic expression of natural processes or leave human beings no 'room to manouevre' in their responses, but it is to recognize how it is nonetheless circumscribed.[1] The point is made with particular clarity by the group of scientists who have spoken of an ecologically 'safe operating space' within which human activities may develop and expand (Rockström et al. 2009). That 'space' is bounded within limits of tolerance identified for the major planetary systems. Human beings engage in activities that cause changes to those systems beyond the limits of tolerance at their peril. The authors have identified boundaries for nine planetary systems: climate change, ocean acidification, stratospheric ozone, the nitrogen and phosphorus cycles, global freshwater use, land system change, the rate of biological diversity loss, chemical pollution, and atmospheric aerosol loading. They estimate that humanity has already transgressed the boundaries for climate change, biodiversity, and nitrogen. This means that we already face the possibility of reaching 'tipping points', where unexpected and uncontrollable change may ensue, including changes thereby caused in other systems.

The planetary boundaries, then, while drawn with some necessary approximateness towards their outer limits, roughly demarcate the degree of ecological change that is consistent with the continuance of life on Earth as human beings know it. (Concerns for other creatures or for less critical ecological features could require respect for more narrowly drawn boundaries.) A point to emphasize is that no conceivable 'technological fix' can be expected to create more operating space beyond the boundaries. Furthermore, the boundaries are interdependent, and transgressing one may shift other boundaries or cause them to be transgressed. The authors also emphasize the distributive dimension of any 'negotiations' within the outer zone of tolerance, for the 'social impacts of transgressing boundaries will be a function of the social–ecological resilience of the affected societies' (Rockström et al. 2009: 31).

Within the 'safe operating space', there can be considerable leeway for humans to make specific and localized decisions whose consequences do not individually threaten planetary systems. Yet the consequences of generalizing such decisions, in the absence of coordination with respect to overarching constraints, could be

[1] In fact, different kinds and degrees of constraint would be highlighted from different normative ecological perspectives, ranging from those that have regard primarily to the sustainability of the economic enterprise itself, through those that embrace a richer variety of distinctively ecological desiderata, to some quite radical biospheric egalitarian positions (see e.g. Hayward 1995, 1998).

critical. This is why ecological problems are sometimes depicted as 'free rider' problems on the model of a 'tragedy of the commons'.[2] For it can be individually rational to exploit a natural resource for localized short-term gain but collectively irrational to do so when the aggregate effect is to undermine the very possibility of anyone gaining anything. The basic problem of political ecology could be regarded as one of institutionalizing collective rationality. In this respect, the task is akin to the kind that political economists undertake, and it is in fact arguable that today we need an approach to political economy that recognizes the task as part of its own (Hayward 1992, 1995: ch. 3).

The theory and practice of political economy involves finding solutions to such collective action problems as arise because the productive capabilities of humans can be developed, utilized, and exploited in a variety of different ways, with different kinds of social impact and with different distributive effects. Technologically advanced societies tend to have more complex and mediated integration into natural systems than is typical in more traditional subsistence economies. They also have power to alter natural processes in quite dramatic, and potentially even devastating, ways. Under the circumstances of advanced global capitalism, technological mediations distance many of us in the developed world from any very clear appreciation of the effects of our economic activities. Natural scientific studies of the material implications of this mode of production nevertheless reveal it to be ecologically disruptive, while social scientific inquiry shows it to involve some egregious maldistribution of costs and benefits.

If financialization processes tend to exacerbate the destructive and unjust tendencies of this problematic mode of production, then even when 'real' economic activity seems to be stagnating, the adverse effects of it could still continue. In other words, it is possible to accept the economists' criticism, that processes of financialization can *inhibit* productivity, while also recognizing that to inhibit economic productivity is not necessarily to inhibit ecological destructiveness.

What has also to be borne in mind, though, is that the possibility of ecological destruction without economic growth does not imply the possibility of economic growth without ecological destruction. To posit the hypothesis of a potential 'decoupling' of 'economic production' from 'ecological consumption' is one thing; it is quite another to demonstrate its application in the world, as Ward et al. (2016) show, especially when the actual trajectory of global economic development has already brought us to critical ecological thresholds and, on current trends, risks pushing us further over them. An underlying concern is that the tendency of 'business as usual' under capitalism is necessarily expansionary, since capitalism is an inherently dynamic system of production, and so there are always likely to be tensions between business goals and ecological constraints. A more

[2] The *locus classicus* of this idea is Hardin (1968); for an insightful discussion see Ostrom (2008).

specific concern about financialization is that it drives businesses to expand while at the same time undermining the abilities of governing institutions to constrain them. The deregulatory tendencies characterizing financialization itself come increasingly to be applied to businesses in productive sectors too. What this means is that ecologically rational constraints can be relaxed or even removed so that the costs to business of exploiting natural resources are reduced. As a consequence, it can become more 'economically viable' to exploit relatively marginal resources at quite considerable ecological expense.

So there is reason to think that processes of financialization *exacerbate* a problem that is inherent in the capitalist mode of production. This view differs from that of the mainstream economists who do not accept that the ecological problem is an unavoidable consequence of the mode of production. Their position is that with the development of appropriate technologies, the connection between economic productivity and ecological destructiveness can be 'decoupled'. A question that remains, however, is if economic growth is measured in terms that do not necessarily relate to any material impacts, then in what sense can it be differentiated from the immaterial sphere of finance? The possibility of clearly differentiating between 'purely financial' activity and 'real' economic productivity presupposes a cogent conceptualization of each of them. In Sections 4.2 and 4.3, respectively, I show how the ecological perspective allows greater conceptual cogency than does the mainstream economic perspective when considering financial activity and economic productivity.

4.2 Money and Finance from an Ecological Perspective

Money, as we have already had occasion to observe, is a strange phenomenon compared to any others of our experience. We experience its effects, and even its lack, as a peculiarly powerful force in the world, and yet in itself it has no intrinsic value, purpose, meaning, or even existence. Sometimes we think of money as *representing* things we value, and this comes quite naturally given our habit of heeding the monetary *price* of things. Yet the correspondence of a token of money and any item in the world is highly contingent, conditional and often even quite fleeting. If the world is described from a purely ecological perspective, there is nothing in it that would be called money. There are printing presses and silicon processors transforming matter and energy; there are tally sticks and metal coins resisting entropic processes over periods of quite some years, even centuries; but these material things qua material things are not money. Money only exists as a phenomenon in our collective mental representations of it.

This fact, that money has what is ultimately a merely *notional* existence, means that conceptually it is quite distinguishable from *wealth* constituted by tangible assets. Of course, we are accustomed to counting money itself as an asset that can be held as wealth, but there is still a significant conceptual distinction between them. It is the thought of such a distinction, after all, that lies at the root of the critique of financialization in the name of economic productivity. Financialization involves processes that tend to treat money as having its own reality and value, quite independently of any collateral in the material world. This, according to the critique, is a mistake, and one that can have harmful consequences.

Money, however, comes in different forms, and they can stand at greater or lesser remove from underlying real assets (Mehrling 2013). For instance, money in the form of gold, a substance quite widely sought after, independently of its use in particular monetary systems, can reasonably be regarded as having a relatively direct basis in real collateral. Banknotes issued as promissory notes against gold held as collateral have a more mediated real basis. Money issued by banks on a fractional reserve basis have a proportionately less direct relation again. A fundamental concern with the financial system today is that, because modern banks, through fractional reserve lending and further instruments of leverage, are permitted to create money by lending vastly in excess of their reserves, indebtedness itself is allowed to count as an asset.

Two points regarding this concern should be noted: one is that to create money as debt is not necessarily to create wealth, since money is itself distinguishable from wealth. The second point is that to create money as debt is to create incentives to engage in activities that bring a monetary return, but without regard to whether anything that could be accounted as real wealth is created in the process. To be sure, when a bank issues credit, this can potentially enable the debtor to produce some wealth that would otherwise not have been possible. However, all that the debtor has a definite requirement, or thus a clear motivation, to do is to get more money in takings than is due to be repaid. Taking more money is not necessarily the same as creating any wealth. If this point may not be obvious from the standpoint of individual agents who can use money they take to buy tangible goods, it becomes evident when thinking about a society as a whole. If you increase the amount of wealth available in a society—understood as the sum value of its goods and services—then you do just that, namely, increase the amount of wealth available in that society. If, by contrast, you increase the amount of money in a society, then you may find that any given sum of it will have the power to command less wealth; if you inflate the amount of money far enough, you can bring it to the point of virtual worthlessness. Merely increasing the amount of money in circulation does nothing to increase society's wealth if it is not absorbed into activities that produce some good or service that otherwise would not have been produced.[3] So, while producing an increase in tangible wealth requires effort

[3] As for money in the form of debts issued by banks, an important point was emphasized some ninety years ago by Frederick Soddy, in a book that presaged the market crash of 1929, about how this differs from real wealth—of the kind represented in buildings, machinery, oil, or livestock:'Debts are

and resources, money can—when credited in leveraged forms—be increased without limit. It is this basic disparity that is exploited to such extraordinarily powerful effect by agents in the financial sector today. Of course, in order for this to work, the money created as debt has to be indistinguishable in practice from the money that is backed by tangible assets. That is made possible by a banking system that allows the intermingling of different forms of money from decidedly different kinds of source.[4]

Insofar as financialization is a process of allowing increasingly leveraged forms of money to enter the financial system, it can be seen as an intensification of tendencies inherent in capitalism. Because capitalism as an economic system is characterized by productive efforts whose aim is to accumulate, it follows that if easier alternative ways of accumulating become possible, then the making of more tangibly productive efforts loses motivation. Hence we have seen an increasing tendency by companies from productive sectors to move into financial business as highlighted by the economic critique of financialization. That critique examines the matter from the standpoint of capitalists' motivations.

A critique from the standpoint of social justice concerns includes the perspective of those whose individual productive efforts have the aim of securing a livelihood. For the more they have to work to pay off debt, in an economy whose productive forces are geared decreasingly to furnishing life's wants for the mass of ordinary people, the harder times become for them. Ordinary people can become materially worse off in the face of an apparently buoyant economy, while in the meantime inequalities intensify. In order to grasp this, the social critique presses substantive concerns about productivity that go beyond what registers from the economic perspective. It emphasizes a difference that can be effaced by economic indicators of productivity, namely, between what really needs to be produced for socially-endorsable reasons and what needs to be produced simply in order to service mounting bank-driven debit–credit arrangements.

A crucial point is that while money may not represent actually existing assets, it does represent claims on those people who have been credited with it as debt. In order that debts be repaid, and with interest, borrowers have to earn more money. Reiterated throughout the economy, this process generates a systemic imperative for the total value of transactions in the economy to perpetually increase. When

subject to the laws of mathematics rather than physics. Unlike wealth, which is subject to the laws of thermodynamics, debts do not rot with old age and are not consumed in the process of living. On the contrary, they grow at so much per cent per annum, by the well-known mathematical laws of simple and compound interest...' (Soddy 1926: 70).

[4] This will be discussed more fully in Chapter 9, which also considers how, in virtue of its control over how money is produced even within notionally sovereign states, the contemporary banking system can perpetuate a dynamic that effectively requires the global economy to pursue the imperative of perpetual growth—regardless of how socially desirable or economically sustainable the pursuit of that goal may be.

the creation of money has the form of credit there will always be people, moving forwards in time, who are obliged together to produce more than was produced previously in order to service the debt.[5] Since every piece of money is itself a piece of debt, then every piece that is destined to be repaid carries with it an additional debt that, as a matter of conceptual logic, will never be repaid; therefore the system has to keep on expanding. And because, along the way, individual repayments become due, stuff does need to be produced on pain of foreclosure against what one has already had. This is regardless of what actual benefits the continuous expansion of economic activity might yield or what damaging consequences it might have for human society or the natural world.

Thus while financial transactions today occur at a scale and velocity such as to exceed any direct correlation with material events beyond the electronic movements that convey them, we are aware that financial crises, and even more routine price fluctuations, can have devastating consequences at a human scale in socio-economic reality. It is something of a tragic irony that occurrences within such a rarefied financial system—and one operated, moreover, by a relative handful of people globally—can have such massive tangible consequences for so many other people.

The critique of financialization from a social justice perspective can thus be seen to align with an ecological critique. For the same tragic dialectic is revealed by both: the impossibility of generating sufficient wealth to redeem all debts—when the process of debt creation is in several ways literally endless—leads to never-ending, and thus ultimately desperate, attempts to generate more wealth. That creates a treadmill for working people and also, we are starting to realize, eventual devastation for the natural world that constitutes the site and materials of the ceaselessly expanding activity. The system of financial debt can thus ultimately yield consequences aptly described as *ecological debt* (Hayward 2008).

The idea of ecological debt need not be understood on the model of quantifiable liabilities on an accountant's balance sheet, or even on the model of legal liabilities of remedy or reparation. The idea was originally invoked by campaigners of developing countries, particularly in Latin America, as a moral counterweight to the external monetary debts they had been saddled with under structural adjustment programmes imposed by international financial institutions. The idea is intended to capture a paradigmatically distinct way of explicating the critical question of *who, as a matter of justice, owes what to whom and why*. In view of how industrialized countries pursue highly indebted developing countries for their financial debts, at great cost to the millions who subsequently go without vital health and education services, the argument refers to a much greater debt: 'the debt accumulated by Northern, industrial countries toward Third World countries on

[5] The problem is compounded by increases in the indebtedness of individuals and families due to having to meet costs resulting from cutbacks in public services.

account of resource plundering, environmental damage, and the free occupation of environmental space to deposit wastes, such as greenhouse gases, from the industrial countries' (Acción Ecológica 2000: 1). With this rhetorical turning of the tables, the challenge is framed as a case for a dramatic shift of perspective on the relations—both economic and moral—between rich and poor.

The concept of ecological debt is thus invoked as a wide-ranging demand for greater justice in relations between rich and poor nations.[6] Ecological concerns are integrated with social ones. If this makes the concept seem unsuitable for application in analytical accountancy, a crucial point of invoking it is to challenge the assumptions about what monetary entries in an account actually represent in the real world. It is to reveal the material and moral shape of the problem that monetary indices will never suffice to grasp. This point has been well-understood by Pope Francis who affirms the applicability of 'a real "ecological debt", particularly between the global North and South, connected to commercial imbalances with consequences in the ecological sphere, as well as the disproportionate use of natural resources made historically by certain countries' (Pope Francis 2015: §51). His critical perspective combines material and moral considerations:

[6] This would include recognizing: 'the historical debt from plundering, destruction, devastation, slave labour and cultural annihilation in the South during the colonial era; debt from the social, environmental, economic and cultural impact of the extraction of natural resources (oil, gas, minerals, marine and forest life); debt from the intellectual appropriation and use of traditional knowledge through biotechnology by agro-business, first in the Green and now in the GMO revolution; debt from the degradation of land, water and air through monocultures, putting the food and cultural sovereignty of communities at risk; debt through pollution of the atmosphere and the appropriation of carbon absorption capacity of oceans, vegetation and forests; debt for the damage caused by chemical, nuclear and biological arms production and depositing of toxic substances' (Goeminne and Paredis 2010: 693).

There are several reasons for comprehending under a single term such a variety of issues. First, the concept of ecological debt is able to draw together comparable experiences from (local) groups all over the South and to unite them under a common banner: 'The term ecological debt seems to be able to articulate the common concerns visible in e.g. protest against shrimp farming, mining, oil and gas exploitation or the overuse of the absorption capacity of the atmosphere. Whether the cases are well-known or not—from Texaco in Ecuador, Union Carbide in Bhopal, Shell in Nigeria over mine exploitations in Peru, South Africa and the Philippines, to shrimp farming in Thailand, biopiracy in Costa Rica, or dumping of toxic waste in India—the pattern is often identical: multinational companies (and often conspiring governments) leave a ravaged land behind, with all its consequences for the local population' (Goeminne and Paredis 2010: 692). This idea is captured under the term *ecologismo popular*, or 'environmentalism of the poor' (Martinez-Alier 2002). Second, ecological debt brings a historical perspective to bear on the concept of sustainable development. While sustainable development, in its canonical formulations, is presented as a concern to meet the needs of present and future generations, it does not attend explicitly to the effects and impacts of the past nor foreground their relevance to the normative demands and political economic constraints of achieving them. 'Ecological debt draws attention to how the present situation has grown out of the—often violent and unjust—past. It points at the collective responsibility of industrialised countries for past and ongoing violations of the right to a clean and safe environment in other countries, in particular in the South…' (Goeminne and Paredis 2010: 693). The third reason concerns the initial link made in the campaigns between external financial debt and ecological debt. As a consequence of this link, a new political perspective is brought to international relations, i.e. 'a reversal of the creditor–debtor relations. From an industrialised country perspective, people are used to thinking in terms of developing countries as debtors of a huge financial debt. The concept of ecological debt shows that countries can be in a creditor–debtor relationship on the basis of physical–ecological relations' (Goeminne and Paredis 2010: 694).

> The foreign debt of the poor countries has been transformed into an instrument of control, but the same thing does not happen with the ecological debt. In their different ways, peoples in developing countries, where the most important reserves of the biosphere are found, continue to feed the development of the richer countries to the cost of their own present and future. The land of the poor in the South is rich and mostly unpolluted, but access to ownership of goods and resources for meeting vital needs is prohibited to them by a system of commercial relations and ownership that is structurally perverse.
>
> (Pope Francis 2015: §52 [*My amended trans.*])

The radically challenging view is that monetary accounts do not simply keep a neutral record of who has undertaken to do what for whom. The financial system is part of a broader exploitative system—called *structurally perverse* by Pope Francis—that coerces some people to do a great deal for others, without any meaningful quid pro quo, and even if it means taking a destructive approach to the environment.

From this perspective, then, there is no contradiction between an ecological and a social view of the problem of financialization. In fact, the two perspectives are integrated at a fundamental level. This integrated perspective is spontaneously adopted by movements around the world whose aim is to reassert claims grounded in lived realities against the abstract and unreasonable dominance of financial capitalist interests. It is this paradigmatically distinct sort of thinking that is engaged in by those who protest against the 'structural reforms' and conditionality of the IMF, for instance; it is what those who are trapped in various kinds of debt spirals have in mind; and it is the thinking that underlies assertions of ecological indebtedness against those claiming financial debt repayments from the poor.

In setting out this case for a radical social ecological critique, the difference between humanly productive activity and purely financial activity is drawn quite clearly and decisively. This perspective serves also to problematize the terms in which the mainstream economists draw that distinction when criticizing financialization for its adverse effects on the 'real economy'. There is a reason for putting this latter term between scare quotes, and it is time to make this explicit.

4.3 What Is the 'Real Economy?'

A distinction between the real economy and finance can be clearly drawn in principle if real economic activity is understood in terms of the production of food, manufacture of goods, and provision of tangible services to people. Finance can then be understood, by contrast, as simply a system of accounting by means of which a tally is kept—in some form or other—of who has undertaken to provide what goods or services to whom in future. When the distinction is drawn in those terms, the reality of the economy is understood to have a material manifestation. This does not mean that all the practices we regard as economic can be reduced to their material elements, but only that there is a reality to the economy that cannot be captured by abstracting from them.

The 'real economy' that is generally referred to by those mainstream economists who are critical of financialization, however, does in a certain sense abstract from material considerations. For what the economists observe and measure are not material transformations of the world but the quantities of 'value' that are attributed through monetary expression to the transactions between people engaged in the various activities of production, exchange, and consumption. Thus, for instance, if one business makes money from environmentally harmful practices and a second makes money from cleaning up some of the first business's mess then there is a double economic benefit, seen from the accountants' perspective. We can thereby appreciate how the mainstream critique of financialization is radically distinct from the ecological critique.

In fact, the ecological critique of economic growth, viewed from the mainstream perspective, involves an elementary confusion of categories. From that perspective, the real economy can deliver benefits to people, via the medium of *value* created, without compromising ecological relationships because the value in question does not necessarily represent any particular ecological goods or services that might happen, contingently, to get caught up in some form of production. For this reason, the conventional mainstream view rejects as naïve confusion the idea that there are natural limits to growth, and it assumes, instead, that economic growth can continue, in principle, indefinitely, without causing ecological devastation. Ecological critics are said to make the mistake of confusing economic growth (as measured through the monetary value of transactions) with the growth of material demands on the planet (as measured materially).

That being so, however, there arises a critical question concerning the mainstream critique of financialization: for if the reality of the 'real economy' is so decidedly immaterial, then on what basis is *this* 'real economy' supposed to be distinguished from finance? The criterion typically invoked for the purpose of the contrast is *productivity*: this is what the economy is held to strive for and financialization to undermine. Orthodox economists take productivity to refer to the volume of economic activity as measured by the value of its net output. That value is calculated, for a firm, as the difference between the cost of inputs and receipts for outputs; for a national economy it is taken as the total value of transactions recorded for 'final goods or services' (i.e. those whose consumption involves the generation of no further economic value to record). To be productive in this sense it is not necessary—and certainly not sufficient—that those engaged in the process work hard or exercise great ingenuity, or that what they produce has particular qualitative worth as judged by criteria other than price achieved; nor does it matter if the productive process imposes harms on the environment, or, indeed, if its purpose is to rectify harms caused by productive processes. What is necessary and sufficient for an enterprise to be considered productive is that it generates net income. On this basis, the relative productivity of different countries around the world can be compared. Interestingly, the rankings of countries according to their GDP (Gross Domestic Product) per capita show the most productive to include Brunei, Kuwait, Luxembourg, Norway, Qatar, Singapore, Switzerland, and the United Arab Emirates; if locations other than full nation-states are allowed a place in the lists, then we also find that Monaco, Liechtenstein, Bermuda, Macau, Jersey, Guernsey, and the Cayman Islands make a strong showing.[7] What this shows is that unless a territory happens to harbour substantial oil deposits or actual casinos, the best predictor of its productivity is the hosting of global financial institutions.

This rather suggests that the conventional economic accounting of productivity does not deliver the clear contrast with finance that the critique appealing to it might have us expect. If global financial centres that lack virtually any significant industrial, agricultural, or technological capacity are the most productive, then evidently the distinction between the financial and the economically productive spheres is not very clear in practice.

In fact, it is arguable that the distinction is illusory (Dillard 1987; Nesvetailova 2015; Palan 2013, 2015). For, as Anastasia Nesvetailova and Ronan Palan (2013), following Thorstein Veblen (1921), have emphasized, both economics and finance are centrally about *business*. The reason people engage in business is for profit, not the social good, or even the production of goods in the sense of things consumers want—except insofar as doing so generates *profit*. An important implication of the centrality of the business perspective, both to the 'real' economy and to finance, can be brought out by reference to the idea that John R. Commons (1931) introduced as *futurity*. This refers not simply to the fact, as noted in Chapter 2, that finance is necessarily concerned with the future, in the sense of facilitating forward planning of enterprise in general. There is also a more specific sense that has come to prominence since the later years of the nineteenth century. Until then, as Palan describes, businesses had generally been valued on the basis of the physical assets they owned at the time of valuation. However, this method of valuation came increasingly to be seen as unrealistic from a business perspective since the point of being in business is not to liquidate assets but to realize future earning capacity. The business interest thus lies in valuing businesses as 'going concerns', factoring in projected future earnings.[8] What has happened in more recent history is that the ways and means of treating future expectations as the

[7] Central Intelligence Agency, 'Country Comparison: GDP—per capita (PPP), *The World Factbook* https://www.cia.gov/library/publications/the-world-factbook/rankorder/2004rank.html Accessed August 2018.

[8] This element was initially captured in accounting by availing of the archaic Common Law concept of 'goodwill', writes Palan (2015), who also notes that more systematic study of 'human expectations in

basis of present valuations have expanded vastly, so that great scope is created for the *leveraging* of asset values. With projections of future earnings included in accounts of current asset values, value can be extracted and set to work independently as if this value were the equivalent of more tangible collateral. Yet since what such added value actually represents is nothing other than estimates of future earning capacity, it essentially reflects market sentiments of optimism and pessimism about the future. These are inherently labile: 'When the mood changes for one reason or another, the same pro-cyclical dynamics that have contributed to an apparent inexorable rise in asset value turn in the opposite direction and wealth literally vanishes' (Palan 2015: 378).

The question, accordingly, is whether there is any determinate basis for establishing a 'real' value of any given asset that could contrast with its nominal value and could, at the same time, be claimed to be commensurate in some way with it. To be sure, a clear distinction can be drawn—as it is, for instance, by Marx—between the realm of economic value as economists construe this, where what registers as value is *exchange value*, and the value tangible things have as useful items in the world and which can be referred to as their *use value*. In an economy oriented to the production of exchange value, as a capitalist economy is, tangible things register as having economic existence only insofar as they partake of the commodity form. Love, housework, giving birth, childraising, and so on, are significant activities in people's lives but they generally do not count as economic activities. When they are commoditized—for example as prostitution, surrogacy, domestic service, and so on—then they can be accounted services and figure as elements of GDP.[9] When something partakes of the commodity form it thus has a dual existence—as is made conspicuous in the contrast between the care one gives to a dependent loved one and the care one purchases from a private clinic. But it would be a mistake to say that the one is real and the other is a representation of that reality.

A commodity can be regarded as manifesting (at least) two kinds of reality—one as a useful thing and the other as convertibility into money. Prices of things are not usefully seen as 'less real' than things viewed under the aspect of their use value; they are more aptly seen as values based on different considerations and perceptions of what matters in the world. Insofar as the material and the monetary are two different realities, it is not self-evident on what basis values assigned in the one might be commensurate with values assigned in the other.

a world dominated by intangible value' was engaged in by Veblen, Commons, and others associated with the Old School of Institutional Economics.

[9] See, for instance, the inclusion of prostitution in the national accounts of the UK to bring them into compliance with European System of National Accounts (Abramsky and Drew 2014).

It would thus seem to be problematic to advance a critique of financialization on the grounds that it allows exchange value to deviate from what it 'should' be. This, in fact, is a point that schools of macroeconomic theory that do not engage in the Keynesian critique of financialization are wont to insist on, namely, that a market price is never other than what it should be. It does not represent some ulterior reality: a real price just is a market price; and that is the only indicator we have of economic value.

So we encounter once more, as in Chapter 3, a matter on which the laissez-faire schools arguably take a position that is conceptually more cogent than that of the broadly Keynesian schools. Yet the normative inference they draw as a basis for policy advice appears to be even less conducive than those of their competitors to either social justice or ecological preservation. For it tends to support the idea that people should learn to adapt to the facts revealed by market forces, rather than seek out some notion of 'real' economic value that happens to suit an ideological preference for social democracy or liberal equality.

This inference drawn by orthodox neoliberal advocates of laissez-faire is not, however, the only inference that can be drawn from the recognition that prices have no ulterior 'reality'. For insofar as the prices are irreducibly real, there can be irreducibly real criticisms of how they are arrived at and of the social effects they can have. So even if market forces are a fact we have to reckon with, given the nature of our economy, this does not mean we have simply to accept their untrammelled exercise, at least when it is in our political power to do otherwise. Hence a core tenet of the Keynesians and post-Keynesians, distinguishing them from the laissez-faire schools, is that economics can and should be consciously governed by political purpose. On this general tenet, ecological economists tend to be in strong agreement; but where they would differ is in understanding what political governance of the economy should aim for. In particular, they attempt to be consistent in understanding the economy's materiality. For a problem with the macroeconomic perspective of the Keynesians and post-Keynesians is that, while emphasizing the *importance* of material considerations, the *nature* of these is assumed to be sufficiently homogeneous and fungible to be represented by monetary equivalents.

Thus a problem with the Keynesian view of economic reality, as Keynes' own influential protégé Ernst F. Schumacher pointed out, is that it 'deals with goods in accordance with their market value and not in accordance with what they really are. The same rules and criteria are applied to primary goods, which man has to win from nature, and secondary goods, which presuppose the existence of primary goods and are manufactured from them. All goods are treated the same, because the point of view is fundamentally that of private profit-making, and this means that it is inherent in the methodology of economics *to ignore man's dependence on the natural world*' (Schumacher 1993: 29 [*emphasis in the original*]). With an understanding of the 'real economy' that is thus selective in its appreciation of the nature of reality, the critique of financialization appears to have no firm anchorage. Thus Schumacher emphasizes how the Keynesian approach to achieving social justice will be undermined in practice by its neglect of ecological conditions. It may be possible, he suggests, to 'overcome the most blatant deficiencies of laissez-faire by means of Keynesian economic management, a bit of redistributive taxation, and the "countervailing power" of the trade unions' (Schumacher 1993: 222). However, he argues, such limited measures are manifestly inadequate to deal with the challenges we now face.

So there are two quite distinct senses in which one might speak of a 'real economy'. The reality of the one resides in the materiality of relationships among humans in their interactions with the natural world, what Marx referred to as the 'human metabolism with nature'; this is the reality studied by interdisciplinary ecological economics, for example. The other is that of market price, where transactions of all material kinds are regarded as qualitatively identical, since the only quality that registers is monetary movement. Analyses of this other reality can be indifferent to what movements of tangible goods and services might accompany the monetary movement; they can thus be indifferent to whether these involve agriculture, manufacture, biotechnology, climate engineering, or the slicing and dicing of loans, options, and various financial derivatives.

The idea of a 'real economy', as understood in the mainstream economics schools does not provide a clear and coherent contrast with the sphere of pure financial activity because it excludes from view what, from an ecological perspective, can be seen as fundamental. The idea that the size and health of an economy can be measured by prices may be a serviceable one within certain parameters, but what is thereby measured only reflects what economic agents, in the various particular positions and relations they occupy, have the ability to pay or the power to demand. In this respect, the idea of an economy is closer to that of pure finance than to the idea of a 'human metabolism with nature'. If prices are, as monetarists insist, simply what they are, and not a representation of any supposedly corresponding state of affairs in the world, then the laws of nature and ecological functionings are simply what they are. That is a conflict of realities that political economy has to deal with. This cannot be achieved by seeking to assimilate or reduce ecological values to economic prices, which, unfortunately, is what mainstream economists attempt to do in their approaches to environmental issues. They characteristically attempt to translate ecological problems into a matter of cost–benefit analysis conducted in relation to a system of prices that are arrived at by methods that use some form or other of market simulation exercise.[10]

[10] For a useful critical overview of the assumptions of standard economic approaches such as cost–benefit analysis see O'Neill and Spash (2000).

It is worth emphasizing, then, that the kind of environmental economics that seeks to determine a proper price for environmental assets takes a perspective that is essentially the same as mainstream economics, and stands in stark contrast to the ecological perspective or ecological economics of the kind that could be endorsed from that perspective.[11] A problem with this is not only that the prices are illusory, but that the illusion can itself add to the difficulty of addressing the major challenges we face. When all ecological aspects of the world are conceptually reduced to discrete 'assets' with prices, they are treated as having a fungibility that, in ecological reality, can never pertain. Yet economists are prepared to treat those prices as sufficiently real to commend various strategies of 'offsetting' and 'compensation' involving the substitution of materially different features of the world on the basis simply of an equivalent imputed price. The fact that these prices are radically arbitrary from an ecological point of view does not appear to register in such a conceptual framework. The illusion can be dangerous because it allows the fostering of unrealistically optimistic ideas about the possibility of 'win–win' scenarios in which doing ecological good can simultaneously be a source of monetary profit. The general idea here, that you can have it both ways—protect the environment and continue growing business—reflects the equivocation in the basic conceptualization of a 'real economy' that is seen as material reality for some purposes and as monetary evaluation for others, with only an unfounded assumption that for relevant purposes the one somehow tracks the other in some non-arbitrary fashion.

The problem is that the real relation between monetary values and material values is not always or necessarily one of representation; monetary values have their own reality as a product of the monetary system. A coin, a banknote, a cheque, a bond, a certificate, a promise, none of these things can function as a site of value without a complex social apparatus of trust, convention, and institutions. That infrastructure has its own reality. It is the reality that makes indebtedness and lack of money real problems for real people.

We need to be aware of this reality of the monetary system when thinking about justice.

4.4 Conclusion

This chapter has shown that with financialization there comes an intensification of the domination of the profit motive in an economy, so that not only human social interests but also ecological concerns are systematically disregarded and materially

[11] For an illuminating discussion of different interpretations of 'ecological economics', from the perspective that is broadly adopted in this book, see Spash (2013). See also Chapter 7, below, for further discussion of the contrast noted in the text here.

compromised. Three major kinds of problem are associated with financialization: it draws wealth and productive capacity out of useful economic activities; the inequality it drives yields distributive injustice, in nations and globally; the cycle of indebtedness it involves drives people to seek ever more desperate interactions with each other and the natural world. It is thus problematic from the perspectives of three concerns: economic, justice, and ecological.

What this chapter has also shown is how it is possible to see beyond the apparent incompatibility of those critiques, particularly concerning tensions between the ecological and the economic. For, at first blush, there seemed to be an evident question: if the economic complaint is that financialization impedes the economy from generating enough useful output, then how can there also be an ecological complaint that the economy engages too much with the material world? The argument that has been developed in response is that although those two propositions appear to be contradictory, in fact the contradiction is between a view of the economy as consisting of material interactions with nature to produce tangible useful things and a view of the economy as represented by values equated with market prices. The former kind of view is consistent with an ecological perspective and provides a clear basis for a contrast with purely financial activity.

On that basis, indeed, one can think beyond the three kinds of *complaint* about financialization to see how they can be integrated into a coherent *critique*. A critique does not only reveal that something is amiss, but seeks to understand the conditions of possibility for the appearance of the problem, doing so the better to understand what might be required of potential solutions to it.

The next part of the book assesses proposals for how the problem might be dealt with in order to make the world more just.

5
Can Giving Money End Severe Poverty?

The first part of this book contrasted the constructive role that finance can in principle play in producing prosperity with the practical effects of the global financial system as presently constituted. These tend not only to hamper the productivity that would support prosperity but also to exacerbate the factors that cause social injustice and ecological destruction.

Given that this global financial system appears to be a significant part of the problem of global injustice, a reasonable inference to draw is that it needs to be significantly transformed. The question then is what kind of transformation would be duly significant. One possible answer would be that while some institutional reform may be required, given that the international institutional order is imperfectly just, it is nevertheless not thoroughly unjust in any more thoroughgoing way (see e.g. the critical discussion in Hayward 2009), and so continued reform, rather than radical transformation, is what is required. Some who take this view argue that even with institutions as they already exist and are evolving internationally, a good deal might be achieved, provided only that there is the will to seek it. Part of this broadly sanguine view of international institutions is a tacit assumption that the global financial system, for all its contingent faults, is at least in principle fit for purpose as a medium through which to effect such transfers of income and wealth as principles of justice might require. It is this assumption that is to be problematized here.

This chapter critically examines some influential proposals advanced by philosophers with the aim of deploying financial means in the pursuit of just ends. Section 5.1 considers the suggested moral obligation of 'earning to give' that was promoted by Peter Singer and has been picked up by the *Effective Altruism* movement. This approach to dealing with the problem of severe global poverty involves using the money generated by those in affluent positions within the world's economy to provide assistance to the disadvantaged. Section 5.2 illustrates, by reference to a case study of a particular charity recommended by effective altruists, some of the limitations of applying the 'earning to give' model for achieving justice. Those difficulties themselves, though, are argued by some defenders of effective altruism to arise only because the monetary donations are not applied sufficiently directly. Accordingly, the key argument considered is that rather than try to use money to solve people's problems, the money itself should simply be sent to the poor in the form of cash transfers. Section 5.3 shows that while cash transfers can certainly bring some benefits to their recipients, questions nevertheless do remain as to whether they are really beneficial, all things considered, for the broader goal of alleviating global poverty.

These questions also go to the overarching question about whether global institutions need minor reforms or radical transformation. For an apparently minor detail about cash transfer schemes is that they do not in fact involve the transfer of cash at all. The transfers are *cashless*. What Section 5.4 then reveals is how investigation of the paradox of *cashless cash* leads us to discern some powerful vested interests that support programmes of 'cash' transfers for reasons that have to do with seeking not justice but profits. This discovery means that those who propose cash transfers as an appropriate response to institutionalize should at the very least do some due diligence. More generally, what this chapter shows is that there are probing questions that can and should be asked about what is actually involved in the sorts of transfer that the philosophers propose as major contributions to achieving global justice.

5.1 *Earning to Give*: Peter Singer and Effective Altruism

A classic starting point for discussions of moral responsibilities regarding the global poor is the famous proposition of Peter Singer:

> if it is in our power to prevent something very bad from happening, without thereby sacrificing anything morally significant, we ought, morally, to do it. An application of this principle would be as follows: if I am walking past a shallow pond and see a child drowning in it, I ought to wade in and pull the child out.
>
> (Singer 1972: 231)

The relevance of this proposition to dealing with global poverty is taken to be that it captures the basic moral shape of the challenge. Its premise is that the problem is one in response to which a little sacrifice on the part of the better off can make a great difference for the worst off. This premise is shared not only by those moral philosophers and philanthropy advisers who are directly influenced by the individualistic ethics of Singer, but also by political theorists who take a more institutionally mediated view of the obligations held by the better off (as will be discussed in Chapter 6).

It seems to me we have good reason to accept the initial moral proposition. If ever one really is in a position to achieve a considerable amount of good for others with a relatively small amount of effort oneself, I believe most people would intuitively decide—in line with what might also be decided on the basis of more systematic reasoning of either consequentialist or deontological kinds—that, other things equal, they should apply that modicum of effort. The question is whether the moral proposition really is so clearly applicable as Singer suggests to meaningful attempts to address the global challenges facing us.

In setting up his analogy, Singer describes a simple situation where a single capable moral agent responds to the need of a single nearby vulnerable moral patient. The very description of the scenario leaves little room for serious moral debate about what the agent should do. The situation does have some particular features that Singer wants us to notice, though: it is not the agent's fault that the child is in the pond; and the agent has no special acquaintance or relationship with the child. If either of those other conditions applied, they might be thought to provide independent grounds for the obligation. Part of Singer's point is that these would not be required to motivate assistance in the drowning child case, since the simple ability to help in the face of clear and present need can be taken as sufficient reason to do so. Another significant feature of the case is the ease assumed to apply for the rescue of the child from the pond. It is thus assumed, by analogy, that with regard to the relief of severe and widespread poverty it would take similarly little effort to do a great deal of good. The analogy, however, is imperfect in several respects that have been discussed in the literature (e.g. Wenar 2011; Wisor 2011). For instance, the 'rescue' of the world's poor cannot be achieved by any agency or means that would be straightforwardly analogous to the modest effort of a single identifiable individual pulling a child from a pond. Among the most minimal requirements it would involve the aggregated commitment of many people, which is liable to require a good deal of coordinated effort to arrange in the first place and then also to sustain for the time needed. Furthermore, because Singer is thinking in terms of voluntary charitable donations made by separate individuals, there is also the difficulty that not everyone will offer to help, and so the effort needed from those who do increases. In the not unlikely event of widespread non-compliance with Singer's moral exhortations, the effort required of those individuals who are determined to achieve the moral goal might be far from minimal. Hence there has been a particular concern in the literature that the position Singer's argument comes to commend is *over-demanding*: for if no individual can ever single-handedly complete the task, there is no inherent limit to the effort any individual might be required to make. Singer himself commends the view that each of us ought to give as much as we dispose of until we reach 'the level at which, by giving more, I would cause as much suffering to myself or my dependents as I would relieve by my gift. This would mean, of course, that one would reduce oneself to very near the material circumstances of a Bengali refugee' (Singer 1972: 241). On a slightly moderated formulation of the principle, it requires us to prevent 'as much suffering as we can without sacrificing something else of comparable moral importance' (Singer 1972: 238). The thought is that nobody in a position of affluence may justly continue to enjoy that affluence until everyone in the world has attained a decent standard of living. The change in lifestyle implied here, for all members of affluent populations, is hardly minor.

Singer is aware of constraints on the feasibility of relying on the sum of individual moral impulses, even in an essentially counterfactual scenario where people are generally ready to accept weighty moral demands. He understands that to enact even the moderate version of his principle 'we would have to give away enough to ensure that the consumer society, dependent as it is on people spending on trivia rather than giving to famine relief, would slow down and perhaps disappear entirely' (Singer 1972: 241). While he has no problem about that per se, he nevertheless thinks, 'looking at the matter purely from the point of view of overseas aid, there must be a limit to the extent to which we should deliberately slow down our economy' (Singer 1972: 241). He illustrates his concern by positing that 'if we gave away, say, forty percent of our Gross National Product, we would slow down the economy so much that in absolute terms we would be giving less than if we gave twenty-five percent of the much larger GNP that we would have if we limited our contribution to this smaller percentage' (Singer 1972: 241–2). He regards this consideration as 'entirely academic', given the improbability of anything remotely like this occurring, but it is interesting to note the economic thinking that lies in the background of his proposals about what people ought to do with money.

Singer appears to anticipate that no matter how much effort 'we'—i.e. the affluent—make to help the poor, it will remain necessary that the economy we are part of continues to grow in order for us to have money to send to those poorer than us. A very basic assumption of his initial analogy is that 'rescuing' the poor involves transferring to them some of the income that 'we' in more affluent parts of the world are able to earn thanks to our more favourable position within the global economy. He does not appear to make theoretical space for the idea that if economic growth is necessary for the poor, then this might be growth of their own economies rather than a side effect of the continued expansion of already developed economies. Nor does he appear to consider that the latter could be a driver of the very problem itself. He argues that individually we should each morally be prepared to give away a significant portion of that income. He does not entertain the idea that the system generating these income differentials could itself be part of the problem. Singer expressly reasons that it is better to let the current economic system generate larger profits unequally, if more can thereby be available for redistribution, than to constrain profits and thereby leave less to redistribute.

Singer's position, then, appears to beg several of the key critical questions that are foregrounded in this book. Most fundamentally, it leaves unaddressed the question of why we should assume our moral obligations are to work within the economic system that is leaving so many so impoverished rather than work to transform that system. Singer tacitly assumes that a liberal understanding of political economy is a satisfactory basis upon which to conduct moral deliberations about obligations of economic reallocation or redistribution. He also tacitly assumes that moral recommendations in this field are not liable to differ depending on what explanatory theory one takes to account for the problem or situation that one has a moral obligation to respond to. He expressly assumes that appropriate assistance centrally involves the donation of money. Before considering the question of how warranted these assumptions might be, however, it is worth examining how his ideas here have recently been taken up as the foundation of the practical ethical approach styled *effective altruism*. For this movement, which has been influential in some quarters, makes even more explicit a recommendation not only of reliance on, but active complicity in, the profit-driven economic system.

The practical philosophy applied in the field of charitable giving by those who style themselves *Effective Altruists* is, simply put, that you should aim to maximize the good you can do by earning as much money as you can so you can donate as much as you can to the charitable programmes that yield 'most bang for your buck' (MacAskill 2015). In practice, this implies two key objectives: first, to get hold of some funds, and then to disburse them to the most cost-effective charitable operator. Accordingly, there will be two interrelated questions to consider. The first is why one should assume that 'earning to give' is better than doing something more directly to help people who need help. The other is how one might decide which charities do the most good for people in need of help.[1]

The first goal, then, for an Effective Altruist, is to maximize the donation they are able to make towards relieving suffering and poverty. This means attending centrally, even if not exclusively, to the question of how to earn the best income one is capable of commanding. If this means taking a job on Wall Street, for instance, the logic follows unfalteringly, as Singer indicates with the observation that a 'high earner in the corporate world who is giving away large sums can create more social gain than if they did charity work'.[2] Some of those influenced by Singer have followed this advice. Thus we may read reports of one of his students, for instance, whose career choices are taken to have exemplified what this would mean in practice. Having come top of his class at Princeton, where he was taught by Singer, he and his friends looked at research which said it costs 'around $3,340' to save a life, and he investigated how best he could set about helping. Taking the view that some people have skills that are better suited to earning money than directly doing good deeds, he decided this applied to him. Accordingly, he took a lucrative job in an arbitrage trading firm on Wall Street, with the explicit purpose of 'earning to give', whereby around half his pre-tax salary would go to those

[1] Some effective altruists have concerns not only about people but also about the ethical treatment of nonhumans, a subject on which Peter Singer has written influentially in the past. However, exploring the question of how such concerns fit with the other elements of their programme would carry us too far from our present focus, so I set it aside here.

[2] The example given in this passage is from Peter Singer as reported in an interview with Joseph D'Urso for Reuters (27 July 2015) http://www.reuters.com/article/global-charities-altruism-idUSKCN0Q10HT20150727

charities which, according to his research, are most efficient. Now I do not suppose that all effective altruists would see their own talents as best deployed in that kind of work, and I dare say some might even have moral reservations about undertaking it; however, the more general principle they do accept is that charity is significantly, if not even primarily, about giving the money that you think morally you should to charities that will do the most good with it. What Singer's teaching—with its focus on moral individualism—did not encourage the young man to question is the set of socio-economic conditions that make it possible for a Princeton graduate to walk into a Wall Street firm and immediately earn so much more than the people he wants to help. Neither teacher nor student appear to have anticipated critical questions about how these Wall Street firms and their employees may 'earn' the massive amounts of money they do not by actually producing anything of value but simply by repackaging various complicated arrangements of others' indebtedness. No account is therefore taken of the literally untold human suffering that may ultimately be generated at the far end of those arrangements for people on the unfortunate side of global inequality. For bright young graduates like this one it perhaps merely appears serendipitous that their particular talents happen to be suited to earning large sums of money in corporate finance so that they can take home 50 per cent of a Wall Street salary, plus any attendant benefits, in addition to the personal satisfaction of believing they are doing the maximum amount of good of which they are capable.

I do not impugn the moral seriousness of such individuals, or of others who approve or commend an approach of this kind. I do however think that if your assumption is that you can achieve a great deal with a little effort, it would be consistent with that seriousness to consider how it can possibly be that so much good can come to you and be done through you in virtue of throwing yourself so fully into the activities of the global 1 per cent that draws so much advantage from the global economy. You may see yourself as giving a little back, perhaps, but have you checked you are not complicit in taking rather more than you return? Perhaps you are content to think that if someone else did your job there might be nothing given back; or perhaps you could argue that critical suggestions about your line of work being exploitative rest on controversial theories? My point is that doing some due diligence concerning the origins of your own income should be part of the process of deliberating about how you can do the most good posssible. For there could be more to the question than that of moving some money within the system of global finance, and this is all I want to observe just now.

The second question is how one knows to whom one should entrust one's money in order to do the most good. Presumably, most of us do not individually know very much about the relative effectiveness of different charities. In fact, according to the Effective Altruists, most charities themselves do not organize information in a way that even makes it knowable. If one knew how to assess the value of different charitable programmes, then making that knowledge available to others would itself be a valuable contribution to a solution of the problem. This is where the charity comparison websites come in. In this recently burgeoning ambit of activity we find a number of individuals who have understood that their own special talents lie not directly in executing good deeds, nor even in directly earning money on their own account, but in figuring out how others can best direct their charitable donations.

A particularly influential website is GiveWell (www.givewell.org). It was founded by two Harvard contemporaries of the Facebook creators, who, inspired by the success of the latter, initially sought their own fortune working for a hedge fund on Wall Street. From 2007/08 they turned their attention and their acquired leveraging skills to figuring out which charities could give most 'bang for the buck' of the major philanthropists of their personal acquaintance and also, sometimes differentially, of smaller donors among the wider public. A lamentable characteristic of the majority of traditional charities, GiveWell claim, is a lack of transparency or systematic reflection on the value for money provided by their programmes. Accordingly, the charities favoured and promoted are a new breed, exemplified by a handful of organizations that conform to the auditing criteria promulgated by GiveWell. In this new milieu, in which meta-charitable philanthropy advisers work to promote charities that are also favoured by advocates of effective altruism, it is taken as axiomatic that effectiveness can and should be measured in terms that can be given monetary expression. For GiveWell, the very methodology that they boast as their unique selling point in the world of charity consultancy depends on it. Charities that are not or cannot be audited for 'bang for the buck' are never recommended to donors.

There are two matters here that I think are worth examining more closely. One is whether there are potential limits to the good that can really be done by following criteria of efficiency that narrowly seek to track bang for donor's buck; the other concerns wider issues about the assumptions relied on when thinking about the good that transferring sums of money can do. Sections 5.2 and 5.3 consider these matters in turn, in each case by reference to the case of a particular charity that comes highly recommended by promoters of effective altruism.

5.2 Doing Good with Money, and the Value of the Marginal Dollar: the Case of Anti-Malarial Bednet Distribution

The purpose of this section is to illustrate how it is possible to be misled about the good actually done by a programme of international charitable giving when assessment of its effectiveness focuses on the impact of the marginal dollar, or 'bang for the buck' more generally.

Of the handful of charities ever to receive the endorsement of GiveWell, one consistently recommended by them, and also singled out for praise by Peter Singer (2013), is the *Against Malaria Foundation (AMF)*. AMF is said to provide outstanding value in terms of 'bang for buck', where this means that deployment of the marginal dollar has an appreciable impact. The headline proposition of this charity, according to its website (www.againstmalaria.com), is that '**100%** of the money buys nets **and** they are put over heads and beds **and** we demonstrate this has happened.' If a few dollars buy a mosquito net, and that net then protects a child from contracting malaria in her sleep, then it is a few dollars very well spent. The moral power of this thought lends apparent support to Singer's argument that we should really give *every dollar* we possibly can—for each dollar we withhold could mean the difference between life and death for a child. Yet this thought has to be tempered by an appreciation of the limiting conditions of its relevance. One is that every dollar the charity collects from the public goes towards *nothing but nets*.[3] While the Effective Altruists laud this as the epitome of efficient charitable spending, what it actually means is that all AMF in practice does is secure shipments of nets from their suppliers in Asia to ports in Africa. For the nets to be 'put over heads' involves extensive logistics of distribution, the effort and coordination of which fall entirely on other agencies. Likewise, the demonstration 'that this has happened' is provided, when it is, by those same agencies who do the actual monitoring of receipt, uptakes, and use over time—across large, remote, and challenging geographical regions. It is these actual distributors, too, that gather all the salient data on uptake and use, for which AMF then accepts credit when stating that impact 'is monitored'.[4] So by far the greater part of the actual effort involved in getting nets over peoples heads and demonstrating that this has happened is performed by traditional charities and NGOs of the kind that the charity websites like GiveWell set aside as unrecommended and thereby implicitly dismiss as inefficient users of people's donations compared to AMF.[5]

[3] This phrase, incidentally, provides the name for a competitor charity to AMF that GiveWell has not reviewed, apparently because it opted (for whatever reason) not to participate in the extensive process GiveWell require of their charities (https://nothingbutnets.net/).

[4] When the distributors fall behind with the requisite paperwork, for whatever reason, AMF is left in an awkward position in relation to those, like GiveWell, who are recommending the charity as giving demonstrable bang for an individual donor's buck. GiveWell have in fact noted that this is one of the areas in which AMF has been proving less than satisfactory (see, for instance, the 'Updates on AMF's transparency and monitoring' at https://blog.givewell.org/2016/09/21/updates-amfs-transparency-monitoring/). The repeated delays and uncertainties that GiveWell have recorded perhaps serve to highlight the fact that AMF is not a major broker of bednet supply and, in a context where other and bigger funders and partners are available, cannot really claim that its activities are greatly scalable. So while those dollars that do get spent on nets distributed may be well spent, there is certainly no reason to think this would be the case for much larger quantities of donations, let alone every last dollar that charitable givers can collectively afford.

[5] GiveWell do not specifically criticize charities other than the handful they recommend, but their general remarks about the lack of transparency and impact monitoring in other charities clearly conveys a negative message that potentially applies to any charity they do not recommend. Most

Whether an organization like GiveWell should really give the praise it does to a charity like AMF is one question. But more general questions concern the kind of business model that is regarded as an archetype of good value by the Effective Altruism movement and its philosopher leaders such as Singer.

A business model that depends so heavily on work done by and at the expense of others is clearly not generalizable as a self-standing model for sustainable development. Moreover, in this kind of context—as where a number of charities vie for partnership with the net distributing agencies that are already straining to absorb the potential supply—it is hard to sustain the argument that a few dollars withheld from a particular charity is a child's life jeopardized. Meanwhile the opportunity costs of sponsoring the warehousing of a large quantity of a commodity like nets could include loss of support to charities that actually get involved with their distribution. This is a point highlighted by Leif Wenar with regard to a similar bednets charity, PSI:[6]

> If PSI had not distributed a bed net that was bought with your donation, would another aid agency have distributed that bed net anyway? And if your private donation had been absent, would the Global Fund or the World Bank have compensated for the deficit? (If that compensatory money was drawn away from other Global Fund projects, what different impacts would *those projects* have had? Or would the Global Fund's own donors have contributed more overall to make up for what you didn't give?) ... It could be that your donation to PSI in 2009 hindered malaria-fighting efforts compared with what another NGO would have done with your money. (Wenar 2011: 125)

In fact, there could also be other significant opportunity costs. If a shortage of bednets in the world, or even in African depots, is not the immediate problem, there would seem to be a case for considering more seriously the benefits of supporting African production rather than simply trying to get the cheapest nets. The majority of nets brokered by charities like AMF are procured from Asia, the reason cited by AMF being that its 'first obligation is to protect as many people as we can with the funds we have available. If the lowest price is therefore from Asian supply, that is where we are likely to buy.'[7] AMF maintain that 'it is not economic, for the cost of the net, to have small or medium sized manufacturing facilities

people relying on the site probably do not look much further than the positive recommendations, and the site prominently publicizes the large sums it drives towards its favoured charities.

[6] What the initials PSI stand for is not clearly indicated on the organization's website, http://www.psi.org/, but the LinkedIn page of its Vice President External Relations and Communications, Marshall Stowell, gives it as *Population Services International*. It is based in Washington DC. Information on its bednets programme is here: http://www.psi.org/program/long-lasting-insecticide-treats-nets/.

[7] https://www.againstmalaria.com/NewsItem.aspx?newsitem=Question-to-AMF-Where-are-your-nets-manufactured Accessed July 2018.

in many different, for example African, countries'.[8] However, the logic of this argument would be more robust if the problem were a shortage of nets. Yet the real constraint—as GiveWell have clearly signalled—is a shortage of capacity locally to deliver nets already available and to support effective uptake of them.[9] Development of that needed capacity requires the kind of labour intensive organisation that does not attract the accolades of the new philanthropy of the Effective Altruists.

It is worth reflecting on what it means to call a cost uneconomic in this context. It is arguable that some labour intensive activities are just what the poorest communities of the world need. Certainly, Dambisa Moyo argues this:

> Say there is a mosquito-net maker in small-town Africa. Say he employs 10 people who together manufacture 500 nets a week. Typically, these 10 employees support upward of 15 relatives each. A Western government-inspired program generously supplies the affected region with 100,000 free mosquito nets. This promptly puts the mosquito net manufacturer out of business, and now his 10 employees can no longer support their 150 dependents. In a couple of years, most of the donated nets will be torn and useless, but now there is no mosquito net maker to go to. They'll have to get more aid. (Moyo 2009a)

Accordingly, she advocates instead 'working towards a sustainable solution where Africans can make their own anti-malaria bed-nets (thereby creating jobs for Africans and a real chance for continent's economic prospects) rather than encouraging all and sundry to dump malaria nets across the continent (which incidentally, put Africans out of business)' (Moyo 2009b).

Indeed, anyone assessing the humanitarian value of a charitable venture such as one engaged in the shipping of anti-malarial nets, should be aware that, operating in partnership with it, are business interests that effectively compete with any nascent local producers. In the case of AMF, the primary manufacturer of the nets is the other key player they rely on, and the impact of the donations they broker depends on insecticidal technology that is the intellectual property of the manufacturer. We should not forget that even if such manufacturing companies style their activities as 'humanitarian entrepreneurship', they are first and foremost engaged in business. This means, as AMF admit, that there are the specific business interests of suppliers to take into account: 'technology transfer is an issue with challenges around training a workforce and guarding against technology intellectual property loss, the latter being a reasonable concern of the primary manufacturer'.[10] Thus while the domestic African economy is hindered from the needed degree of protection in starting up its own production processes, organizations like

[8] https://www.againstmalaria.com/Newsitem.aspx?NewsItem=Where-do-we-buy-our-nets-from Accessed July 2018.

[9] GiveWell notes regarding AMF that there is 'significant uncertainty as to its ability to scale up'. (http://www.givewell.org/international/top-charities/amf Accessed July 2018.

[10] https://www.againstmalaria.com/NewsItem.aspx?newsitem=Where-do-we-buy-our-nets-from

AMF work with manufacturers based in more developed economies and are even obliged to consider the business interests that enable them to be globally competitive in terms of quality and price. The integration of private enterprise into humanitarian action is inherently conditional on profits being achieved, somewhat irrespective of actual benefits being yielded to those in need. A for-profit business cannot be expected to surrender the rights that underpin its profits. How far a charity's procurement decisions should be dictated by the logic of profit-making enterprises is, of course, another question. Furthermore, as Moyo emphasizes, this is the kind of question that a host nation ought to be able to decide for itself. It should not be obliged to find itself potentially flooded with products produced elsewhere that may serve to reinforce its own condition of economic dependency.

The problem of continued dependency, we already noted, is something that Singer does not foreground as a concern, yet it is clearly relevant to thinking about how money might serve the ends of poverty relief or justice more widely. Among the effective altruists are some who think it can be addressed on their approach.

5.3 Cash Transfers as a Solution to the Dependency of the Poor?

It has been claimed on behalf of effective altruism that its principles can be applied in ways that need not reproduce problems of dependency. Timothy Weidel (2016), for instance, has acknowledged that there are real concerns on this score. These include the point made by Dale Jamieson (2005), that we should be working to make it less likely for the poor to fall into the pond, rather than donating money to pull them out, and the related point of Andrew Kuper (2002) that we should be thinking not merely about providing symptomatic relief but about supporting potential solutions at an institutional level. Weidel also acknowledges the influential argument of Thomas Pogge (2002) for attending to the underlying structural causes of poverty, since individual philanthropy would have little effect if it only meant some individuals amongst the poor get some money while there remained an economic system rigged against them as a whole. So while not denying that an institutional strategy is important, Weidel claims that it is not inherently opposed to the philanthropic approach that is characteristic of effective altruism.

In order to illustrate this claim Weidel highlights the example of GiveDirectly, another of the charities that comes strongly recommended by GiveWell. It is a different kind of charity from those that might create dependency, he believes, because its approach is to make direct cash transfers to the poor:

> GiveDirectly avoids a neocolonialist approach, wherein the poor in developing countries are given aid only according to what benevolent Western citizens/governments/NGOs deem the 'rational' choice. Instead, it is the poor persons

> themselves who are able to make decisions about how to spend the money, engaging in practical reasoning on their own terms. (Weidel 2016: 176)

Accordingly, this charity, and the approach it champions, will be the focus of critical discussion in what follows.

The question to be addressed, however, is not simply whether a programme of cash transfers can provide some symptomatic relief without having adverse effects on structural programmes. On this point I propose simply to assume Weidel might be right. For it may well be the case that substracting from a substantial reconstruction and development budget a small amount of ring-fenced funds for disbursal to a particular set of people may enhance the lives of the latter more than it detracts from the benefit of any individual in the larger society. The question is whether individualized cash transfers could play more than this marginal role without creating serious opportunity costs against a more comprehensive programme of structural reform. In other words, the question is not whether an operation like GiveDirectly might do some good at the margins, but whether its approach is even in principle sufficiently scalable to make any appreciable impact on global injustice. The question is whether a contribution of cash transfers on a scale sufficient to register effects on the workings of structural programmes is necessarily going to be *supportive* of the latter or whether attempts to scale it are liable to be counterproductive to that end. It would be a serious limitation of the effective altruist approach, and of GiveDirectly specifically, if it turned out to be the case that it could only achieve its own stated goals on condition that it were *not* part of a serious, widespread, and sustainable attempt to redress global poverty. Certainly, it would undermine Weidel's claim that this application of effective altruism need not reproduce problems of dependency if we discover that if attempted at scale it would risk *augmenting* problems of dependency.

When considering the general case in favour of cash transfers, it should be noted that cash transfer programmes can be either conditional or unconditional, and that they can be run by voluntary agencies or by governments. Whereas programmes run by host governments are often conditional, programmes established by international charities or NGOs tend to be unconditional, as is that of GiveDirectly.

The benefits of unconditional transfers for their immediate recipients, as ascertained through evidence reviewed by Richard Ballard (2013), include: reducing the extent and depth of poverty; improving household consumption, nutrition, and expenditure on children; lowering rates of child labour; improving school attendance, health and nutrition measures; and supporting the empowerment of women in households. Not only are there many things poor people are immediately enabled to do by receiving a windfall of cash, there can also be positive spillovers for their communities through the injection of new spending power and investment capacity. Appreciating these benefits of them, Kieran

Oberman has likened charitable transfers received from affluent strangers to remittances sent home by family emigrants: 'Cash transfers, like remittances, bypass middlemen, allowing the poor to decide how resources are spent' (Oberman 2015a: 248). Indeed, they even compare favourably in that, unlike remittances, 'they do not require desperately poor people to migrate abroad' (Oberman 2015a, 248). This line of comparison may be instructive in further ways too. For both sorts of funding stream—cash transfers and remittances—may in principle bypass the global financial system: money earned in one national economy is sent via an interpersonal conduit as cash to be directly converted into a locally accepted currency and handed to its individual or familial recipient. In both cases the arrangement is voluntary and informal; success in both cases depends on the earned currency being stable; in both cases, the central premise is that the earner is economically advantaged in comparison to the recipients.[11] Both remittances and charitable donations are forms of voluntary action; they are not directed or governed by any state organization. Both may reasonably be perceived as practical responses to injustices in transnational economic relations.

Unconditional cash transfers are most clearly beneficial when deployed in expenditures that directly serve a household's immediate identifiable needs, particularly those of the most vulnerable (Hall 2008). Achieving some of the other goals of poverty relief involves more complex or mediated arrangements, and evaluating success is less straightforward in areas like improvements in health and education where these depend on socially organized provision. In fact, as the benefits of cash transfers have become increasingly apparent to national governments of developing countries (Levy 2013), the uptake of them as an instrument of social policy has generally involved attaching certain conditions.

Conditionality makes it possible to aim at specific objectives of social policy for poverty alleviation. For although the available evidence does not suggest that poor people make irresponsible use of cash that is granted unconditionally, their different kinds of use do have different effects, not only for the recipients, but also for wider communities. Conditions on transfers steer recipients towards behaviours that administrators of the scheme judge to be the most appropriate (see e.g. Schubert and Slater 2006). Insofar as conditions are intended to direct the demand of recipients for goods or services, the success of the scheme also depends on availability or provisioning from the supply side. So, for instance, the clearest evidence of benefits in the fields of education and access to health services, according to Sudha Narayanan (2011), is found in circumstances where there is extensive public provisioning of services. Mihir Shah (2008) argues, in an Indian context, that cash transfers cannot be more than a part of a solution to poverty since various public expenditures are essential to lift people out of poverty. As

[11] This is true even though remittances are often also sent from family members in one affluent country to another (Kapur 2004).

Devesh Kapur similarly emphasizes, 'it is critical to work out the complementary state actions that will ensure that cash transfers serve their purpose. If cash transfers are seen as a substitute for state actions, they are unlikely to achieve their long-term goals' (Kapur 2011: 80).

As well as appreciating how social infrastructure plays a causal role in the success of cash transfers, we should also recognize how transfer may in turn have effects on social infrastructure. Thus, Narendar Pani (2012) recommends attending to the potentially adverse macroeconomic effects and the diverse impacts transfers may have on households in view of their different kinds of vulnerability. Regarding macroeconomic effects, one would not necessarily expect these to show up on the basis of relatively small-scale transfer programmes, but studying a relevantly comparable cash-for-resources scheme in Mongolia, Ying Yeung and Stephen Howes (2015) found it 'likely, and certainly widely believed, that the cash transfers contributed to higher inflation'. (They also noted that public external debt rose noticeably when the scheme came into operation.) There is evidently a risk that if demand is enhanced by an influx of cash, and local supply is unable or slow to respond, then prices will rise, particularly of the items most likely to be sought in greater quantities: so food price rises are likely to erode the real value of transfers for recipients and to make non-recipients in the community worse off (Rachel Sabates-Wheeler and Stephen Devereux 2010; see also Kebede 2006). Other adverse effects potentially include the worsening of critical under-nutrition by the shift to cash transfers, if these are taken to substitute direct nutritional interventions (Pani 2012). This is because often the most vulnerable have the most particular nutritional requirements. They, '(the very young, pregnant and lactating women, the sick—especially those with HIV/AIDS—and elderly) may not be able to locate the kinds of food they specifically need in local markets' (Farrington and Slater 2006: 507–8). Provision for such needs is liable to require governmental direction rather than to be reliably expected from private initiatives.

It is even possible that one of the apparently strongest grounds of support for cash transfers may in fact not support them after all. I refer to the general assumption found in much of the literature that it is desirable for poor people to be given cash—as opposed to goods or support in some other form—because this enables them to find their own best solution to their own economic problems. It may certainly be salutary to heed what some recipients themselves think. For instance, a recent poll of Tanzanians reported by Sandefur et al. (2015) showed that about two-thirds preferred funds drawn from oil revenues to be spent on government services rather than on cash transfers. Surprised at this result, the researchers sought to check that the poll had not been skewed in some way by how the question had been framed or interpreted. So they followed up with an intensive process of deliberation to get a fuller understanding of what the people thought. The outcome of this further deliberation was that the number of respondents who preferred cash fell still further (from 28 per cent to 18 per cent). 'In short, the more people heard and talked about cash transfers, the less they liked the idea.' A similar lack of grassroots support has been reported in response to the 'resources-to-cash' scheme attempted in Mongolia (Yeung and Howes 2015).[12]

Why this unexpected reaction? Various explanations are possible. One is that cash transfers can be divisive. This can be so, moreover, regardless of whether or not they are targeted at specific categories of recipient. If they are untargeted, they may go to people who do not need them, while failing to reach some who do, which is arbitrary and can create tensions in a community. Yet targeting may not eliminate this problem: 'in Malawi, farmers rejected the notion of targeting in relation to subsidised inputs on the grounds that they were all poor, and that it would be divisive' (Farrington and Slater 2006: 508). Relatedly, Ian MacAuslan and Nils Riemenschneider note that while cash transfers leave recipients materially richer, they can also leave them resented. So not only material impacts but also 'symbolic, and in particular relational impacts should be taken more strongly into consideration' (MacAuslan and Riemenschneider 2011: 20). For cash transfers 'are not apolitical top-ups with impact only on income, but social and political processes with social and political consequences' (MacAuslan and Riemenschneider 2011: 21). Sandefur et al. (2015) note anecdotal evidence to suggest a concern that, while social services encourage a collective voice that helps increase accountability, cash transfers would focus people on private interests and leave room for corruption. It seems that people may have greater trust—and perhaps a stronger interest—in tangible assets such as schools and health clinics that are supported by real people in the community than in the abstraction of a currency. This is particularly so when it is not clear what net balance of benefits and costs (including local inflation and resentments) will result from an influx of gratuitous cash into the community.

How generally applicable any of those, or other possible, explanations may be is a matter for further research. But in order to know what such research needs to discover it could also be helpful to reflect on what actually needs explaining. We might usefully reflect on why we find it surprising that people have reservations about the value of cash. After all, why do we not instead find it strange that cash has a more tangible or persuasive value to us than do actual communal goods or public services? Since we cannot eat, wear, or do anything else with cash, our attachment to it is due to our faith in its marvellous abilities to transmogrify into whatever we want. We perhaps tend to forget that what we want still has to be

[12] 'Even at the height of its popularity, direct disbursement has received much less support than the use of funds for either "invested by state" or for "long term social development", and these gaps have widened over time. The latter two options are now about four times as popular as direct disbursement' (Yeung and Howes 2015: 22).

produced somewhere by someone, and in timely fashion. Perhaps in places like Tanzania and Mongolia it is not so easy to forget this.[13]

To sum up, we cannot be sure that a system of cash transfers could amount to an effective means of achieving freedom from dependency for the countries most in need of economic development. We cannot simply assume that giving extra spending power to some individual families means that a society as a whole thereby becomes less dependent. It is not even certain that the wider effect could not be to worsen the situation, for there seems to be a possibility that cash transfers might do more harm than good for those they are supposed to help. These are only cautionary observations, however, and relate to matters that would take further research to settle more definitively.

Meanwhile, there is a more fundamental concern to highlight about the very nature of cash transfers, as these are understood to operate in the kinds of scheme in question. Up to now, we have left unchallenged the assumption that what is being transferred is, indeed, *cash*. Yet the programmes implemented by organizations such as GiveDirectly and endorsed by the effective altruists do not in fact transfer *cash* at all! This is because they depend on the technology of cashlessness, and it is only due to the technological feasibility of doing so that they are viable at all. While this may seem a mere technical detail to those who are broadly persuaded of the value of cash transfers, it does manifest a paradox that, at the very least, requires some comment.

5.4 The Paradox of Cashless Cash

The idea of *cashless cash* is certainly paradoxical, in the abstract, but what about in reality? A question is whether the use of electronic payments systems alters in any significant way the nature of what we understand as cash. Certainly, compared to the use of banknotes and coins, cashless payments have some general advantages in terms of convenience and versatility. More specifically, they make possible the sort of cash transfer programme operated by organizations like GiveDirectly. The technology now available allows them to dispense spending power instantaneously, across geographical distance, and at a significant scale of

[13] Sandefur et al. (2015) found it 'interesting that in a low-income democracy like Tanzania, cash transfers remain a fairly technocratic fad, rather than a movement with popular, grassroots support. In Tanzania, people appear to trust their government more than economists do.' But this is not just a matter of people trusting a government because they support it politically: 'Based on conversations with opposition politicians in Dar es Salaam, we speculated that people who trust the current government less would be more supportive of cash. What we found is the opposite: more trust in government yields more support for direct distribution, although this correlation is not statistically significant. We can only speculate after the fact as to why. Perhaps respondents preferred the known to the unknown: schools and health clinics have, after all, been built in most villages in rural Tanzania in the last 30 years. During deliberation, participants questioned the mechanisms required to channel cash directly to households. Who would be in charge of accounting for that transfer?'

operations. The transfers can reach intended recipients without the attrition of bureaucratic waste, corruption, and chiselling that more traditional forms of cash transportation would have incurred. The use of electronic payments eliminates various intermediaries that otherwise could each have been taking a cut at the various stages along the route from donor to recipient.

The advantages, however, are not unalloyed or unqualified, and there is a particular qualification to note in relation to proposals for unconditional cash transfers as a medium for alleviating poverty. This is that the possibility of cashlessness depends on the fulfilment of certain conditions. These may or may not be regarded as onerous or problematic by senders and recipients of the transfers, but they do need to be understood by those who aim to appraise such schemes. Although these days we may tend to take for granted the advances made in technology, we should not lose sight of the significant achievement represented by the creation of electronic payments systems. Nor is it merely the technical infrastructure involved, for this can only serve to transfer spending power around the world when harnessed to an immense and complex set of organizational arrangements.

It is no simple matter to operate payments systems in regions that still lie beyond the reach of the global banking system. It is because *GiveDirectly*'s operation has developed a workable solution to this practical challenge that it has won the enthusiastic support of an array of influential backers including philanthro-capitalists like *Good Ventures*, a partner venture to GiveWell,[14] who are fulsome in praise: 'The *GiveDirectly* team is outstanding, and their tool—unrestricted cash transfers—has the potential to become a new standard of comparison for efforts to help the global poor.'[15] Thus while ordinary charitable donors to GiveDirectly can appreciate the simple fact of being able to make instantaneous efficient transfers, what particularly impresses the backers is the technology that makes it possible.[16]

The way the system works, when donors make their payments of earned dollars these are not then transferred directly to the poor. Donors first make electronic payments to GiveDirectly, and recipients subsequently access payments by means of a mobile money system operated in their own vicinity. In between these two occurrences are several intermediary steps. The initial donation comes from a

[14] *Good Ventures* (http://www.goodventures.org/) is a philanthropic foundation established by Cari Tuna and her husband, the Facebook co-founder Dustin Moskovitz. It has a close association with GiveWell, and is one of the funders of GiveDirectly.

[15] http://www.goodventures.org/about-us/press/good-ventures-announces-5-million-in-matching-funds-for-givedirectly Accessed June 2018.

[16] An early backer of GiveDirectly was Google, whose endorsement mentions that 'GiveDirectly's *potential* moving forward is massive' and promises 'impact *outside the confines of their own program*' (https://www.givedirectly.org/funders-and-partners Accessed June 2018). Other major investors include two Facebook co-founders—Chris Hughes, who is on GiveDirectly's board, and Dustin Moskovitz—and the Omidyar Network, established by eBay billionaire Pierre Omidyar (https://www.omidyar.com/blog/why-we-invested-givedirectly Accessed June 2018).

person's bank account and is transferred via the established banking system to an account held by GiveDirectly. It is thus entered as a credit into a digital transmission system. GiveDirectly's bank can send the credit to a bank account within the jurisdiction and currency area of the intended recipient. The credit then has to be forwarded to an account held with a mobile money system. In the case of Kenya, which has led the way in developing mobile money systems in Africa, the local mobile currency is M-Pesa (for the origins of which see Hughes and Lonie 2007). Such a system needs to be in place—complete with branches or agents that can convert electronic credits into local cash currency—in order for the recipients to access the payment. For that purpose, the recipients need to be registered with the system and also to have access to a mobile phone in order to collect the electronic record of their entitlement to the payment.

As thus described, that is from the perspective of the users, the steps may seem quite straightforward. However, in order for a monetary credit in some international currency to become a credit on someone's M-Pesa account, as accessed via mobile phone, some further technical intermediation has been required. Even if it is not noticed by users, this is critical in making the system work so that transfers can be seamlessly made right to the 'last mile', where the digital signal leaves the global banking highway and has to negotiate one of the myriad windy tracks of local money systems in economically remote regions. This service of 'last mile' conveyance is supplied by what are known as 'third party aggregators'. These are technical companies that specialize in providing a secure interface between the various different global banking systems, on the one hand, and the local mobile money providers like M-Pesa, on the other. What a third party aggregator provides, in terms of technology, is a flexible API (Application Programming Interface) that runs in the background to make possible the smooth and secure transfer of funds from the sender's money system to the mobile system of payment (McKay and Pillai 2016). In Kenya, for instance, the company Cellulant is an established third party aggregator; and among newer players to enter this burgeoning field of business, in 2014, was a company called Segovia Tech.

Segovia Tech provides the technological interface GiveDirectly relies on to effect its cash transfers. The founders of Segovia Tech, Paul Niehaus and Michael Faye, were also the founding directors of GiveDirectly. There are clearly synergies between these directors' for-profit and non-profit activities.[17] For the distinctive

[17] Isobel Coleman (2014), wrote that 'Segovia's potential market is enormous. A World Economic Forum report estimates that government cash transfers to the unbanked in emerging markets are nearing $550 billion. India's cash transfer program to workers alone is $14 billion. Already, approximately a billion people are reached by cash transfers in emerging markets, and that figure is only likely to grow'. By 2015 Segovia had secured substantial backing: '$15 million from investors like LinkedIn founder Reid Hoffman, the Omidyar Network and the Global Innovation Fund' (Cutler 2015). Elizabeth MacBride (2016) wrote of Segovia as part of a new business development that is 'potentially defining a new financial system, one that may include banks but may not rely on them, one that is less regulated and more accessible, and one that serves as a conduit between the developed world

selling point of the charitable venture is the 'skilled management' and 'scalable technical tools' it brings, which are provided by the for-profit company. In its early days, Segovia provided something like a *pro bono* service to GiveDirectly, but subsequently shifted its costings onto a more business-like basis.[18] Meanwhile the wider business opportunity illustrated by the charitable trials of the cash transfer technology did not go unappreciated by their wealthy backers or the business press:

> Faye and Niehaus don't see their company as solely limited to non-profits either. They're also very interested in the hundreds of billions of dollars in remittances that flow through global markets every year. Then, there are also lots of corporations operating in emerging markets with hundreds of suppliers.' (Cutler 2015)

Their experience of arranging cash transfers in Kenya and Uganda is presented in their early business pitches as proof of concept for the potential of their innovations to exploit a major untapped market in the field of mobile finance. For the dramatic growth of mobile phone use in developing countries, especially in Africa, was seen to furnish 'the foundational architecture—technology and policy—to connect nearly all of the world's poor to the financial network' (Faye and Niehaus 2015: 2). This opportunity was still greatly under-exploited, they could point out in 2014, since 'only 8 percent of mobile connections have an associated financial account; in other words, while the foundation is there, widespread usage is not' (Faye and Niehaus 2015: 2). In making their case to a business audience they highlight how their cash transfer programmes 'drive the adoption of digital payments' and how the process of delivering funds to the poor, 'has required us to register up to 1,200 households per week with local financial institutions' (Faye and Niehaus 2015: 2).

This, then, gives a sense of the intermediation involved in the actual process of effecting cash transfers, and it also gives some interesting perspective on the idea that these are *unconditional* cash transfers. For they in fact depend on the fulfilment of a demanding and extensive set of conditions. These include massive investments on the part of players in communications and banking sectors, investments on which a return will be expected.

It is therefore not self-evident that the business of facilitating remittances and donations from abroad will necessarily contribute to ending dependency. For it seems to be premised on structural arrangements that might be thought to have a

and emerging markets'. Sangwon Yoon (2015) noted that a 'fundamental challenge facing Faye and Niehaus is how quickly the $25 billion humanitarian aid industry, with its 4,480 organizations and 450,000 workers, is willing to diversify from a system it has relied on for decades'.

[18] These arrangements, and questions about potential conflicts of interest, have been a subject of discussion on the GiveWell website in a passage on 'Segovia' dated November 2016: https://www.givewell.org/charities/give-directly/supplementary-information#Segovia Accessed June 2018. That page also links to pages documenting earlier discussions.

tendency to perpetuate it. In fact, we now appreciate, 'cash transfer' schemes such as those utilized by entities like GiveDirectly, can be viewed as part of a massive global business. Given the potential for conflict between interests in promoting the well-being of the poor and interests in generating profits for corporations, there is some reason to be cautious about the potential contribution of cashless cash transfers to the goals of global justice.

What has become clear is that 'cashless cash' is paradoxical not merely in the abstract. In practice, we find the more material paradox that organizations like GiveDirectly, while claiming to cut out the middleman in making cash transfers, in fact rely on new and systemically more powerful middlemen. Furthermore, operative within this system, viewed from a purely objective standpoint, there is an evident conflict between interests in promoting the well-being of the poor and interests in generating profits for corporations. In the best-case scenario, of course, there could be a happy synergy between the two sets of interest which yields a win–win outcome. But far less happy scenarios can also very plausibly be imagined.

In fact, this brings us to consider a deeper reason still for concern about the real tensions underlying cashless cash. These are such that today there is serious discussion of a *war on cash.*

For some academics, this is a just and necessary war. A leading exponent of this view is the economist Kenneth Rogoff, author of *The Curse of Cash* (2016). The justice of the cause is proclaimed in relation to the vices that cash readily facilitates. These include various elicit practices of the shadow economy and tax evasion as well as criminal activities such as drug trading, human trafficking, money laundering, bribery, and terrorism. The necessity of the war, for Rogoff, relates to what he sees as a need of monetary policy for central banks to be able to impose negative interest rates, not only on bank reserves but on the public's money holdings too. Critics, however, have questioned both the proportionality of this response to the stated problems[19] and the legitimacy of central banks or governments adopting a strategy involving what could be seen as tantamount to theft, in exposing people's money holdings to the attrition of negative interest rates.[20] In short, the case for a war on cash is controversial.

[19] For instance, the idea that cash is peculiarly prone to criminal misuse simply disregards the extraordinary amount of fraud and illicit transactions that occur in movements among accounts in banking and finance (see e.g. Scott 2017).

[20] 'In the absence of cash, everyone must keep their money in the form of digital bank deposits. During recessions central banks could then use the banking system to deliberately corrode people's deposits via negative charges, 'inspiring' them to spend rather than hoard' (Scott 2016a). Indeed, it has been explicitly argued by Andrew Haldane, Chief Economist at the Bank of England 'that the presence of cash constrained central banks from setting negative rates to stimulate a depressed economy. In a future economic or financial crisis, current low rates would restrict the effectiveness of monetary policy. Enhancing the ability to use negative rates would provide central banks with additional flexibility and tools to deal with a slowdown. It would be an imaginative, rapid, and durable mechanism for levying negative rates to confiscate savings' (Das 2017: 24).

The fact is, nonetheless, that whatever normative arguments might be mustered for or against, digital payment systems are now being strongly promoted around the world as part of a wider move towards a *cashless* future. Currently, Western governments and NGOs 'are working hand-in-hand with banks, telecom companies and local authorities to replace cash with mobile money alternatives. The organizations involved include Citi Group, Mastercard, VISA, Vodafone, USAID, and the Bill and Melinda Gates Foundation' (Quijones 2015). Working to coordinate this is the *Better Than Cash Alliance*,[21] a consortium that promotes the idea of a cashless society based on the premise that eliminating cash would stimulate entrepreneurship among the poor. It is possible this move could yield benefits conducive to greater justice in the world. For, in principle, the extension and refinement of electronic payments systems could open new opportunities for innovative projects aimed at poverty relief and social justice. It is nevertheless prudent to be aware that this is not their primary goal and that the drive to eliminate cash could lead to other kinds of consequence as well, or even instead.

Some observers are indeed sceptical concerning both the intentions and the prognosis for the 'Better Than Cash' proposition. For one thing, cash does have its distinctive uses, which can be especially important for people in precarious circumstances.

> In reality, the elimination of cash would reduce a great many opportunities for entrepreneurship for people of few means. Gone would be the informal businesses the working poor often operate: roadside produce stands, street performances, handicraft tables, and day labor.... a cash-free society would limit entrepreneurship to those with the means to incorporate a business, afford the proprietary system required to accept payments, and understand the local, state, and federal tax burden the payment system would create. (Mason 2015)

For another thing, it is not only that the loss of cash could have problematic consequences, because the fall of cash is likely to mean the rise of something else, and this could bring its own problems. Brett Scott is alert to these when considering the reasons why such powerful interests are aligned behind the push for a 'cashless society'—or, as Scott suggests it would be more aptly named—the *bank payments society*. The dominant interests are aligned between three major sectors:

> The first is the banking industry, which controls the core digital fiat money system that our public system of cash currently competes with.... The cashless society, in their eyes, is a utopia where money cannot leave—or even *exist*—

[21] 'Based at the UN, the Alliance has 60 members, collaborates closely with other global organizations, and is an implementing partner for the G20 Global Partnership for Financial Inclusion. The Alliance is funded by the Bill & Melinda Gates Foundation, Citi Foundation, MasterCard, Omidyar Network, United States Agency for International Development, and Visa Inc. The United Nations Capital Development Fund serves as the secretariat.' https://www.betterthancash.org/about Accessed 17 June 2018.

> outside the banking system, but can only be transferred from bank to bank. The second is the private payments industry—the likes of Mastercard—that profits from running the infrastructure that services that bank system.... Cash transactions are peer-to-peer, requiring no intermediary, and are thus transactions that Visa cannot skim a cut off. The third—perhaps ironically—is the state, and quasi-state entities such as central banks.... cash's 'offline' nature... hampers central banks in implementing 'innovative' monetary policies, such as setting negative interest rates that slowly edit away bank deposits in order to coerce people into spending. (Scott 2017)

Scott also notes the supporting role of economists, pundits, and academics in the battle to win hearts and minds to the cause of cashlessness.

It is therefore also worth asking a question about the role of political philosophers. Although to date there has not been extensive debate about the possible normative and institutional contours of a cashless society, the idea of one is at least implicit in those proposals of applied philosophy that centre on comprehensive systems for the distribution of money or credit. A prominent example would be the burgeoning literature on unconditional basic income (UBI). Although the normative principles underpinning schemes of this kind do not necessarily entail cashless distribution, the political philosophers' discussions of basic income tend to assume it. Already in an early survey of the emerging literature on UBI, De Wispelaere and Stirton (2004) noted that 'most universal basic income schemes will rely on cash transfers'. They also observed that, in fact, '[f]ew researchers seem to fully appreciate how many distinctive forms cash transfers can take' (De Wispelaere and Stirton 2004: 270), despite there being considerable differences, for instance, between the grant of a postal cheque, a debit card with automatic top-up, and a refundable tax credit.[22] By 2012, they were in a position to suggest that 'the most promising technological advances can be found in the use of cell phones and various types of smart cards as electronic delivery systems for cash transfers' (De Wispelaere and Stirton 2012: 114n9). Meanwhile, Philippe Van Parijs, one of the leading proponents of UBI, had long assumed 'a computerised and efficient tax-collection and transfer-payment technology' (Van Parijs 2004: 20), and he appears confident that a 'fair and efficient distribution of cash' can be achieved with 'relative ease' in this 'era of electronic benefit delivery' (Van Parijs and Vanderborght 2017). The literature thus appears to accept the use of cashless cash without attending closely to the sorts of critical question raised here, or to the

[22] 'Discussions of UBI usually propose one of the following payment schemes: UBI can be implemented through existing tax-credit schemes (such an implementation turns UBI into a refundable tax credit); UBI proponents alternatively advance the idea of a basic income debit card from which recipients draw their grant. The card functions just like a bank card; a recipient uses it to make a cash withdrawal' (De Wispelaere and Stirton 2007: 538). For an overview of these modalities in Africa, see Vincent and Cull (2011), and on other technological aspects, particularly biometrics (albeit without particularly critical perspective) Gelb and Decker (2012).

case for addressing concerns about such practical matters before advocating institutional arrangements that will depend on them. So while it is unobjectionable to explore the conceivable benefits of such schemes, when thinking innovatively about principles of distributive justice in a new era of changing work patterns, I believe it is quite another to support practical experiments involving them without doing due diligence regarding the possible risks of cashless cash.

5.5 Conclusion

Recent philosophical thinking as applied to the problem of global justice has generated a number of proposals that are assumed to be realizable through more equitable distributions of money. In principle, and in the abstract, it is easy to understand why. But proposals intended to have real application in the world need to take into account practical complications that bear critically on the possibility of success. This chapter has considered some of these, showing that while potentially disruptive effects of relatively small-scale transfers to poor communities may be transient, larger-scale transfers could bring further problems. These could include reinforcing rather than reducing dependency in recipient countries, particularly if one condition for the transfers is integration into the global banking and communications systems.

Insufficient attention to the complications could lead to excessive confidence in the power of money as a carrier of potential good outcomes and in its power to amplify those good effects by being transferred from richer people to poorer people globally, at little cost to the former and great benefit to the latter. Confidence is sometimes expressed by effective altruists with striking claims such as that '[i]f we all donated a percentage of our income to the most effective charities, together we could actually end extreme poverty in this lifetime'.[23] It is encouraged by some of their favoured charities, as here, by the directors of GiveDirectly:

> from a purely fiscal perspective cash transfers could end extreme poverty today. In a world with ubiquitous payments, the amount of money needed to end extreme poverty would be within reach even under conservative assumptions.'
>
> (Faye and Niehaus 2015)

Yet we have seen that attempting to achieve a world of ubiquitous payments by means of the kind of distributional system they operate is not without its potential pitfalls.

Of course, given that the cautionary questions raised have not so far been thoroughly examined in the literature, it is conceivable that reassuring answers might yet be supplied. However, even if one supposes that all the concerns

[23] https://www.givingwhatwecan.org/get-involved/myths-about-aid/ Accessed August 2018.

articulated in this chapter could be assuaged, with the paradox of cashless cash proving innocuous, and money proving successfully transferable without adverse effects, there would still be other questions to consider. These bear, in particular, on the belief—shared by effective altruists and proponents of taxes for global justice—that a little money provided by the world's relatively small affluent population can help the much larger poor population a very great deal. Questions about the basis of this belief and its presuppositions are thus to be considered next. For a deeper potential objection to the possibility of eradicating poverty by means of monetary transfers is not that nominal sums of money cannot be made to arrive; it is that in virtue of the processes enabling them to arrive, *and in amounts needed to eradicate poverty*, those nominal sums may not have the value expected.

6
Can Benign Leverage Be Relied on to Make the World More Just?

Where Peter Singer and the Effective Altruists advance moral arguments about why affluent individuals should give to the poor, proponents of tax and fund approaches to global justice provide a fuller description of the problem of global poverty, in particular by integrating an understanding of the role of institutions in supporting practices and normative regimes that are harmful for the poor. Thus Thomas Pogge and others emphasize that we should not simply think in terms of offering assistance to the poor, but that we should take more seriously our obligations to avoid our institutionally mediated complicity in keeping them poor. They nevertheless share the view that the extent of the adjustment required, in relation to the size of the global economy, is remarkably small, because the duty we have can be discharged through the transfer of a relatively small amount of money. This is to rely on an effect that I shall refer to as *benign leverage*. The question for this chapter is whether those who premise on this their proposals for relieving global poverty take sufficient notice of the conditions that make it possible.

Section 6.1 explicates the idea of *benign leverage* and examines the question of what makes it possible. An answer presupposed by some liberal philosophers would allude to the superior industriousness of affluent countries that has enabled them to leverage greater value through their material economic interactions with the world;[1] on this basis they posit, as Peter Singer does, a charitable obligation to help the less successful peoples of the world. Cosmopolitan liberal theorists of justice like Pogge, however, are aware that the advantages of liberal nations are somewhat inseparable from their colonial history, as well as from their inequitable exploitation of the world's natural resources and their domination of international institutions. In light of these factors, it is held that there is not merely a charitable obligation, but an obligation of *justice*, to mitigate their adverse effects on those

[1] John Rawls (1999), for instance, refers to the view of economic history offered by David Landes (1998), which was influential for his liberal contemporaries. As Landes would have it, the remarkable economic transition in modern Europe was a matter of '*buildup*—the accumulation of knowledge and knowhow; and *breakthrough*—reaching and passing thresholds' (Landes 1998: 200). Rawls endorses the explanatory emphasis on 'good political culture', even if with certain qualms about the extent of Landes' Euro-centricity. For a contrasting view, which takes greater account of the materiality of the West's colonial history, see Kenneth Pomeranz (2000).

disadvantaged by them. This position, however, still only takes the current international institutional arrangements to be imperfectly just, rather than fundamentally unjust. The existing institutions are broadly serviceable, structurally speaking, but just require better safeguards to prevent abuses by the corrupt, criminal, and irresponsible agents that acquire power within them. If only the requisite good political will can be brought to prevail, justice can be achieved. Pogge's view of what would be required for its achievement is similar to Singer's in that it assumes a little effort on the part of the affluent would be sufficient to alleviate severe poverty globally.

Section 6.2 considers how tenable is this assumption of benign leverage by considering the preconditions for its applicability. We note first that there could be technical difficulties in operationalizing it to the ends of eradicating poverty globally, but we then also consider that, even if those difficulties may be surmountable, there is a more fundamental problem. I introduce this by reference to what I call *the paradox of benign leverage*. This arises in circumstances where what happens is that the more successfully the leverage is used to benefit the poor, the more difficult it becomes to achieve further success or even to consolidate the gains already made. This scenario is presented only hypothetically in the present chapter, and this is to leave open the possibility that in reality the paradox may not indicate a fatal flaw in programmes relying on benign leverage. Nevertheless, reasons are given for thinking that the concern is real and strong enough to warrant reserving endorsement of such programmes pending the assessment of the assumptions they rely on about how benign leveraging operates in the world.

6.1 The Benign Leverage Assumption

If tax and fund proposals are advanced on the basis that a modest shift of income or wealth from the affluent to the poorest may suffice to eradicate severe poverty in the world, then considered support for them should be able to refer to what, more concretely, makes the impressive leverage possible. One quite familiar and classic liberal view—influentially formulated by John Locke in the seventeenth century and endorsed in work as recent as Landes (1998)—is that some countries are more affluent than others due to a happy combination of good fortune and efficiency that work to their advantage. The idea, in simple terms, is along the lines that the more industrious, better organized, and more innovative political economies of developed countries have made much more efficient use of labour power and natural resources than poorer countries have. Because these rich countries are more efficient in extracting value from their material interactions with the world, so the thought goes, they can with less effort produce much more; and so for this reason they can afford to share some of their surplus with those less fortunate in the political economic conditions they have inherited from their less industrious or innovative forebears.

Reasons not simply to accept an account that rests so heavily on assumptions about the West's great 'unilateral' successes, however, include observations about the history and legacies of colonialism, slavery, and exploitation of worldwide resources. The Western liberal economies may have been well-organized in their practices, able to harness great industriousness and to stimulate innovation, but that is not the whole story. It is not only a case of the West forging ahead of the rest, economically, in the modern era, for there has also been profound exploitative injustice as well as a great deal of violence done on the part of the more powerful against the more vulnerable. Nor is it only historical legacies at issue, since exploitative and violent injustice persists to this day. The deeper causes of the continuing patterns of violence and exploitation worldwide may be a matter for debate, but what can be observed is that the rules of the game as enforced in international law, through treaties and institutions relating particularly to trade and investment, are very much shaped by those who have the greatest wealth and power. Since the international institutions also tend to serve those interests better than those of the economically weaker, it is thus possible to take a critical view of them as playing a causal role in maintaining global patterns of inequality. The prevailing norms appear to be functional for allowing the vested interests of those with financial power to draw further advantage over those disadvantaged by the system. This view would contribute to explaining the increasingly extreme polarization of wealth and income in the world.

Pogge highlights three interrelated factors that are fundamental in making the current global order less than just: the common and violent history that has shaped it; the shared institutional order globally that is imposed by, and in the interests of, those who have the greatest wealth and power; and the fact that, meanwhile, the poorer and more vulnerable of the world are excluded, without compensation, from access to the natural resources with which to make decent livelihoods. He thus conveys that we are dealing with a great material problem and one that is institutionally embedded globally. In his judgement, nevertheless, international institutions today are imperfectly just, rather than radically unjust, and they could, with appropriate reform, become more just. The thrust of his proposals is to ensure that funds are raised, protected, and directed so as to be used to the benefit of the poor rather than siphoned off by the rich, the powerful, and the corrupt. If flows are channelled through robust brokerage mechanisms, so that real net sums of funds can arrive where they are needed, then extreme poverty might be eradicated by using the global institutions that already exist. We do not need new institutions or even a new political philosophy, on Pogge's view; what is needed is more thorough and consistent application of the liberal principles that international institutions already purport to embody.

Furthermore, while recognizing the need for an institutional approach to achieving the redistribution that would eradicate poverty, Pogge—along with tax and fund proponents more generally—shares with Effective Altruists two assumptions about the role of money transfers in the alleviation of poverty. One assumption, which was discussed in Chapter 5, is that transferring money equates to a relatively straightforward transfer of effective spending power and thus also of a net benefit in terms of the freedom this brings with it. The further assumption, which is to be examined now, is that any given sum of money raised by the affluent is going to have much greater purchasing power for the poor than it does for the rich. This assumption plays a critical role in arguments for the feasibility of reform to the existing institutions. For it supports the view that with only a modest amount of reform, the problem can be solved.

This second assumption I shall refer to as that of *benign leverage*. The assumption has an intuitively compelling element, namely, the general idea that the marginal utility of any given dollar is greater for the poor than for the affluent. The assumption certainly seems tenable as a proposition of microeconomics: for instance, the marginal utility of a dollar is clearly greater for the hungry family that can use it to buy a second bag of rice than it would be for anyone in an affluent society. Yet we still need to keep in mind the question of whether what is true for a selection of individuals and families can also be true for an entire society. If the goal is poverty relief for all, then some very basic questions of macroeconomics arise. If everyone in society can now buy twice as much rice as before, where is all the extra rice going to come from? Why should we assume its price would not be affected? What might be the knock-on effects of adjusting to different production schedules and/or prices?

When Pogge claims that his tax and fund proposal is a *feasible* solution to the problem of extreme poverty, it is arguable that his notion of feasibility does not involve sufficiently robust criteria. Mathias Risse has challenged the assumptions of Pogge on this score:

> Pogge seems to think 'feasibility' is primarily a matter of allocating money to developing countries, money that could and should be provided by rich countries. He calculates that it would just take 1.2% of the income of the rich economies, $312 billion annually, to bridge the aggregate shortfall of those living on less than $1 per day from the $2 line. (Risse 2005: 371)

Risse does not think this is an adequate account of feasibility, for 'while Pogge's calculation shows that at least abject poverty would not be insurmountable *if* closing such a gap were merely a matter of transferring money, this if-clause is highly problematic' (Risse 2005: 371). Risse points out that further necessary conditions for achieving the goal include 'reliable ways of distributing the funds to individuals who, after all, do not simply have bank accounts they can securely and regularly access (and to which money can be transferred without interference by local strongmen who would rather channel the funds to benefit their own purposes), as well as an environment in which individuals can actually spend the money' (Risse 2005: 372). Securing such conditions, moreover, requires institutional capacity and infrastructural investment. To effect transfers at scale 'one would need either a trustworthy banking system, or some other network for distribution' (Risse 2005: 372). Risse's points here are in line with what I have been arguing. But he stops short of making a further point I would emphasize, for he still assumes that money transfers in principle would do the job.

From Risse's point of view, the problem is essentially a technical one. Yet if the problem were only a technical one, it need not be insurmountable; and if it were not insurmountable, then a reformist approach to global institutions—as envisaged by Pogge and others—might indeed turn out to be feasible. Reasons to be sanguine about a technical answer were indicated in Chapter 5, where we noted that a key practical selling point of the new breed of charities that fit the Effective Altruism mould is that they have technical solutions to the money transfer problem. In explicitly addressing the issue of establishing a network for circulating cashless cash, the problem of corrupt intermediaries siphoning off funds is potentially circumvented too. It thus does seem possible that a central objection of Risse's could be met.

If there is any impediment to the efficacy of cash transfers, then, it would not seem to be of a technical kind. If reservations might be in order, it would be for different reasons. For instance, we know from Chapter 5 that the cash transfers effected by the means identified are conditional on their recipient opening an account with a particular financial delivery system and having access to a mobile phone. This is not the kind of condition that is usually associated with conditional cash transfers, for those are specified as a matter of social policy and require participation in some activity of directly social value such as promoting nutrition, health, or education. There is an evident difference in that the uptake of financial services is not inherently any part of the primary ethical objective of the transfers but merely a means for facilitating it. The reasons to accept the condition do not follow directly from the purpose of the transfers. Whereas conditions of participation in practices related to nutrition, health, and education encourage people to do things that are expected to contribute directly to accomplishment of the policy goal, it is not so evident that being drawn into a digital payments system is such an inherently beneficial thing. In fact, we noted some reasons to be concerned about this. Certainly, the justification of the means thus does not follow in a comparably direct way from arguments supporting the ends. Nevertheless, even assuming that inclusion in the global financial system is or could be an acceptable means, the question remains as to whether the transfer of money that it makes possible can necessarily be expected to achieve the end of eradicating severe poverty.

Here we approach a deeper sort of problem than the technical one concerning the feasibility of modest reforms having very substantial impacts on global poverty. It tends to be supposed by their advocates that given the means for effecting transfers, achieving the eradication of severe poverty would just depend on effecting transfers of a sufficient amount. In Pogge's estimate, we noted, such transfers would be in the order of 1–2 per cent of gross income from the affluent. It is assumed that, provided only that the channels of delivery can effectively be kept open, money can flow through and achieve the desired ends. Yet, certain other conditions are tacitly assumed to hold. One obvious condition necessary for the successful transfer of a small percentage—say 2 per cent—of global income to the poorest is that the rest of the world's economic and financial actors do not meanwhile engage in any activities that would increase their aggregate share to more than 98 per cent of global income or affect prices or purchasing power in ways that would render 2 per cent insufficient in real terms. Another condition is that new and different patterns of inequality, other than those at which funds are directed, do not materialize in the interim. A concern has to be that a change significant enough to lift substantial numbers of people out of severe poverty could involve a good deal of other changes in the financial system, and these changes are likely to work in favour of those with greatest power and influence over it. This is the deeper concern about the feasibility of benign leverage working as straightforwardly as supposed by the proposals that rely on it.

6.2 The Paradox of Benign Leverage

So far we have seen that good arguments can be advanced for believing that cash transfers are desirable in principle, have some proven efficacy at small scale, and are technically achievable by electronic means. We have also taken note of the sums of money it is reckoned would need to be transferred from the affluent to the poorest in order to eliminate severe poverty from the world, and we have understood that these are of a magnitude that it is supposed could potentially be raised by means of some reasonable revenue-raising scheme such as various philosophers have proposed. On the basis of these considerations, proponents of tax and fund suggest that what remains is to get political commitment from the governments of the world to take the modest steps required to establish the requisite scheme or schemes. To this end, they may deploy moral arguments, quite similar to those of Effective Altruists, designed to coax and motivate governments, and those who elect them, to do what is needed. A key factor in establishing the moral persuasiveness of these arguments is the claim that a great deal of good can be done at a very modest cost. This is based on arithmetical calculations about the sums of money that would assure success.

However, for the arithmetic to have application to the matter at hand, it has to be assumed that the 'real value' of each sum entered into the calculations remains broadly constant throughout the course of all the transactions involved in effecting a transfer in the world. This presupposition is seldom made explicit, and I am aware of no argument that has been offered to support it. And yet the core moral argument appealed to depends on its being warranted. So can it be?

When benign leverage operates, a relatively modest monetary sacrifice on the part of the affluent can do a very great deal for the world's poorest people. In the situation assumed, the cost—and thus the effort—of helping is low for the donor, relative both to their own resources and to the effort that would be required of the recipient to attain the amount of spending power the donation confers on them. A factor that makes benign leverage possible, then, is the low monetary cost of the basic necessities whose supply would suffice to alleviate the severest effects on them of poverty. As was highlighted in Chapter 5, however, an influx of spending power into a poor community can have adverse effects in terms of rising prices and possible strains on social cohesion. A reply to such concerns would be that local inflationary pressures experienced in the short term could actually stimulate local economic growth and thus provide the basis for a longer-term benefit. However, if that would be a solution to the first problem it could be the cause of another.

The problem here is something akin to a paradox, sharing certain features of both the 'paradox of thrift' and the 'paradox of deleveraging'. The paradox of thrift, as explained by Keynes (1936: ch. 23.vii), can appear when the virtuous conduct of a thrifty individual is generalized into a pattern of behaviour among the wider population. If all individuals lead thrifty lives, consumption and aggregate demand falls, meaning that production diminishes. So the outcome of individuals working hard and saving rather than spending leads to a situation in which the society ends up being less productive than if individuals had been more profligate. The paradox of deleveraging arises as the generalization of the virtuous deed of paying down one's debts. For to pay off a debt one needs to liquidate assets; if everyone starts putting assets on the market at the same time, prices will fall, so the more everyone tries to get money to pay off their debts, the less able will everyone be to do so. Both kinds of scenario appear as paradoxes due to failure to beware of a *fallacy of composition*: this is the fallacy of assuming that what is true for an individual case is necessarily also true for a collective case. There is a comparable and related fallacy of composition, I want to suggest, at the heart of the thinking about what it would take to eliminate global poverty. It resides in the assumptions made about the arithmetic involved. The assumptions are quite explicit in Singer's account of how he came to adopt estimates provided by a United Nations task force headed by Jeffrey Sachs, which costed achievement of the millennium development goals at $121 billion in 2006, rising to $189 billion by 2015. 'When we take account of existing official development aid promises,' Singer calculates, 'the additional amount needed each year to meet the goals is only $48 billion for 2006 and $74 billion for 2015' (Singer 2006). He declares: 'I double-checked the figures and asked a research assistant to check them as well. But they were right. Measured against our capacity, the Millennium Development Goals are indecently, shockingly modest.' Until doing these calculations, he says, he had never before 'fully understood how easy it would be for the world's rich to eliminate, or virtually eliminate, global poverty' (Singer 2006). By what methods he checked the calculations I don't know, but nor do I think we can simply assume that this is the sort of problem that can be grasped with simple arithmetic. A very basic criticism that others, including Barry and Øverland (2009), have levelled at Singer is that he does not look especially carefully at harms that can be done by aid. They point out, too, that one needs to be cautious when making claims about the effectiveness of aid for poverty relief because, in debates about this matter, little is settled. Given the real possibility that aid can do harm rather than good under certain conditions, they argue that more attention needs to be paid to the empirical questions than is paid by Singer. While institutionalists like Pogge heed a wider range of conditions, they still advance similarly simple quantitative proposals on the basis of monetary estimates. Pogge has calculated that $312bn per year could eliminate global poverty by lifting everybody above the $2 a day threshold; this would involve a transfer in the order of just 1 or 2 per cent of total global annual income. So although Pogge may improve on the description of the problem, he stops short of examining the conditions that have to be assumed as existing in order for benign leverage to be possible. Yet even if we set aside issues concerning the immense and complex qualitative questions about what is practically involved in real poverty relief in particular situations, it is still possible to challenge the assumption of benign leverage even in its own terms. The challenge arises from a concern that, as the use of leverage brings achievement of the goal closer, it may at the same time push it further from attainment. This is what I refer to as the *paradox of benign leverage.*

Benign leverage can in principle be brought to bear in situations of great inequality such as may be illustrated by taking a simplified example whereby one group of people earn, say, a median $100 per day and another earn less than $2, as denominated in a convertible international currency. If we assume a situation where $2 is required for a minimally decent life and where 100 million people try to subsist on $1.50, then transforming the lives of those people would cost $50 million dollars. Given a population in the order of a billion in Western Europe and North America, if only 5 per cent of them gave up just $1 a day, a situation of severe mass poverty could be alleviated. The numbers here are intended very roughly to depict the kind of situation assumed in the literature influenced by Singer and Pogge. Given the nature of the situation, it is reasonable to assume that the additional daily $0.50 received by the poor is mostly spent on subsistence goods, particularly food. One consequence of this is that aggregate demand for food in the regions receiving the assistance will increase significantly, and it is hard to imagine food production rapidly increasing by a comparable amount, so prices are likely to rise. Accordingly, transfers that stimulate economic demand are liable to have inflationary effects that reduce the spending power of those transfers. Of course, the aggregate increase in demand is likely to flatten out as people's most basic needs are satisfied, which could ease the inflationary pressure. At the same time, though, it is also possible that as people's immiseration starts to ease they can better resist pressure to perform some of the more intensely unpleasant and arduous jobs for such low wages that they were formerly constrained by desperation to accept. So we might expect some inflation in wage levels would feed through into prices. The net effect of these responses would be to diminish the ratio of leverage in the process of applying it.

Furthermore, we might expect changes to the leverage ratio to come not only from the recipients' end but also from that of the donors. For if any inflationary erosion of payments received is to be offset, that means increasing donations, which would add pressures in the donors' economy. One of the starting assumptions for proposals relying on benign leverage is that the donation of a small portion of an individual's income would not be experienced as a great loss, for it is 'spare cash'; but at least part of that cash might otherwise have been spent on something else, and so the aggregate economic effect of domestic spending forgone could be somewhat deflationary. Such an effect may not be appreciable at a small scale, but it would be magnified if and when significant steps towards more complete accomplishment of the goal were achieved.

The 'paradox of benign leverage', then, can be summed up as follows. Starting from an assumption that circumstances of benign leverage apply, as Effective Altruists and proponents of taxes for global justice do, then the initial situation is one of high leverage, with each small donation potentially achieving proportionately great good. Once cumulative donations begin to scale up, however, and money starts achieving its goal in the target community, we may expect upward pressures on prices in that community. Concomitantly, as the amount being sent from the donor community increases, we may expect a reduction of domestic spending power in the domestic economy, which will exert downward pressure on demand, meaning some contraction of earned income. In this way, the leverage ratio is reduced by movements on both sides. The more extensive and successful the programme of transfers is, the more the ratio is liable to reduce. The paradoxical element here is not the simple fact that gains come more easily at the outset than later. This is a phenomenon familiar from many kinds of task that figuratively involve first picking some low hanging fruit and then confronting harder-to-reach rewards of effort. The paradox is that the achievement of gains can *cause* further gains to be harder to achieve. In other words, the operation of benign leverage tends to undermine the conditions of its own possibility.

This, of course, is simply to unfold a logic that follows from some elementary premises of economic theory, and how exactly it would play out in practice is a matter that could only be settled on the basis of practical evidence—which we do not have in advance. Meanwhile, though, there are significant points, both methodological and substantive, to highlight about reliance on benign leverage to assist the challenge of remedying severe widespread poverty.

One methodological point is that it could be a mistake to suppose that the magnitude of the challenge of relieving global poverty can meaningfully be represented by means of *arithmetical* calculations. It was noted that such calculations sufficed to convince Singer that the goal of eliminating severe poverty was within reach; Pogge likewise uses arithmetic to calculate that the global poor could be lifted out of extreme poverty by means of transfers amounting to 1.2 per cent of the aggregate annual gross national incomes of the high-income economies (Pogge 2002: 7). However, if the logic of benign leverage operates as understood here, then we can see why the difficulties bound up with the challenge could become *exponentially* greater along the way to meeting it. Given this possibility, the methodological basis of calculations for benign leverage needs to be made explicit and defended.

The substantive point is that arguments relying on monetary proxies to depict the scale of the challenge can miss what is really at issue, namely, the material question of how it is possible for all the people in the world to have at least the basics they need for a minimally decent life. These are things like food, fuel, shelter, clothes, and medicines; money, as such, is not one of them. So what a leverage ratio ultimately relates to is the difference of effort or resource required from people in dramatically different circumstances on this planet to achieve a minimally decent life. This necessarily involves productive activity and not simply monetary transfers. When an affluent donor gives up the price of a lunch to feed a poor family for a day, s/he does not experience this as a loss of food, but the gain in food has to come from somewhere. If we think about the material dimension of what is required, we see that assumptions about benign leverage are out of place. If they can appear to hold good for money transfers, this is because of differences in the prices of money in the different parts of the world. So care needs to be taken when drawing more material inferences about eliminating the real problems of poverty.

At the end of Chapter 5, we noted the confident claim of cash transfer advocates that, since the amount of money needed to end extreme poverty was easily within reach, one could infer that 'from a purely fiscal perspective cash transfers could end extreme poverty today' (Faye and Niehaus 2015: 6). This reference to a *purely fiscal perspective* is telling. The idea conveyed by the expression lies at the very heart not only of Effective Altruist strategies, as we noted, but also of tax and fund approaches to global justice. The *purity* of the perspective is the simple and context-free idea of income and expenditure entries balanced in a ledger: no actual economic or financial facts need to be considered. For this reason it can be regarded as a matter of simple arithmetical calculation of the kind called into question in this chapter. What is missing is an adequate understanding of how the entries on the fiscal ledger are supposed to relate to what is happening in the world. This is a matter that will be discussed more fully in Chapter 9, but here I want to flag the basic point that the 'purely fiscal perspective' from which such figures are projected could only yield a verifiable view of a budgetary situation under circumstances in which the institutions and instruments of taxation and spending are fully established. Such a situation would apply only within a fiscally unified political entity. Mere hypotheses about alternative uses of a given sum of money, particularly when the different uses could occur in entirely different economic contexts, do not generate a *fiscal* perspective as such. An actual fiscal perspective must take into account how any spending decision may have effects on revenues raised and how any significant redistributive measures—such as would remove extreme poverty—may involve significant structural shifts in society and the economy, which in turn can generate complex financial adjustments that affect the very value of revenues. Complex considerations of these kinds, moreover, arise even within the relatively contained context of a single economic region with its own currency. The variables and uncertainties will multiply significantly in transfers between different regions or currency areas. A fiscal perspective, in short, presupposes the institutional preconditions that would have to apply for effective tax and fund measures to be possible—and these are conditions that are precisely absent from global relations today.

So the claim that from a 'purely fiscal' perspective there is no impediment to ending extreme poverty today may be true, and yet its relevance is limited insofar as that perspective not only abstracts from, but effectively presupposes a denial of, the actual circumstances that exist today or in any currently foreseeable future. In real fiscal budgeting processes, estimates have to be made in relation to the particulars of circumstances and likely real eventualities; concerns have to be addressed about who will be expected to pay the tax, how compliance will be ensured, what the political fallout might be, how the shift of a tax burden might alter the currency values, wages, or prices, or thus how the expenditure might achieve the goals for which it was estimated. To aim to balance a budget on the basis of entirely unknown future prices and exchange rates, by contrast, is not to make an informed calculation so much as a rather random guess.

6.3 Conclusion

This chapter has examined the assumption that, with just the will to apply a relatively modest amount of effort, the more fortunate inhabitants of this planet can relieve the most severe suffering of the mass of their least fortunate cohabitants. An assumption left unchallenged is that the natural world provides a sufficient resource for human beings today to achieve that goal. Indeed, the problem under discussion is not one of nature's making but an outcome of the strategies that various sections of humanity have pursued in developing their relationship with the world of nature and with each other. To put it another way, the circumstances of justice are assumed to pertain: the world has moderately scarce resources relative to human needs, and human beings have 'limited sympathies' for their fellows; but there is also a general acceptance of a need for workable cooperative arrangements between people and peoples.[2] Given the reasons to believe humans have a fundamental interest in seeking justice in their relationships with each other, optimism about the possible will concerning its achievement is appropriate. Optimism alone, however, will not suffice for its achievement, and without due intellectual precaution there is a risk that overconfidence could generate illusory hopes.

Accordingly, critical questions have been asked about the presumed robustness of estimates of how much money needs to be raised, and of how readily what is needed can be raised by the affluent, in order to end extreme poverty. This is not to say the estimates are necessarily wrong. But it is to say that rather than simply allow the assumptions generated from the optimistic perspective, proposals that depend on benign leverage should acknowledge a duty of due diligence in the matter.

In discharging that duty, it is conceivable that a warrant in reality for the optimistic assumptions might be found. This might be anticipated, in particular, in two kinds of scenario. In one scenario where benign leverage is being applied, any decrease in the ratio would take place sufficiently gradually that alleviation of severe poverty is reached *before* the effort of leveraging becomes so demanding as to be problematic. In the other, even if the leverage ratio decreases less gradually, the increase of effort required to make improving gains for the poor can still be achieved by the affluent on the basis of their own commensurate economic growth.

A major problem under such scenarios, however, is presented by ecological constraints. Even continuing the current trajectory of global economic development, on whose maintenance the former scenario would depend, the ecological effects are expected to be unsustainable. The second scenario, which depends on continued economic *growth*, thus appears still more problematic. Accordingly, there are questions to be picked up in Chapter 7 about the preconditions that must be assumed to apply for anticipation of an optimistic scenario to be credible.

[2] Discussions of the 'circumstances of justice' in the political philosophy literature generally take their bearings from Hume's idea (Hume [1739] Bk III, Pt II, sec.ii) as adapted by Rawls (1971: 127), which is roughly glossed in the text here. In commenting on the literature, however, Peter Vanderschraaf suggests that the standard account might be supplemented by a further condition that Hobbes would emphasize, namely, 'that the parties all live under the rule of a commonwealth' (Vanderschraaf 2006: 337). The thinking here has something in common with the Rawlsian objection to cosmopolitanism that there is no relevant 'scheme of cooperation' to make distributive principles applicable. But the Hobbesian augmentation of their specification also brings into focus a factor that links concerns about the necessary conditions of fiscal arrangements with the concern to be discussed in Chapter 11 about securing the circumstances of justice necessarily preceding any attempt to implement the principles of justice.

7
Can Money Transfers Serve to Offset Ecological Harms?

The idea that the relief of global poverty can be achieved by means of some quite modest redistributive measures appears to depend, for reasons outlined in Chapter 6, on a background assumption of continuing economic growth. For on this basis it is conceivable that the requisite redistribution need not be experienced as problematically costly by the affluent. There need then be no strong resistance to minor institutional reforms that could nevertheless achieve for the global poor something akin to what was achieved by the modern welfare state for the poor in developed countries. Yet among reasons for caution about the prospects of such a remarkable achievement is the consideration that indefinitely growing the global economy may not be a viable option. As was shown in Chapter 4, it is reasonable to accept that there are ecological limits to real growth in the economy. In fact, under the circumstances now prevailing, it is even possible that the pressures referred to as financialization drive a disregard for ecological constraints in a way that does not even guarantee economic growth as a result. The concern to be examined in this chapter, however, is that the problem may be still more intractable than that. For not only can financialization be a driver of ecological unsustainability, ecological unsustainability in turn can present challenges of financial instability.

This possibility is introduced in Section 7.1 by reference to a significant speech delivered by Mark Carney in 2015, as Governor of the Bank of England. Financial stability matters, he affirmed, because maintaining low, stable, and predictable inflation is a public good. If strategies for economic growth are constrained by the requirement of maintaining financial stability, he showed, the situation is further complicated by ecological constraints. There are various ways in which transformations in the natural environment—and Carney considers specifically the effects of climate change—can affect the value of assets and the costs of insurance. These factors can influence all the prices of money and can thus potentially generate considerable financial instability. With the prospects of climate change becoming more serious in the longer run, and with markets becoming increasingly uncertain about future movements, even the mere anticipation of future problems can be destabilizing in the shorter run too. Thus we find that not only can financial developments drive adverse ecological consequences, the converse may be true too. So just as the value of money can be affected by ecological changes, so the cost of dealing with adverse ecological circumstances can be affected by financial instabilities. Since financial instability predictably has adverse effects on productivity and the prospects of reducing egregious inequalities, this risks driving still further ecological irresponsibility—in what could become a deleterious feedback loop.

Given, then, the prospect for feedback between the two sides of the process, the unpredictability of both material ecological costs and monetary estimates of their value can be amplified and rendered more radically uncertain. This situation, I shall suggest in Section 7.2, compounds the problems that have already been mentioned about projecting valuations of costs and benefits into the future. Chapter 3 showed that the projection of values on the basis of futurity is part of the big problem that constitutes financialization, since it has inescapably speculative aspects. This renders problematic such ideas as that money can serve to express economic comparisons of costs and benefits over time. Given that the basis for commensurating various kinds of ecological impact so as to then measure them in terms of economic costs and benefits is uncertain in the here and now, then any attempt to project such measurements into the future compounds the uncertainties involved. This ought to be a reason for caution about thinking that pro-ecological policies can rely on projections of that kind. Thus one might question the assumption apparent in Simon Caney's (2011) suggestion, for instance, that progress towards the goals of climate justice could be made by distributing the revenues raised from selling permits to emit greenhouse gases when those revenues are spent on mitigating and adapting to climate change. The assumption in question, to be clear, is distinct from others that might be challenged, such as whether any substantive loss or harm can ever meaningfully be compensated by money or, indeed, by any kind of substitute, given that in human lives, as in ecosystems, some important things are non-replaceable. The question applies even in relation to situations that could in principle be rectified through compensation or substitution: it concerns the conditions under which financial flows can in fact convey stable monetary value from one place to another in the way that has to be assumed for a strategy of compensatory funding to work. For it is not definite that money can serve as a suitably reliable store and transmitter of value. If it is the case that the allocation of money can in general not be regarded as a neutral, independent, and reliable proxy for substantive goals, it is a fortiori the case with regard to ecological goals.

The argument of this chapter, then, is that proposals involving monetary compensation for environmental problems, like proposals relying on possibilities of benign leverage, put faith in money necessarily having certain properties or powers that in fact it only has under certain conditions. It is arguable that those conditions are unlikely to be fulfilled in the circumstances the hypotheses are invoked to apply to. This is a reason to be cautious about the use of tax and fund proposals in relation to environmental challenges. More generally, in view of the worrying dialectic of financial instability and ecological unsustainability that underlies the radical uncertainty of monetary values, we need to be cautious about arguments that generate hopes of strategies based on profit-seeking leading to outcomes that enhance social justice or ecological sustainability.

7.1 Financial Stability as an Ecological Challenge

Financial stability in a market economy is something that cannot be assumed as a given but has to be achieved and maintained. If maintaining stability is already a challenge under ordinary economic circumstances, the challenge may be significantly enhanced when ecological circumstances also enter into play. To explicate this point I shall make reference to a carefully explained warning provided by Mark Carney, speaking as the Governor of the Bank of England, not to assume that money can maintain stable value in the face of a significant ecological challenge like climate change. Climate change is one of the best known and most significant of the ecological problems we face, and it can be taken to be indicative of the still wider and more complex problem that the full range of ecological challenges present us with today.

Addressing a gathering of insurers in 2015, Carney emphasized the unpredictability of climate impacts on financial stability. He highlighted three ways in which climate change can affect financial stability, namely, through: (i) impacts on insurance liabilities and the value of financial assets arising from climate-related disasters; (ii) potential liability risks if those affected seek to hold people responsible in future for causing harms; (iii) transition risks—that is, transition to a different economic basis can entail a radical reassessment of value of some kinds of asset. Let us briefly consider the reasoning in each case.

(i) Environmental change generally, and climate change particularly, can affect the value of financial assets—either directly, by damaging property or disrupting operations, or indirectly, by disrupting operations of major customers or suppliers. It can also affect insurance claims and liabilities. The value of financial assets is intimately bound up with the cost of insurance, and the costs of insurance are sensitive to material circumstances of risk. Although not all physical risks of climate change are a threat to financial stability, some can be, as Brett Christophers illustrates:

> The risk of rising seas engulfing a Pacific island whose inhabitants and public institutions are essentially isolated from the global financial system is potentially a human tragedy but is not likely to be a threat to financial stability. If, though, for example, those inhabitants have property insurance and their government

> raises finance by issuing debt in the international capital markets, then, if the numbers involved are big enough, the threat to financial stability represented by rising sea levels could be a very real one indeed. (Christophers 2017: 1114L)

Physical risks from climate change, Carney notes, will become increasingly relevant to the asset side of insurer's balance sheets. For although insurers can re-price or withdraw cover, they 'need to be wary of cognitive dissonance within their organisations whereby prudent decisions by underwriters lead to falls in the value of properties held by the firm's asset managers' (Carney 2015: 7). This can have considerable significance given that the insurance sector in the UK, and worldwide, manages trillions' worth of assets to match liabilities that often span decades. 'While a given physical manifestation of climate change—a flood or storm—may not directly affect a corporate bond's value, policy action to promote the transition towards a low-carbon economy could spark a fundamental reassessment' (Carney 2015: 7).

(ii) Meanwhile, the idea that businesses in the future may be held retrospectively liable for harms they have in precedence played a causal role in creating can exert downward pressure on the valuation of a business. Liability risks, Christophers notes, include 'tort litigation (coastal flooding allegedly was already being contemplated by certain island populations as grounds for claims against emitters), criminal litigation (where the state, rather than individuals, would take corporations to court, potentially on the basis of damages to human health), or environmental justice litigation (given . . . the disparity between those who contribute most to global warming and those who must bear the worst of its consequences . . .)' (Christophers 2017: 1112R). Noting that such litigation could be enormously disruptive financially, Christophers adds that there could be further potential claims raised against fossil fuel companies on the basis of misleading statements to investors and other financial stakeholders they may have made in the past. The potential for such cases of liability to succeed is likely to increase if and when courts lend growing support to the idea that every human being has a right to an adequate environment (on which see e.g. Hayward 2005, 2017). In fact, the mere possibility of this development could have a dampening effect on confidence in future values. Furthermore, Carney points out, a result of such impacts that might be anticipated is an 'upward trend in losses that arise indirectly through second-order events like the disruption of global supply chains' (Carney 2015: 5). He is keenly aware how insurers can—and for their own sake must—be at the cutting edge of a holistic understanding of the emerging threats. He illustrates how these can give rise to major crises and political questions. For instance: 'In some extreme cases, householders in the Caribbean have found storm patterns render them unable to get private cover, prompting mortgage lending to dry up, values to collapse and neighbourhoods to become abandoned' (Carney 2015: 6). Carney notes that precedents are being set for potentially unmanageable liability claims, including failures in fiduciary duties to heed financial risks attendant on climate change.

(iii) Carney points out that the necessary transition to a new kind of economy, one no longer based on energy wrested from the burning of fossil fuels, will inevitably involve the reassessment of financial assets insofar as their value is grounded in holdings related to the fossil fuel industry. As fossil fuel companies come under increasing public criticism, this can deter suppliers, subcontractors, potential employees, and customers; it can also provoke shareholders into activism; it can alienate political support, with firms even being barred from competing for public tenders, acquiring licences or property rights for business expansion. Crucially, if campaigners can create an expectation that government might introduce a carbon tax, this could depress demand and increase uncertainties about future cash flows of fossil fuel companies. As Christophers notes, 'a large and rapid revaluation could very well be destabilizing and spark 'a pro-cyclical crystallisation of losses' (2017: 11). These transition risks have been assessed in a report of The Stranded Assets Programme at Oxford University's Smith School of Enterprise and the Environment (Ansar et al. 2013), which finds likely that they 'will indirectly influence all investors... to go underweight on fossil fuel stocks and debt in their portfolios' (Ansar, Caldecott and Tilbury 2013: 14). Institutional investors, they believe, are likely to begin by liquidating coal stocks, while 'banks, particularly multilateral institutions such as the World Bank, may stop lending to fossil fuel companies, particularly coal' (Ansar et al. 2013: 70). As confidence in the future of fossil fuel companies ebbs away, they risk being left with *stranded assets*. Ultimately, Carney warns, 'a wholesale reassessment of prospects, especially if it were to occur suddenly, could potentially destabilise markets, spark a pro-cyclical crystallisation of losses and a persistent tightening of financial conditions' (Carney 2015: 8).

The overarching thesis expounded by Carney, then, is that risks relating to climate change—and, potentially, by implication, to environmental changes more generally—can undermine financial stability. But would this necessarily be an unmanageable problem? Those in favour of business as usual being allowed to continue with as little interference as possible propose that it could be managed through light touch voluntary regulation, with firms and organizations being transparent about their exposure to the sorts of risk Carney has indicated. Critical commentators are less sanguine, however. It is not just a matter of whether they will really be transparent, but even whether they can in principle *know* the extent of the risk they are exposed to. For, as Brett Christophers points out, even if such a regime were to be participated in with scrupulous honesty—which it might not be prudent to rely upon—it would still come up against limits of possible knowledge of the risks at issue.

Here it is worth observing a clear conceptual distinction. The very concept of a 'risk' admits of different interpretations. Generically speaking, Christophers suggests, 'risk refers to exposure to the possibility, but not certainty, of some adverse or unwelcome future circumstance'; and, correspondingly, the similarly generic idea of financial risk 'refers to exposure to the possibility of future financial loss' (Christophers 2017: 12L). The concept of 'risk' can more specifically be distinguished from that of 'uncertainty', as explained in the seminal work of Frank Knight (1921).

> The practical difference between the two categories, risk and uncertainty, is that in the former the distribution of the outcome in a group of instances is known (either through calculation a priori or from statistics of past experience), while in the case of uncertainty this is not true,... because the situation dealt with is in a high degree unique. The best example of uncertainty is in connection with the exercise of judgment or the formation of those opinions as to the future course of events.... (Knight 1921: 233)

We can straightforwardly understand that the insurance industry has the financial viability it does insofar as it deals with risks rather than uncertainties, on these definitions. Insurable risks are calculable: for although outcomes are randomly distributed amongst insured parties, those outcomes are of knowable probability. In circumstances of uncertainty, by contrast, probabilities are unknowable. In circumstances of what might be described as deep or *radical* uncertainty, the nature of possible outcomes is also unknown. A special kind of radical uncertainty concerns a range of possible outcomes that is known to include some that might be catastrophic or 'game-changing'. This is the kind of outcome that scientists predict as possibilities when ecological 'tipping points' are reached: for what will happen thereupon is unknowable in advance. In response to radical uncertainty of this troubling kind—which we might refer to as *dangerous* uncertainty—it is rational to consider the case for applying the *precautionary principle.* This principle is not a simple one, either to conceptualize or to apply,[1] but the general idea is that some possible outcomes of a course of action would be so unacceptable that they should simply be avoided, irrespective of the cost. This kind of reasoning is quite unlike that of insurers calculating risks: for neither the probability of the outcome nor the cost of its consequences can be known or therefore quantified or calculated.

Categorized in terms of that distinction, Christophers points out, regulators take what climate change poses to financial stability to be risk in Knight's sense, that is, as a set of futures with knowable probabilities; and yet 'it is a very long way from certain that the financial stability risks associated with climate change can be measured, that they are indeed "risks" rather than "uncertainties"' (Christophers 2017: 12R). He believes that 'if any development in human history renders the future inherently uncertain and unknowable, it is climate change, a phenomenon

[1] For an overview of different interpretations of the principle see Hayward 2005:104ff.

wholly without precedent' (Christophers 2017: 12R). In fact, as he points out, numerous scholars have argued that with the unprecedented ecological transformations of our time we are entering a realm of radical uncertainty (e.g. Kandlikar et al. 2005). Certain kinds of disaster may be so catastrophic that we can have little idea in advance of all the serious consequences that might follow from them. When the consequences include setting in train large-scale feedback loops, as can happen with severe ecological crises, and as is possible as a result of climate change reaching certain tipping points and crossing 'planetary boundaries', then those consequences are radically incalculable.

There is no way to contemplate compensating for such game-changing events, since we cannot even know what material processes, let alone human actions, might be able to reverse them or serve as adaptation to them. A point that Carney alerts us to is that once game-changing events become a discernible possibility—even if of radically uncertain likelihood or consequence—they can have a dampening effect on the readiness of insurers to cover risks that lie in the general direction of those incalculable threats. Thus once the ecological realities are understood to impinge on the factors that finance in the last analysis depends on, a holistic view becomes a chastening necessity.

Interesting to note, then, is how the pragmatic perspective of the head of a central bank coincides with quite a radical socio-ecological analysis. For his perspective is a little longer-sighted than that of government or profit-seeking corporate leaders. Indeed his remarks to insurers include the rueful observation: *given the short term horizon of monetary policy, it is likely that* 'once climate change becomes a defining issue for financial stability, it may already be too late' (Carney 2015: 3).

7.2 The Limits of Liberal Environmental Economics

It is interesting to note how the perspective taken by Mark Carney contrasts with another that informs policy advice and even philosophical discussion of approaches to dealing with climate change. Some influential contributions have placed considerable implicit reliance on financial stability as a premise of their discussions of strategic options. These have been based on the general idea that incremental steps to address environmental challenges can be taken by raising and applying monetary funds. This idea is characteristic of the broad school of thought that we might refer to as environmental liberalism, and it has an evident parallel in the cosmopolitan liberal idea that a similar approach is appropriate for dealing with global poverty. Of course, as has already been noted, reliance on money as a solution to the world's ills can be criticized from a number of familiar perspectives, including those that emphasize the incommensurability of various environmental goods and the impossibility of compensating for irreversible environmental harms.

The focus here is on one particular presupposition of money-raising approaches that has to be considered even in cases where money in principle could contribute to solving an environmental problem. Necessarily presupposed by the possibility of money being able to do at least a little good, and no harm, are conditions of financial stability. This presupposition is evident in assumptions made both about the possibility of using finance to compensate for environmental harms and also in discussions of discount rates. In what follows I shall consider reasons for doubt on each score in turn.

Financial Compensation for Environmental Harm

Revenues raised from greenhouse gas emission charges, Simon Caney (2011) has suggested, can be used to fund compensation for dangerous climate change. This suggestion not only tacitly endorses the idea that climate harms can be compensated for by some sort of offsetting—which is itself controversial—but also assumes that the value of money can be preserved so that whatever offsetting is envisaged can be reliably costed. The kind of thinking reflected in such philosophical contributions has been influential in discussions under the auspices of the Intergovernmental Panel on Climate Change (IPCC). At its basis are the ideas of the group of economists, who, commissioned by the UK Government and led by ex-Chief Economist of the World Bank, Nicholas Stern, produced the influential Stern Review (Stern et al. 2006). That report may be taken to exemplify the kind of framework of understanding that comes from liberal economics. In what follows I shall indicate how it is problematic in putting unwarranted faith in the stability and neutrality of money.

The Stern Review emphasizes the importance of taking action to mitigate climate change, not only as an environmental imperative, but also as a matter of good business sense. Thus it seeks to add specifically economic weight to the case for mitigating climate change by arguing that there are monetary costs of failure to act:

> Using the results from formal economic models, the Review estimates that if we don't act, the overall costs and risks of climate change will be equivalent to losing at least 5% of global GDP each year, now and forever. If a wider range of risks and impacts is taken into account, the estimates of damage could rise to 20% of GDP or more. In contrast, the costs of action—reducing greenhouse gas emissions to avoid the worst impacts of climate change—can be limited to around 1% of global GDP each year. (Stern et al. 2006: vi)

If engaging in these sorts of projection were to be understood as just a way of 'painting a picture' to urge publics and policy-makers to recognize the need for action, then it could be of some service. However, the numbers themselves can be criticized for being arbitrary. As Clive Spash points out, 'precise GDP numbers on climate change control costs and benefits may be precisely wrong' (Spash 2007: 707): 'Drawing precise inferences is notoriously difficult and various monetary numbers are based on a variety of ad hoc assumptions...' (Spash 2007: 708). The Stern Review does in fact acknowledge that there are large uncertainties, that models are merely illustrative, and that the model results 'should be treated with great circumspection'; it even warns of 'a danger that, because they are quantitative, they will be taken too literally. They should not be' (Stern et al. 2006: 144). Despite all the caveats, however, the authors maintain that 'if the model is to quantify the full range of effects, it must place monetary values on health and the environment...' (Stern et al. 2006: 144). Their significant caveats are not emphasized in summaries, conclusions or the launch speech, which focus on aggregate changes in GDP.

Thus the problems of spurious quantification and premature precision are acknowledged but not resolved by the report's authors. This leaves its credibility vulnerable to attack by those promoting the interests of climate scepticism. A criticism I would press, though, is not about the estimates of the costs of inaction, for I believe we know that there will be serious costs even without calculating particular numeric claims. Rather, I wish to direct critical attention to the further claim by Stern that action is not only needed to solve the problem but will be profitable in its own right. The objection to be pressed is obviously not to the general principle of adopting a win–win solution to a problem where one is available; the objection concerns the basis for assuming that a win–win solution of climate change problems is *available*. The control of greenhouse gas emissions is presented as a good investment with positive returns. Climate change, according to the Stern Review authors, 'presents opportunities for financial markets. Capital markets, banks and other financial institutions will have a vital role in raising and allocating the trillions of dollars needed to finance investment in low-carbon technology and the companies producing the new technologies.' (Stern et al. 2006: 270) 'The development of carbon trading markets also presents an important opportunity to the financial sector. Trading on global carbon markets is now worth over $10bn annually' (Stern et al. 2006: 270). The authors point out that it could grow considerably beyond this if the markets are expanded and linked. They suggest this would promote cost-effective reductions in emissions and bring forward action in developing countries, making it possible to 'drive flows amounting to tens of billions of dollars each year to support the transition to low-carbon development paths' (Stern et al. 2006: 575).

Yet to work out estimates of transition costs and quantities of flows potentially mobilized is not the same as ensuring that the money raised will be dedicated to meeting the ends in question. The fact that there are profits to be made by some economic actors cannot be regarded as equivalent to a claim that appropriate compensatory benefits for others will be achieved. While financial institutions may make billions, along with carbon traders, energy suppliers, and other entrepreneurs who spot opportunities, it is another matter whether substantial amounts would be ploughed into productive low carbon developments. Meanwhile, carbon markets themselves work to redistribute emissions rather than necessarily to reduce them.

The grounds for concern here are not simply that profiteering and rent seeking may trump real investment in transitional technology and infrastructure. There is also a concern that, even if the flows generated were directed in the right direction, they cannot simply be assumed to have the same value—the same purchasing power—as they are taken to have at source. The raising and the deployment happen in different times and places; and we know it takes very little for the value of money itself to fluctuate in the real world of time and space. Yet assumptions about the reliability of the value of money are deeply embedded in the thinking exemplified by Stern. Not only is it assumed that the money raised would be devoted to the needed works, the broader economic context of this is assumed to permit reasonable budgetary assumptions to be stable around the world and over time.

Just to be clear, these assumptions can be challenged on two distinct bases: they can be criticized for erroneously assuming that all costs and benefits can be commensurated in any non-arbitrary way at all, or therefore expressed non-arbitrarily in monetary terms; but they can also be criticized on the grounds that even if monetary commensurabilities could be agreed, the possible changes in the value of money over time are so unpredicable that any evaluation system incorporating estimates of future evaluations would be arbitrary for that reason alone. The first of these criticisms is well established in the literature on using cost–benefit analysis in relation to environmental values (see e.g. O'Neill and Spash 2000). Stern's case for the positive economic value of tackling climate change follows in a tradition of environmental economics that seeks to attach value or price to unpriced or undervalued environmental 'services' (e.g. Costanza et al. 1997). The many problems with this approach have been exhaustively discussed in the literature, and these are not what I shall focus on here. The concern here is with the second criticism, that regarding the projection of monetary valuations into the future.

The Indeterminacy of Discounting

Any valuation relating to future costs and benefits is crucially dependent on the discount rate used.[2] This is because prices of assets can vary over time, and makers

[2] This refers to what is known as the social discount rate, which, as Simon Caney explains, 'determines the extent to which resources should be devoted to people's interests now in preference to people's interests at a later date. The higher the positive social discount rate the less should be spent on the future' (Caney 2009: 164).

of policy decisions will seek information as to whether it is less costly to act now or wait until later in order to achieve some particular future benefit. With respect to the cost of achieving carbon emissions reductions, for instance, a high discount rate tends to favour decisions to postpone action. Of course, the value of the benefit can also change over time, and so arriving at a particular discount rate involves a good deal of discretionary assumptions. Thus we find some strikingly different discount rates assumed by different economists. In advancing an upbeat case for a win–win combination of economic growth and climate protection, Stern's determination of the 'correct' current price for carbon employs a discount rate (1.4 per cent) that is significantly lower than used by some other mainstream economists, notably the influential William Nordhaus (5.5 per cent). This difference implies dramatically different policy advice, particularly regarding appropriate levels of taxation: Stern's emissions reductions target is consistent with an estimated tax rate of US$300 per tonne on carbon emissions; by contrast, Nordhaus supports a carbon tax of only around US$30 per tonne, rising to US$85 per tonne by 2050. This difference is almost entirely the result of the different assumptions made when calculating the social discount rate (Broome 2008).

Of course, there is no such thing as a 'correct' discount rate. One reason is that the rate chosen is inextricably linked to normative value judgements. It was attention to ethical issues that led Stern to arrive at a significantly lower discount rate than Nordhaus, whose higher rate arguably implies a low level of concern for our descendents (Quiggin 2008). Yet although the Stern Review focus takes ethical issues more seriously into consideration than do some more standard economic analyses, they have only a limited impact on its findings and recommendations. Indeed, as Clive Spash has pointed out, if we combine the discounting assumption with the growth projections, then even Stern's lower-than-typical discount rate still implies a quite rapidly diminishing concern for the welfare of future generations. The standard business practice of factoring in the value of expected future growth may thus be said to find its correlate in Stern's readiness to discount the impacts of future harms.

In fact, it is not only future impacts we should be concerned about. In thinking dominated by standard mainstream economic assumptions, it is possible to lose sight of the material nature of problems through placing too much emphasis on their monetary proxies in the present too. Spash thinks that the Stern Review falls prey to this tendency, particularly in that its purported attention to the ethical aspects of the question treats a variety of substantive human concerns as commensurable with the economic value of consumption. For instance the displacement of people in developing countries is priced at three times per capita income by Stern, but Spash wonders why. 'How has someone decided this? What do we do about the fact that the poor sell cheaply (Martinez-Alier 2002), and that millions live on $2 a day or less? Is a couple of thousand dollars meant to compensate forced relocation?' (Spash 2007: 709R).

Something that is illustrated by this is how the assessment of costs and benefits, and thus of possible compensation too, presupposes settling prior questions about whose interests, needs, and perspective are to provide points of reference in calculating them. Such calculations can have very different bases in different collocations within global political economic and ecological systems. The main point I want to make here, however, concerns a deeper problem for the possibility of *any* calculation of costs and benefits, regardless of whose interests or perspective might be the basis for it. This is the problem of *radical uncertainty.*

Even if everyone could agree today on current ethical values and future discounting rates, this would not eliminate uncertainty, even of radically strong kinds, regarding the possible future scenarios in which such framing assumptions would have to retain applicability. For one thing, we cannot simply assume there could be no 'game changing' events, events that bring such momentous alterations to our material circumstances that no preparation on the basis of prior knowledge can equip us adequately to preserve our way of life in the face of them. The possibility of their occurrence is something that awareness of climate change and the transgression of other planetary boundaries cautions us about. Interdisciplinary scientific research into the biophysical tolerances of our planet has identified at least nine so-called 'planetary boundaries', the overstepping of which may tip our ecological circumstances into unprecedented and unpredictable changes of kinds potentially liable even to render our species, and many others, extinct.

Even excluding consideration of possible game-changing events, though, ecological unpredictabilities about the future still compound uncertainties about other factors affecting the value of money, particularly when insurance costs become impossible to calculate with actuarial confidence. In seeking to quantify the costs of climate change and the economic benefits of tackling it, there is ineliminable arbitrariness in the selection of basic material assumptions about the state of the world and possible future developments.

So with regard to the prospects of either compensating for actual harms or determining appropriate discounting rates for the evaluation of potential harms, we face the problem of the radical uncertainty of monetary values.

7.3 The Radical Uncertainty of Prices, and its Implications

The idea that price fluctuations can be regarded as manageable is presupposed by discussions of compensation and discounting. It is relied on, in particular, for the claim highlighted in the Stern Review—without regard to the significant caveats contained in its detailed presentation of data—that tackling climate change 'can be done in a way that does not cap the aspirations for growth of rich or poor countries' (Stern et al. 2006: viii).

However, the idea that risks and their attendant liabilities can be reliably priced rests on questionable assumptions. One would be that financial markets are rationally competitive and function as reliable information processors. Yet, as Paul Krugman observes, 'many real-world investors bear little resemblance to the cool calculators of efficient-market theory: they're all too subject to herd behavior, to bouts of irrational exuberance and unwarranted panic' and 'even those who try to base their decisions on cool calculation often find that they can't, that problems of trust, credibility and limited collateral force them to run with the herd' (Krugman 2009). The fact is that prices of money, in the kind of system that exists globally today, can undergo changes that bear no very direct correlation to humanly or ecologically needed changes in the world.

It is not just that those tangible needs have complex social and ethical dimensions, for the more basic point is that market prices cannot closely track even economic values. George Soros has highlighted the practical significance of Knight's distinction between risk and uncertainty in explaining this. Where modern mainstream economists discuss economies in terms of models that assume all relevant factors can be quantified, Soros is clear—like Keynes, Hayek, and other earlier theorists who still recognized the ineliminable significance of qualitative variables—that economic reality is constituted by uncertainties, with calculable risks being but a small subset of situations about which decisions must be made. In this connection he has applied his theory of *reflexivity* to the operation of financial markets. The idea of reflexivity Soros (2003) explicates in terms of a two-way feedback mechanism between the participants' expectations and the actual course of events. Negative feedback serves to correct participants' miscalculations and brings their views closer to the actual state of affairs. In a situation of positive feedback, however, participants' misjudgements cause mispricing in financial markets, and this in turn affects the underlying economy in a self-reinforcing fashion, thus driving the participants' views and the actual state of affairs ever further apart. What renders the outcome uncertain is that although positive feedback cannot continue indefinitely, the exact point at which it may turn negative is inherently unpredictable. Soros also notes, however, that elements of the situation are nevertheless more predictable for some than for others because markets confer the ability 'to transfer risk to counterparties, not merely to hedge it or speculate on it in a level playing field'. Therefore prices always tend to reflect the ability of skilled market players to maximize profit prospects at the expense of weaker players.

The approach of Stern—acquiescing as it does in the continuance of a system that tends to polarize holdings of income and wealth—is also liable to allow distributive inequalities to become more deeply entrenched. It aims to achieve the public good of climate protection by stimulating action on the basis of its profitability. But the logic of profit seeking in practice involves the discovery of unintended opportunities, the exploitation of which can readily subvert the good intentions of policy advisors. In this light, one might think caution an appropriate response to what Stern appraises as 'the great opportunities for banks and the financial sector in funding pollution reduction (that is, defensive expenditures) and partaking in carbon trading' (Stern et al. 2006: 270). Financial interests draw considerable benefit from the opportunities opened by having a whole new commodity over which the distribution of rights represents a new income stream. Critical commentators in fact suggest that the reason carbon trading is being promoted so strongly as the dominant approach to climate change, and the reason for 'the sheer prominence of the financial sector in the carbon business' (Lohmann 2012), is that 'speculators and bankers see permits as financial instruments which provide money-making opportunities' (Spash 2010: 177). Indeed, we have to be concerned that this new method of profiteering may not only further disadvantage the global poor but could even involve an ideological deflection onto them of responsibility for causing the climate problem in the first place:

> carbon project sponsors and managers are pictured as creating value (it is they who 'avoid' emissions that otherwise were 'inevitable'), while nonprofessional actors in already low-emitting contexts or social movements actively working to reduce use of fossil fuels are demoted into passive objects of deterministic calculation or even global warming culprits.' (Lohmann 2012: 100)

If financial interests benefit from the opportunities opened by having a whole new commodity over which the distribution of rights represents a new income stream, those interests should not be mistaken for wider interests reflecting the public good, either now or in the future.

Accordingly, we should be cautious regarding *ethical* arguments that are premised on assumptions about the neutrality or even desirability of allowing markets to decide values. Market movements can have distributive effects regarding who has a right to consume which environmental resources, potentially leaving the worst off without access to a basic minimum necessary to meet their basic needs. Meanwhile, a market contains no inherent principle or motivation to restrain their consumption by those with money. This is not conducive to the ends either of justice or of environmental protection.

On the basis of these considerations, one might infer that, instead of attempting to estimate costs and benefits of future assets or future harms, or to measure these against similar analyses in the future, it could be better to think of the challenges in more directly qualitative terms. The advocacy of remedial strategies involving monetary proxies seems to be something of an unhelpful diversion.

A general point to emphasize, therefore, is that there are limits to the extent to which monetary accounting can credibly be invoked as a proxy for the real world delivery of substantive goods, whether these are to provide for the day-to-day economic requirements of a decent livelihood or for the longer-term utilization of ecological resources.

If the activities we materially engage in lead to ecological harm that becomes increasingly hard to repair, then the needed response is going to be considerable and may entail quite unpredictable demands. To suppose that our capacities to devise solutions will keep pace with the ecological problems we cause is not only to assume that science and technology could continue to deliver. It is also to assume that there is sufficient political will in operation, as well as a dedicated commitment to directing the development of technology so as to serve the longer-term public interest over and above more immediate private gain.

My argument is that we should consider it a matter of due diligence to investigate how good the reasons are to grant such assumptions, and to consider what would be the implications of their being unwarranted. We have also seen reasons to doubt the tenability of the idea, as appears in some philosophical arguments concerning forward-looking proposals for justice or welfare, that money can be 'set aside' today for use to achieve some goal we may have in mind that will need to be achieved in the future. The problem is not just that we cannot be certain about future circumstances, but that we cannot be certain about the value of money, even in the shorter, let alone the longer, term.

In fact, even to speak of the 'value' of money, is to use an expression that itself is simply shorthand for a very complex reality. Money does not have value itself, but what is designated as money has such value for people as they are practically prepared to recognize when treating it as an appropriate substitute for things they actually want and need. Although we often think for practical purposes of money as if it was inherent value-bearing stuff, its credibility and value ultimately rest on the fact that people are willing to do things in exchange for it. Money is thus a proxy that can help solve a problem only as long as the transactions using it command real commitments by real people or agencies to perform such actions as would constitute its solution. If we think of funds raised as somehow representing a set of actions undertaken or agreed, then for those funds to solve a problem as intended, the various commitments represented by the funds have to be conveyed intact. So in order to address any substantive problem concerning poverty or environmental change, substantive action needs to be taken. (We may thus notice how the situation regarding avoiding ecological harms is akin to that, previously examined, regarding the relief of poverty. In each case, a supposition that the problem can be dealt with by using a monetary proxy—via a transfer or compensation—appears questionable on the grounds that contributing some money serves merely as a way to avoid making the actual contribution, in terms of effort and sacrifice, materially required for dealing with the problem.) Money itself does not act; it merely symbolizes contracted agreements involving action.

7.4 Conclusion

This chapter has shown that ecological change can drive financial instability and that we cannot reliably put a monetary value on ecological costs and benefits across time. This brief consideration of the ecological context has alerted us to the radical uncertainties that underlie the non-reliability of money as a medium for transferring value over time as well as across geopolitical space. In order for money to serve as a store of value, as it would have to, certain conditions must be satisfied. Savers, investors, and spenders of money need to be related to one another through institutions in whose stability they can all place reliance. Those institutions require the efforts of good governance to maintain even within a well-ordered economic area. Between different economic areas, the institutions require additional efforts to maintain. Over periods of time, the efforts may be so great that certain kinds of volatility are all but inescapable. We are now further aware that if the effects of natural resource depletion and environmental change are added in, then the sources of volatility may become radically uncertain.

If there is volatility in the value of money, nonetheless, it still ultimately has to do with behaviours and expectations of people in dynamic interaction with others. The expression 'market sentiments' is taken for granted in the business world as a description of a key driver of changes in market conditions. These sentiments, to a certain extent, make money what it is: bullish sentiments make it active and expansive; bearish ones make it coy and recalcitrant. To say this is not to fetishize money, but, on the contrary, to emphasize how money 'is' nothing other than what social norms, practices, institutions, and even sentiments make it: thus people are more reticent to do things for money when market sentiments make it seem riskier to hold what are essentially promises rather than tangible goods; they are eager to do things when they believe the money they get will help them receive or achieve even more than it takes to get the money.

At this point, therefore, it is worth stopping to take stock more explicitly of what exactly money is. At the start of the chapter we recognized the point that monetary stability is a public good; this presupposes that the availability of money is itself a public good. But we might usefully reflect on what kind of good money is—that is to inquire, not only in what ways is it good, but even what kind of 'thing' it is.

8
What Is the Good of Money?

This book is not an expert treatise on money; it is an essay reflecting on how a political philosopher, who is not an expert on money, should think about it when addressing questions of justice. The questions about money that are prompted by the investigations of Chapters 5–7 concern the paradoxical aspects of benign leverage and cashless cash, and, more generally, radical uncertainties about the value of money in different circumstances. If a theory of global justice aims to understand how given circumstances ought to be altered, and if money is envisaged to play any role at all, then uncertainties about money have to be taken into account. Yet the problem with uncertainties, of course, is that they leave one not knowing exactly what to take into account or how! In situations of uncertainty, circumstances are experienced as beyond our control. A question worth exploring, therefore, is whether there are ways of bringing circumstances within our control—where by '*our*' I am thinking in terms of the basic set of collective human interests that were invoked as the benchmark for concern when setting up the fundamental problem of global justice and finance in the opening chapters. What I propose from here on—in this and coming chapters—is to look at money from perspectives that can help us discern the questions of control and bring them within the purview of social and political theory.

In order to approach such questions, it is necessary to have some conceptual clarity about what we have in mind when we refer to money. The present chapter serves as a prelude to the inquiries of Chapters 8 and 9 by explicitly reflecting on the general conceptualization of money that has been developing up to this point and will inform the discussion.

Section 8.1, accordingly, considers *what kind of thing* money is, asking, in particular, how we should conceptualize or imagine money when we think of it 'flowing' to or from one person or place to another. Although often referred to by an analogy with water, there are respects in which money's flow is more like that of an electric current, and seeing it in this way can help us understand the limitations of some inherited assumptions about it. For money is not simply found 'there', in a given amount and determinate place, to be directed or redirected this way or that. Its supply depends on the existence of complex and deeply embedded social practices and its 'flow' can be generated or shut off by those who have control of the generation and transmissions systems.

Whatever analogy we find helpful in thinking about it, though, a second question is *what kind of good* this complex thing is. We know it can be regarded as an *economic* good, both in the sense of being sought after by economic agents and in the sense of facilitating economic activity as such. In fact, however, once we start to elaborate the ways in which it can be an economic good, we find that they are multifarious. As Section 8.2 shows, money can be categorized, from different perspectives, in terms of a variety of kinds of economic good. Given that different people occupy various economic positions, the good that money is cannot necessarily be regarded as uniform across a society, let alone the globe. Nor, therefore, can money be regarded as a neutral instrument for policy purposes. In its various different forms it can function differently for different purposes, any adequate account of which would have a sociological dimension. For money is available to be used only on certain terms as set by those who control the institutions. Thus the question of 'where money comes from' is also of notable normative significance: powers to create money and to control the conditions of its creation are powers that people have good reason to want to be subject to legitimate political authority. Unless the production and management of the monetary system are under legitimate political control, it may not be realistic to suppose that its functions can be pressed into service of the strategic goals of global justice.

8.1 What 'Kind of Thing' Should We Think of Money as Being?

One thing we know is that money needs to circulate in order to support a productive economy. Money that is saved (neither spent nor invested) does not circulate, and is unavailable *as* money in the economy. Money that does nothing is, economically speaking, no good. Circulation is driven by all the particular transactions that money facilitates. Ensuring good circulation is thus good in aggregate and also for all the particular transactions that are facilitated by it. However, ensuring circulation is something that takes some achieving. This is highlighted in an analogy drawn by Segovia, the software company that set up the cashless cash transfer management system mentioned in Chapter 5. Segovia was named by its directors after one of the largest aqueducts of the Roman Empire—an engineering feat that carried water for two thousand years. 'At Segovia we are building aqueducts for today's social programs', reads their publicity, which explains the symbolism:

> Before aqueducts, moving water was a slow, costly, and leaky process. Aqueducts made it faster, cheaper, and more secure. The Aqueduct of Segovia—one of the oldest and largest—epitomized these benefits and was a symbol of effective governance.[1]

[1] https://hired.com/company/segovia or http://www.truevaluemetrics.org/DBadmin/DBtxt001.php?vv1=txt00010513

To talk about money flows by analogy with flows of water is to tap into a quite standard traditional way of thinking. The assumption operates in philosophical arguments for a tax and fund approach to global justice insofar as these take financial flows to convey money in much the way that water can be brought to flow, with the value of money, analogous to the volume of water, remaining roughly constant. To transfer stable amounts of value from the richer to the poorer, on this view, is a matter of ensuring clear conduits and honest brokers. It is as if the richer have a substantial reservoir from which appropriate channels can allow small amounts to be withdrawn so as to irrigate a wide expanse of poverty sufficient to allow at least minimally decent livelihoods. With financial flows considered in the same way as water flows, then, assuming there are no leaks or blockages, and no siphoning off elsewhere, it is expected that the amount that leaves the source will reach the destination. Its marginal utility may thereby be vastly enhanced as irrigation for numerous livelihoods rather than sitting idle in a reservoir.

Yet we should be aware of important disanalogies between movements of money and movements of water. One point about water is that, however complex and extensive may be the hydrologic cycle globally, the total amount of it in the biosphere as a whole remains close to constant. Money does not have the same objective existence that water does; and it thus also does not exist in a fixed or even determinate quantity.

Perhaps a more satisfactory metaphor, as Anne Mayhew (2011) points out, would be electricity. On this point she commends the advice of the economist, Morris Copeland, who actually invented the 'flow of funds' method used in US national accounting.[2] Thus where '[t]he hydraulic analogy likens the money circuit to a system of reservoirs and connecting conduits (pipes or canals).... [i]n the electrical analogy the reservoirs become batteries and the conduits become wires' (quoted in Mayhew 2011: 247). A key difference reflected by the more appropriate analogy is this: if you switch off the current, no electricity flows; without movement, there is, for practical purposes, no electricity. And that is the situation with money: if people for some reason stop accepting it in exchange, or if credit lines are cut, it effectively ceases to exist. Mayhew offers an historical illustration of the conceptual difficulties with the hydraulic analogy and the advantages of thinking in terms of electricity:

> Between 1929 and 1933 the total money supply in the United States decreased. Students and the public ask: where did the money go? If we think of money

[2] 'In 1952, a now rarely remembered economist, one Morris Copeland, published, under the aegis of the highly respected National Bureau of Economic Research, annual estimates of money flows in the United States for the years 1936–1942. These were the first such estimates and were important because they were the basis for the now widely used flow-of-funds accounts that are compiled and published quarterly by the Federal Reserve System. Copeland's publication was also important because, well before digital forms became the norm, he proposed using electricity rather than water as a metaphor for money. This proposal was quite radical—too radical as it turns out—to displace the textbook and quasi-official hydraulic money metaphor of the United States' (Mayhew 2011, 245).

> as water, what happened to it? Economists can explain that the velocity of use of money decreased so that more money simply sat in the pipes and they can explain the leveraging of 'high-powered money' (currency held by the public and banks as well as commercial bank deposits in Federal Reserve Banks) was reduced. It is easier, however, to say that households and business firms did not turn on the switch that causes money, thought of as electricity, to be generated. Money did not sit in hypothetical reservoirs; it simply was not generated.
>
> (Mayhew 2011: 248)

On Copeland's conceptualization, financial flows can be modelled with sectors of the economy having credit and debit poles. The poles are given their 'charge' through transactions whereby 'the crediting of an account automatically generates a debit in like amount to another account and the two are simultaneous. This is the process of our economy and the electrical metaphor closely approximates it' (Mayhew 2011: 247). 'The credited sector acquires funds and the debited sector acquires assets in the form of promises to pay in the future.' Thus total inflows and outflows will always be equal, 'but the total quantity of flows may vary from period to period and will do so through the discretionary action of participants in each of the different sectors' (Mayhew 2011: 247).

If this metaphor did not catch on, Mayhew surmises, this is because it falls foul of an objection, to be anticipated from economists, that what Copeland is talking about is credit, not money. Mayhew cites this account of that distinction from a standard economics textbook:

> It might seem natural to include credit cards as part of the economy's stock of money. After all, people use credit cards to make many of their purchases. But, credit cards are not really a method of payment but a method of *deferring* payment.... When the time comes to pay your credit card bill, you will probably do so by writing a check against your checking account. The balance in this checking account is part of the economy's stock of money.
>
> (Mankiw 2004: 456 [cited in Mayhew 2011: 249])

In response, Mayhew points out:

> bank accounts against which checks are written also have to be restored.... Toward the end of each month bank accounts typically dwindle in size and are refunded (or recharged) when paychecks or pension payments are deposited. The process is the same as that which occurs when a payment is made to a credit card issuer though the labels that we put on the flows of funds differ. I receive the *income* which is *mine* from employer or pension fund in the one case and in the other, make a *payment* to *discharge a debt* and the increase in my allowable acquisition of new debt increases. While there are some legal and accounting differences and perhaps even moral differences between the two processes, in terms of the macroeconomy, the effects are the same. My batteries are recharged and I can spend. (Mayhew 2011: 249–50)

If we are to account for the insistence on a qualitative distinction between money and credit, she suggests, it is because most economists, and those who respect their authority, tend to regard money as a class of 'stuff' rather than 'a charge that causes changes in ownership of many different kinds of stuff' (Mayhew 2011, 250).

That money is not any class of 'stuff' at all is a crucial point that has, in fact, been appreciated by some leading economists. They include both Hayek and Keynes, whose respective economic views are so opposed in other ways. Hayek is explicit in arguing that while we may usually assume there is 'a sharp line of distinction between what is money and what is not', in fact, 'so far as the causal effects of monetary events are concerned, there is no such clear difference. What we find is rather a continuum in which objects of various degrees of liquidity, or with values which can fluctuate independently of each other, shade into each other in the degree to which they function as money' (Hayek 1990:56). He even reflects that it could be 'rather a misfortune that we describe money by a noun, and that it would be more helpful for the explanation of monetary phenomena if "money" were an adjective describing a property which different things could possess to varying *degrees*' (Hayek 1990: 56). Keynes, in similar vein, observed 'that "liquidity" and "carrying-costs" are both a matter of degree; and that it is only in having the former high relatively to the latter that the peculiarity of "money" consists' (Keynes 1936: ch. 17§5). He pointed out, moreover, that there is 'no absolute standard of "liquidity" but merely a scale of liquidity—a varying premium of which account has to be taken' (Keynes 1936: ch. 17§5)[3]. J. P. Koning suggests that, to avoid the mistake of thinking of money as stuff, we could think of the property he calls 'moneyness', something that various different things may possess in different measures, and different ways. He explains this thought:

> Certain characteristics of a good allow it to become more money-like, including durability, verifiability, fungibility, and portability.... The moneyness of an object can be improved by manufacturing these characteristics. Gold, for instance, is rendered more money-like by incurring coinage costs in order to promote verifiability. Adding copper to a gold coin increases its durability. Network effects can be harnessed through marketing. As long as the expected returns of boosting an object's moneyness are higher than the costs, liquidity providers will happily bear the costs' (Koning 2014)

Not only can different things have moneyness in different degrees, they can, because money actually refers to several distinct functions, have different degrees of moneyness in respect of their different functional aspects. Sometimes, we can do unexpected things with money to bring into clearer relief how it has these

[3] See also discussion of the problem of illusory liquidity in Chapter 9, below.

different aspects. This is nicely illustrated by the following anecdote about collector's coins and whether or not they do or should circulate at face value:

> From 1997 to 2003 Robert Kahre, a resident of Las Vegas and owner of 6 construction companies, ran a scheme in which he paid wages with gold eagles at their legal tender face value. Rather than hiring someone for say $50,000 a year payable by check, Kahre paid with 45 ounces of Eagles with a total face value of $2,250 or so. Their declared income of $2,250 was so low that Kahre's workers didn't have to report their income to the IRS. At the same time, Kahre saved on payroll tax. Win–win. Except for the IRS. In May 2003, Kahre's businesses were raided by the tax authorities. (Koning 2013)

That the case was not authoritatively clear cut, however, was indicated by the uncertainties of verdicts: although Kahre was at first acquitted in 2007, in 2009 he was found guilty of tax evasion and sent to prison. The conceptual point here is that in the case of these gold coins the function of being a unit of currency (their face value) comes apart from their function as a store of value; so their deployment as a means of exchange has very different socially perceptible effects depending on which of the other functions is taken to be legitimately fulfilled in a given context.

To ask what is the good of money, then, is to ask what money is and what is good about it under various different descriptions. The question admits of no unique or simple answer even in principle and at the most abstract conceptual level. Empirical considerations are also difficult to disentangle from normative ones due to the role that expectations of a normative kind have in maintaining its empirical presence. So having made some observations about what kind of *thing* this presumptive good we know as money is, we should also consider what kind of *good* this complex thing is.

8.2 Money as an Economic Good

In earlier chapters it has been pointed out that money is only a reliable store of value if certain necessary conditions are in place. A similar point can be made about all of its functions, although the conditions for fulfilling each will vary. That different social and institutional factors differently affect different kinds of money in different contexts is of relevance when thinking normatively about distributive issues. To assume money in any given form is straightforwardly a neutral medium of exchange and stable store of value is to risk missing normatively relevant features of financial realities. As a complex social phenomenon, the money of a financial system is a complex good that can serve in different ways people who have different kinds of power in, through, and over it. Accordingly, when thinking about the demands of justice it is helpful to be aware of the distinct kinds of good money can serve as, and for different people in different situations.

Money as a kind of good can be analysed by reference to established economic categories of goods—in particular, private goods, collective goods, club goods, and common pool goods. For different purposes, it can appear to have characteristics of all these kinds (as well, quite likely, as of others). Jack Birner (2012) has helpfully distinguished various perspectives on the social functions of money and on the 'kind of good' money is. He demonstrates that what type of economic good money can be considered as depends on what aspect of the monetary system one is considering and from what perspective. It involves a multitude of heterogeneous relationships, at different levels of interaction, involving individuals, private banks, central banks, governments, international monetary institutions, and the Bank for International Settlements. Thus, from an everyday perspective, one might think that money is a private good, insofar as it is rivalrous and excludable; but the spending power that is privately captured in money is due to the fact that money can serve the functions through which alone such power can be realized. Thus financial stability can be regarded as a public or collective good: for all can benefit from it while the benefits for one do not diminish those available for others; it is also the opposite of rivalrous because one agent's stability increases the stability for other agents with all its positive effects. Of course stability is a feature of the monetary *system*, and while the institution of money can be regarded as a collective good, meaningful access to it depends on having some money, so in that sense money is more like a club good—that is, it is still non-rivalrous but it is excludable. But if access to the use of money is a club good, the actual use of it is limited by the extent of your buy-in; so in that sense it is not a club good:

> At the level of relationships between individuals, the money I have in my pocket cannot at the same time be in somebody else's pocket. But then money is not only not an excludable good but it would also be subject to rivalry in use (be subtractable). (Birner 2012: 19)

So what kind of good is it? He points out that the analysis of goods that are both rivalrous and subtractable is the focus of Elinor Ostrom's work on common pool goods. Birner suggests that the way private banks together, and together with central banks, create money, means that what is provided is a particular type of common pool good. But whereas those are typically natural resources found in the world in given determinate quantities, money is a social construction and is, in principle, unbounded in quantity, so this model, like the others, is of limited applicability.

The purpose of that swift and highly compressed survey is not to indicate even the full agenda of a definitive analysis of the kinds of good money can be, but just to underscore the fact that money is a complex and variable kind of good. For the possibility is that any particular form of it may not fulfil all the standard functions as another, at least not in the same way, to the same degree, or in all circumstances. An implication is that it would be a mistake to rely on purely theoretical propositions concerning the functions of money when devising policy recommendations. Certainly, the idea that money is somehow a neutral measure of what happens in socio-economic reality rests on important simplifications and abstractions with respect to the systemic realities.

One point to emphasize, then, is that the financial *system* is much more, and something other, than simply a sum of flows. It is a complex *apparatus*. Money exists as a phenomenon in and of that apparatus.

For the purposes of thinking about the requirements of global justice, accordingly, one should understand money as an aspect of a major system of norms that govern some of the most basic relationships that make up humanity's collective life. This can mean taking critical distance from some of the simplified assumptions that are sometimes found in mainstream economics. In particular, there is a need to see through the idea of 'neutral money'. This is the idea that the role of money in economic life can be modelled in terms of an idealized barter system, so that money is thought to exist for no other reason than to make trade easier. That idea is not confined to economics but has permeated social and political thought since the mid-twentieth century. It was quite clearly set out by Joseph Schumpeter:

> Real analysis proceeds from the principle that all the essential phenomena of economic life are capable of being described in terms of goods and services, of decisions about them, and of relations between them. Money enters the picture only in the modest role of a technical device that has been adopted in order to facilitate transactions... so long as it functions normally, it does not affect the economic process, which behaves the same as it would in a barter economy: this is essentially what the concept of Neutral Money implies.
>
> (Schumpeter [1954] 1994: 277, quoted in Ingham 1998: 4R)

Yet it is sociologically mistaken to suppose that all the important features of economics can be understood in terms of the barter exchange of goods and services, with money serving just as a form of expression of the terms of exchange. As we have seen, money does not only serve as a medium of exchange, but has a number of other important functions which can be fulfilled in different ways, depending on where power lies. Thus, as Geoffrey Ingham argues, social scientists have an important role to play in developing an appropriate understanding of money. Sociology, in particular, should recover 'some responsibility for what are seen as "economic" problems, such as inflation, the supply of credit, the determination of interest rates and so on' (Ingham 1998: 14R). This is to emphasize that the money system has a reality that needs to be understood in its own terms and not mistaken for any sort of neutral representation of some supposedly ulterior reality.

This fuller sociological understanding of money is directly relevant to understanding the challenges of achieving justice in the world. For in order to determine what it would mean for the world to become more just, one needs an appropriately clear understanding of the ways in which the world is currently unjust. Confronted by the stark situation where many people are devastatingly poor and a few are incredibly rich, a question to reflect on is how it can be that money is so much easier to come by for some than for others. The assumptions of liberal political economy tend to abstract quite systematically from the concrete realities of a common violent history, asymmetrically imposed worldwide institutions, and unjust access to natural resources. Recent theories of global justice, particularly since Pogge's contribution, have accepted a need to acknowledge those realities. But, as I have argued elsewhere (Hayward 2008), it is necessary to go beyond just including them in a description of the context in which normative principles are to be applied. We have to be ready to consider that the normative principles we find justified may imply a need to transform that context. That means taking due cognizance of how it came to be formed and what sustains it. That includes consideration of questions about the social reality of money. The institutions of a globalizing market economy have not emerged as the product of any kind of democratic constitutional convention or socialized planning process; rather, they have resulted from historical processes of political economic activity involving competition and conflict of myriad kinds among different classes of socio-economic agent. Concomitantly, since money has its existence only by virtue of the authoritative institutions that underwrite its value, money is available to be used only on certain terms that are set—directly or indirectly—by those who control the institutions. Money has a determinate nature—in terms of the particular functions it fulfils—depending on the particular set of practices and institutions where it operates. It should not be thought of as a neutral medium for the facilitation of productive economic activity. Powers to create money and to control the conditions of its creation are powers that people have good reason to wish to be subject to legitimate political authority. In the hands of unaccountable protectors of predatory business interests, those powers can be exercised with anti-social effects. Unless those powers are brought under legitimate political control, it seems unrealistic to suppose that the system of money creation can be pressed to the ends of justice.

8.3 Conclusion

What, then, is the good of money, considered as a social phenomenon, for people and planet? We have noted that it can be many kinds of good for different people. Its various uses depend on dense and complex social relations. A central message of this chapter is that money has to be recognized as a complex sociological phenomenon that exists as a system in which a variety of structural and agential factors interact. Political philosophers' questions about how money might or might not be used in the pursuit of justice need to be integrated with an understanding of the sociological realities of money and the conditions under which it can be relied upon to fulfil any of its functions.

Regarding the question of what money is, the opening clarification was that to think of money as something that flows in the manner of a water supply from some source to some end use is to take not just an overly simplified view but a view that, in crucial respects, is misleading. It is necessary to recognize that money as it circulates in the world today is not appropriately thought of in terms of a simple, stable quantity like the ocean; nor are its availability or prices under any particular package of terms set by natural conditions; nor even are the different forms it assumes indifferent to the uses to be made of it.

In asking then what kind of good money is, this chapter has emphasised the need to appreciate how money is neither a phenomenon with inherent value in itself and nor is it the representation of some other kind of value; money is a social phenomenon constituted as a system of norms that has its own reality as such. Money is a product of complex social arrangements and normative orders, whose directions and differentiations manifest deep-seated power relations. It is here that an important source of injustice is rooted, and an adequate understanding of this is a pre-requisite for proposals to rectify the injustices emanating from it. Money, in the forms of it that actually exist today, is not neutral with respect to power relations, and understanding this is vital to a better understanding of the problems that have been highlighted thus far in the book and in formulating plausible solutions.

9
The Monetary Constraints on Tax Justice

This chapter examines a problem that fundamentally affects the prospects of pursuing global justice by means of taxes raised in the context of the global institutions that currently exist. The problem can be introduced by way of a hypothesis that follows from what has been said about how the financial system globally holds so much sway over the pursuit of common economic goods. The hypothesis would be that a global shift of economic relations in favour of the poor could elicit market responses on the part of dominant financial actors that precipitate a countermovement of asset values in the opposite direction. It is conceivable, in other words, that a shift in the order of 1 per cent or 2 per cent of global income and/or wealth could induce financial reactions whose effect is to annul the gain, or even worse. This hypothesis is, of course, speculative,[1] but in considering how it might be put to the test we become aware of certain critical issues that bear on the conditions of any potential success of using money transfers to promote global justice.

The original tax and fund proposals for global justice tended to regard the non-existence of a global tax order as a matter that can largely be set aside when thinking through normative principles. More recently, philosophers concerned with global justice have come to focus greater attention on the need for international cooperation on tax as part of any serious normative proposal; they have also highlighted how funds already flow away from the poorer countries, notwithstanding inward aid and foreign investment. This is due in part to companies taking advantage of tax competition and tax havens, as well as through various kinds of illicit transaction via Offshore Financial Centres (OFCs). It is generally recognized that these various 'illicit flows' probably exceed the inward flows. If this situation cannot be redressed, then proposals for innovative international taxes are unlikely to see successful implementation or contribute as hoped to the practical realization of global justice. These considerations are discussed in Section 9.1.

A fundamental obstacle to dealing effectively with illicit flows, however, is that these are not necessarily *illegal*, which means that steps to prohibit or even

[1] There is nevertheless some evidence of such processes occurring, as, for instance, when post-Apartheid South Africa found its economic success being undermined by speculative attacks on its currency (LiPuma and Koelble 2009).

regulate them are hampered by lack of conceptual clarity and legal authority. In fact, so far are they from being illegal, as Section 9.2 shows, that a very substantial part of the global financial structure supports them. With the practices of so-called shadow banking now well integrated into it, licit and illicit flows are thoroughly intermingled in global finance. An especially problematic aspect of these practices is the generation—particularly through the creation of various financial derivatives—of illusory forms of liquidity. It is these that, while making it possible for some to become very rich, can ultimately destabilize the financial system and wreak havoc with productive economies and ordinary people's livelihoods. As we see in Section 9.3, they make it possible for global finance to be overrun by 'mad money'—money backed by little real collateral but having a very real capacity to increase indebtedness around the world—and this is something that would clearly need to be brought under accountable political control in order for anything approaching justice to be possible in relation to global finance.

What we thus discover in the course of the chapter is not only that there are reasons to take seriously the hypothesis that significant progressive transfers might be offset by financial market responses. We will also see that the regressive effects of market tendencies are independently a cause for concern.

9.1 Tax Justice and Illicit Financial Flows

Recent philosophical literature on tax justice has gone beyond offering normative proposals for particular taxes to consider questions about the institutional conditions required in order to implement them.[2] Among the critical objectives identified is that of stemming the illicit financial flows that tend to drain away control of resources from those who most need them into the hands of a wealthy elite. Currently, taxes are circumvented by the rich and powerful in a variety of ways and on a vast scale. Some of this involves outright tax evasion, particularly as assisted by the secrecy offered by offshore financial centres; but some of it involves tax avoidance strategies that remain compliant with the letter of relevant laws. In view of these challenges, the attention of a number of political philosophers has accordingly shifted from particular substantive tax proposals or more general distributive principles to consideration of how to ensure that any taxes, including those already formally in force, are properly administered. Gillian Brock, for instance, believes that 'reform of our international tax regime could be a very important vehicle by which we can begin to realize global justice' (Brock 2008: 177). For ensuring that

[2] The literature is extensive, but works that are indicative of its themes and approaches include: Cappelen (2001); Brock (2008); Ronzoni (2009); Brock and Pogge (2014); Dietsch and Rixen (2014a, 2014b); Pogge and Mehta (2016).

transnational corporations pay their fair share of taxes 'is crucial to ensuring that all countries, especially developing countries, are able to fund education, job training, infrastructural development, and so forth, thereby enabling poor countries to help themselves better' (Brock 2008: 177).

A basic step towards successfully using fiscal means to the ends of global justice is to ensure that taxes are collected where due in the first place. A challenge for any tax regime is thus to ensure its requirements cannot be *evaded*. The category of tax evasion serves to mark out cases of nonpayment in which rules have clearly been broken, in letter as in spirit. A practical problem, though, is that sometimes it is hard to identify who exactly is evading payment or to what extent. One particular obstacle to effective governance of an existing financial system is the amount of secrecy that is permitted to operate within it. Secrecy is considerably facilitated by the system of Offshore Centres, which play a very significant role in the global economy. It can render obscure the extent to which prudent tax planning shades into aggressive tax avoidance or even outright evasion, as well as allowing proceeds of inherently criminal activities to be integrated into tax free holdings of anonymized members of the global elite. Thus, according to Pogge, rich countries 'run a global financial system that enables shell companies, tax havens and secrecy jurisdictions to be important elements of how millionaires and multinational corporations run their operations' (Pogge 2013). Yet although removing secrecy may help reduce tax evasion, along with other kinds of financial crime, it will not necessarily help tpo address problems of legal tax avoidance. Thus, while there may be good reasons for distinguishing between evasion and avoidance (Brock and Pogge 2014), the application of that distinction depends on how clearly given laws can be applied in given cases, and this can sometimes be a matter of genuine legal uncertainty (Forstater 2015).

In fact, however, *avoidance* of taxes by transnational corporations is itself one of the major problems. Avoidance does not involve unequivocally illegal strategies so much as exploitation of ambiguities and loopholes within tax regimes or discrepancies between them. It is especially egregious, at least from an ethical perspective, in the practice of transfer (mis-)pricing. This involves artificially manipulating prices in trades between subsidiaries of a single corporation based in different jurisdictions so as to minimize or eliminate tax liabilities. Legitimate business optimization can thereby shade into more illicit kinds of behaviour, without necessarily crossing the line of legality. In fact, part of the underlying problem, and why so-called illicit flows do not always involve illegality, is that a legitimate aspect of tax avoidance for firms is simply to take advantage of how nations compete to offer lower rates. 'One long-standing obstacle to global tax reform is the way countries compete with each other to offer preferential tax deals in order to attract investment from multinationals' (Chonghaile 2016).

Hence tax competition between states is a central issue discussed by a number of authors. Because this drives a race to the bottom as far as corporate tax rates go

(Ronzoni 2009), the world's poor necessarily are further disadvantaged in the process. Dietsch and Rixen explain:

> Tax competition between states puts pressure on domestic fiscal regimes. Mobile factors of production have the opportunity to 'shop around' to minimize their tax burden. This interdependence of national tax regimes generates external effects that undermine the *de facto* sovereignty of states. As a consequence, tax competition tends to exacerbate inequalities of income and wealth both within countries and across borders. (Dietsch and Rixen 2014a: 151)

One way for philosophers to address these issues, the authors note, would be to propose redistributive policies for correcting what are perceived to be unjust inequalities. However, they recommend an approach geared towards preventing injustice arising in the first place. Its aim would be to examine 'the rules of the game' of international taxation with a view particularly to seeing how it might be possible to 'delineate legitimate fiscal interdependence from illegitimate tax competition' (Dietsch and Rixen 2014a: 151). Following Miriam Ronzoni (2009) they present this as a discussion of the conditions of *global background justice* that need to be met to guarantee rules of international taxation that are free from unjust bias. Ronzoni's normative assessment of the problem of tax competition leads her to propose that there is, internationally, a 'requirement to establish new practices (that is, supranational regulatory institutions) in order to maintain old practices (states) just' (Ronzoni 2009: 251). She does not assume that the new practices should be governed by the same principles that would be appropriate in the domestic context of a well-ordered state. For Ronzoni considers it likely that 'the supranational institutions that are needed to tackle tax competition will need to engage in *regulatory*, rather than *distributive*, tasks' (Ronzoni 2009: 251).

Ronzoni is thus concerned to emphasize 'the need for normative theory to pay more attention to problems of *empowerment* in global institutional design' (Ronzoni 2009: 231). She recommends thinking about what would be involved in 'the establishment of international institutions that could tackle problematic *power-relationships* between global actors' (Ronzoni 2009: 255). This, it seems to me, is an important point, and, in particular, it is hard to imagine the needed improvements to global tax governance without addressing the governance of the global financial system.

So it is understandable that philosophers concerned with global tax justice are making common cause with promoters of reforms to the financial sector. Thus both Brock and Pogge, for instance, have endorsed the objective of combatting flows of 'illicit money',[3] which has been central to the campaigning of

[3] Brock (2015) speaks in terms of illicit money, as do signatories, who include Pogge, of the 'New Haven Declaration On Human Rights and Financial Integrity' according to which 'large outflows of illicit money—many times larger than all development assistance—greatly aggravate poverty and oppression in many developing countries. Illicit money leaves poorer countries through a global

Washington-based advocacy group *Global Financial Integrity* (GFI), headed by Raymond Baker. He argues that 'we in the West have built and expanded an entire global structure to facilitate the movement of illicit money across borders' (Baker 2007). GFI identifies the core of the problem:

> More money flows illegally out of developing and emerging countries each year—facilitated by secrecy in the global financial system—than they receive in foreign direct investment and foreign aid combined. Beyond bleeding the world's poorest economies, this propels crime, corruption, and tax evasion globally.[4]

It will be noticed that Baker defines 'illicit money' in terms of illegality: 'Illicit money is money that is illegally earned, illegally transferred, or illegally utilized. If it breaks laws in its origin, movement, or use, it merits the label' (Baker 2007). He distinguishes three broad categories of cross-border 'illicit money': the proceeds of bribery or theft by government officials; the proceeds of criminal activities including drugs, racketeering, and terrorist financing; or the proceeds of tax evasion and laundered commercial transactions.[5] Baker notes that '[t]he commercial component, driven by falsified pricing of imports and exports, is by far the largest component, at some 60 to 65 percent of the global total' (Baker 2007). What we might additionally note is that it is also the component that least clearly fits his definition of *illicit*. Practices associated with Baker's first two categories of 'illicit money' are clearly bound up with illegality: bribery is in illegal form of commission payment, theft is illegal, and so are dealing in illegal drugs, racketeering, or being involved in terrorism. By contrast, commercial activity is of course not illegal. Nor is it necessarily clear which of the commercial practices that involve the use of 'illicit money' would themselves be illegal. Certainly, taking advantage of legal loopholes or of jurisdictional differences in tax rates can be regarded as prudent business planning through which companies fulfil their fiduciary duty with regard to shareholders. The use of the term 'illicit' was perhaps lighted upon in the first place because of the difficulty in making a case for the actual illegality of the problematic practices that have become so deeply institutionalized. It signals a sense of moral disapproval, and a desire to use the force of law to sanction the practices, while at the same time indicating a tacit admission that nothing *more practically normative* than moral indignation is conveyed.

So this leaves us to consider the status of the weighty claim that the world now has 'an entire integrated global financial structure the basic purpose of which is to shift illicit money from poor to rich' (Baker 2007). If the whole global structure of

shadow financial system...' https://globaljustice.yale.edu/sites/default/files/files/NewHaven Declaration.pdf Accessed July 2018.

[4] This is from the homepage of the GFI website https://www.gfintegrity.org/ Accessed August 2018.

[5] The proceeds of the first category amount to only about 3 per cent of the global total, and those of the second to about 30 to 35 per cent.

finance is so ordered as to support illicit flows, then this is clearly a problem that would need to be dealt with before global taxation could be a meaningful proposition in practice. Measures for dealing with it would include eliminating tax havens and the corrosive secrecy of Offshore Financial Centres, while also reducing the scope for laundering the proceeds of inherently abhorrent practices and the evasion of legitimate taxes. Insofar as 'illicit flows' carry the spoils of criminal activities and straightforwardly illegal transactions, they can in principle be identified and staunched by implementing effective and appropriate legal measures. However, the most substantial flows do not necessarily involve any clearly determinable illegality, but tend, rather, to involve the exploitation of loopholes in legal frameworks and discrepancies between different jurisdictions and tax regimes.

With regard to Baker's weighty claim, I would point to the importance of seeking conceptual clarity concerning the idea of 'illicit money'. For we need to be aware of how the global financial architecture defies analysis in terms of a clear operable distinction between the licit and the illicit, even if there is a definite moral sense that some such distinction ought to be drawn. Thus, rather than affirming that the global financial structure serves 'to shift illicit money from poor to rich', I would suggest that what the financial system today tends to do is shift *licit* money from poor to rich by means that are morally illicit yet legally permitted. To put it this way is to acknowledge the difficulty that the very concept 'illicit' is analytically elusive, being appropriately rendered by the vague paraphrase 'unethical and often illegal'.[6] A substantively more important point implicit in this conceptualization is the fact that, in the way the financial system operates, there is a meaningful sense in which 'bad money drives out the good'—to the detriment of the worse off and to the enrichment of the already rich. This can happen due to a further real difficulty that stands in need of analysis, namely, that money regarded as 'illicit' can mingle indistinguishably with more 'licit' kinds of money in the global financial system.

9.2 How Licit and Illicit Flows Intermingle in Shadow Banking Institutions

The distinction between licit and illicit flows is hard to apply, given that what is licit—or otherwise—is what is allowed, and it is not always perfectly clear, even as a matter of law, what is allowed with regard to financial manoeuvres. A particularly intractable problem is that money of various different forms and origins intermingles in the global financial system so that separating out those that are less 'licit' than others, even where criteria for determining this are in principle

[6] As Forstater notes of illicit transactions, 'it is generally understood the issues and behaviours occupy a spectrum between illegal and legally condoned behavior' (Forstater 2015: 5).

clear, may be difficult if not impossible. This problem goes beyond dealing with the elements of secrecy and evasiveness that are permitted by Offshore Financial Centres, for it involves transactions that also go on 'in plain sight'. Indeed, so far from being illegal are these practices that a whole institutional infrastructure has developed that gives them support. This is commonly referred to as *shadow banking*, and it greatly increases the scope for leveraging in financial markets.[7] In particular, it permits considerable leveraging of futurity, through the securitization and trade of debt, and thus deals in inherently somewhat unstable assets, which makes the system prone to volatility and to intensified pro-cyclical trends with resultant crises.

The normative aspect of the problem here is not simply that such a system tends to incentivize illicit and questionable kinds of business conduct, which can, in itself, be corrosive of justice in socio-economic arrangements quite generally. There are also two quite distinct and specific concerns of *social* justice, with both domestic and global reach. (In fact, I shall argue, this system can be criticized as *doubly exploitative* of the worst off.) The first way that social injustice arises is through the aggregate effects of a financial system that permits the intermingling of different kinds of financial instrument representing radically different forms of money at source. For what occurs in the process of this mixing is that the financial assets generated by the hard labour and valuable resources of ordinary people, including the worst off, are siphoned off by the securitized instruments created by powerful financial players. This is a significant source of injustice itself, but it is not the only one, and the system that supports such a process could be regarded as doubly exploitative of those who earn their income through work. Not only are they liable to suffer the general adverse effects on economic productivity that may be caused by financial instability; the second distinct concern is that they may then also suffer the more particular consequences of their own personal debt burden. What this burden entails in terms of particular obligations and what sacrifices redeeming it will require of ordinary people can itself manifest profound injustice.

If it is the case that the way global finance works really does produce such a systemic injustice, it is important to know. That would give serious reason to doubt that its institutions are merely 'imperfectly just' as opposed to standing in need of quite radical transformation.

The first thing to establish, then, is whether there is good reason to think the problem is a systemic one rather than one that could be addressed by more modest regulatory means. An aspect of the problem of distinguishing licit from illicit financial flows is that the kinds of transaction that critics want to characterize as

[7] As Nesvetailova explains: 'shadow banking instruments helped to increase leverage in financial markets in three ways: by providing new instruments for borrowing, by increasing economic leverage and by creating embedded leverage.... The layering of securitisation upon securitisation or the hedging and re-hedging of investments with credit derivatives means that the leverage of individual investments can be multiplied many times over' (Nesvetailova 2015: 448).

'illicit' are, in fact, supported by legal norms and practices. The difference between mainstream banking and shadow banking, on a basic account of it, is that the former is supported by the state, its treasury and government, and ultimately by the tax-paying public; shadow banking, by contrast, is supposed to be a purely private system of arrangements dealing informally in 'secondary' forms of money.[8] Yet shadow banking is perhaps rather misleadingly so called given the part it plays within the current financial system. While the workings of this sector may indeed be obscure, in virtue of both the secrecy of Offshore Financial Centres and the complexity of the new sorts of highly leveraged investment vehicles traded, it is hardly of 'outlaw' status. All the contracts that comprise the financial instruments and the dealings in them are drawn up and enforced in rigorously legal terms. The fact is, shadow banking plays an integral role in the financial system as currently constituted.

> Today, behind the facade of any major banking conglomerate, there is a plethora of entities, transactions and quasi-legal cells, many of which are 'orphaned' from the visible part of the bank by complex legal and financial operations, yet which have become absolutely integral to the functioning of our banks. These practices and cells of credit creation include the rather obscure entities such as special purpose entities (SPEs) or structured investment vehicles (SIVs), structures of collateralised debt obligations (CDOs) and asset-backed commercial paper (ABCP), as well as more established institutions and practices, such as asset-backed securities (ABSs), hedge funds, funds of funds, money-market funds and government sponsored financial institutions like the US mortgage giants, Fannie Mae and Freddie Mac. (Nesvetailova 2015: 432)

Thriving on complexity and opacity as it does, Nesvetailova argues, 'the shadow banking system has evolved as a largely undetected yet vital "infrastructure of the infrastructure" of the economy driven by search for high-quality assets…' (Nesvetailova 2015: 432–3). Shadow banking, then, is neither illegal nor 'external' to the global financial system, but can be seen, rather, as 'the financial industry's institutionalised response to investors' search for yield and investables' (Nesvetailova 2015: 450).

A contributory reason for the very distinction between licit and illicit flows being suffused with uncertainty in practice is thus that the creativity of the financial sector makes even questions of legality hard to test:

> financial markets are always innovating—creating new financial products, new markets in which to trade them and finding new clients to use them. As a result,

[8] Shadow banking can be understood as 'a system of unregulated off-bank balance sheet credit intermediation and maturity and liquidity transformation activities conducted by bank owned or sponsored entities in the capital and money market domains for the primary purpose of expanding the rate of production of yield bearing debt securities required by the global investor community' (Lysandrou and Nesvetailova 2014: 260).

> even with the reformed financial regulatory regime there will always be new, and not easily recognized, incentives for regulatory arbitrage in the search for financial market profits. (Knight, M 2014: 14)

Regarding this difficulty, Nesvetailova cites some telling words of a senior French banker whom she interviewed: 'It takes me about two hours to assemble a team of finance geeks and lawyers to devise a product or a transaction that would bypass any new rule or regulation coming our way' (Nesvetailova 2014: 6). If that is the reality, then it indicates a degree of futility in relying on regulation to deal with the social dysfunctionality of the financial sector.

There is thus good reason for thinking critically about the problem at the level of the system itself, rather than simply in relation to particular norms that might be altered by regulation within it. What has made it possible for shadow banking to grow to the extent it has—estimated to account for up to a third of the world's financial system (Nesvetailova 2015: 449)—is how the legal framework has allowed such extensive freedom to treat debt as a saleable commodity.[9] This is a critical factor. It has been driven, as noted earlier, by how the economy has shifted increasingly to valuations grounded in *futurity*. This means, as Mehrling (2013) puts it, that the present valuations of capital assets are dependent entirely on imagined future cash flows projected back into the present. When the expectations of future gains come to be treated as assets, then the system comes to be increasingly a business of dealing in debts.

The fact that debt can be traded as a commodity is the fundamental premise of the shadow banking system. Yet the more that securitized assets are permitted to function like money—that is, including being treated as a medium of exchange and a store of value—the greater is the range of risks opened against the society or societies permitting it. There is, in particular, the risk that financial innovations can reduce the liquidity in the economy while appearing to increase it.

A problem with treating debt as an asset is that, of its nature, it cannot generally be as liquid as cash or more tangible assets can. For it is when liquidity most crucially *matters*—as when one wants to be able to 'deleverage' one's financial position by converting to tangible assets—that a counterparty is least likely to be ready to accept an IOU in lieu. Therefore we should not assume that the ease and speed with which an asset might in a certain period be traded necessarily indicates its liquidity (Warburton 2003). As Hyman Minsky put it, 'the ultimately liquid

[9] Nesvetailova cites Henry MacLeod's observation that the discovery to have 'most deeply affected the fortunes of the human race' is probably the 'discovery that a Debt is a Saleable Commodity'. If credit 'has done more a thousand times to enrich nations than all the mines of all the world' that is because it 'may be used like Money: and produce all the effect of Money'. Nesvetailova updates the observation by adding: 'The discovery that debt, especially low-quality debt, may not only be sold, but deferred into the future and divorced from the underlying risks, and thus become a vehicle for value extraction today, may well be seen as one of the most important political-economic discoveries of late twentieth century.' (The quotes from MacLeod are found in Nesvetailova 2015: 449.)

assets of the economy consist of those assets whose nominal value is independent of the functioning of the economy' (Minsky 1982: 9). The apparent liquidity of debt-assets can be a dangerous illusion that arises in times of buoyancy.

The danger of illusory liquidity lies in mistaking a part of the truth for the whole of it. There may be nothing illusory in the perception that, for a time, an individual investor in debt-based assets can find it advantageous to leverage up; yet where this practice is engaged in by a number of other investors doing likewise the situation eventually reveals itself to be collectively irrational (Adrian and Shin 2010). For the sum of individual actions leads to the inflation of a bubble that will in due course burst—with adverse consequences for all who are then left holding discounted IOUs. So although highly leveraged financial instruments may for some periods seem very liquid, because trade in them is brisk, they are not fundamentally stable. In fact, Nesvetailova says, 'liquidity may be perceived as highest precisely when it is most vulnerable', for when markets are over-heating '[t]he success of leveraged trading generates high profits, adds to market-making capacity, and lulls participants into a false sense of security' (Nesvetailova 2007: 82). Already prior to the 2008 crash, she had warned that the wide accessibility of new credit lines was a particularly worrying development: 'instability arises because financial intermediaries issue new kinds of financial instruments which, as long as the market judges them "liquid," serve as "effective" money without increasing required reserves' (Nesvetailova 2006: 46). Debts grow without any increase in real assets, so '[a]s a result of a perpetual chain of financial innovation, "even an accumulation of debts" (in the form of intricately packaged financial instruments) can appear as an accumulation of capital' (Nesvetailova 2006: 46). This creates problems because it tends to amplify expansionary tendencies in the economy during good times and to exacerbate the fall in values during down times, contributing significantly to the precipitation of crises. In other words, the shadow banking system has a structural tendency to work in a pro-cyclical direction.

A reason this tendency is particularly problematic from the perspective of a concern with justice is that the profits taken during buoyant times are subtracted by private investors; the losses that come with crises have their primary effects on the rest of society, and, furthermore, the costs of making them good may be socialized via state bailouts too. This redistributive effect is regressive, exacerbating the inequalities between the minority in the global elite who draw benefit from their market activities and the greater majority of humankind.

For the majority of humankind, the system can be experienced as doubly exploitative. For one thing, as a result of treating debt as an asset, financial volatility and crises ensue, which in turn have adverse effects on the economy, and it is the worst off who suffer hardest from these. Since it is they who can least afford additional hardship and have done the least to deserve it, whereas those who have caused it draw benefit from it, this can, in my view, be regarded as exploitative. The second exploitative aspect is the specific burden loaded onto those who find themselves drawn into the cycle of debt, in its lower and outer reaches, that the system is increasingly dependent on. As incomes sink and debts rise, the most disadvantaged people, whose only asset is the labour they can sell, at whatever price it will fetch, may become so pressed that they find themselves left with such options as renting out their bodies for others to use, or selling their organs, or their children, or bonding their families into servitude. I characterize this situation as *exploitative* since the process involves diluting hard-earned cash with unearned credits thereby leaching value from those contributing the former to the mix. The logic of the situation is that when debt is treated as a saleable asset this creates a market for trade in people's obligations to render future services; in consequence, the more financial profit is extracted from such trade, the more extensive become the bonds of those obligations. A comparable logic operates even at the level of a national economy when a debt crisis results in the demands of creditors for the imposition of austerity measures. Peripheral economies, in particular, which already generally tend to be fragile with respect to international economic forces, can be subjected to demands for 'structural adjustment' programmes that can exacerbate situations of poverty and injustice. These in turn further reinforce impacts on individuals and families.

The implications for global justice of the mingling of leveraged financial instruments with money that represents the hard-earned fruits of labour are accordingly serious. It has, of course, to be recognized that not all cash flows in licit ways, that not all leveraged financial instruments involve illicit transactions, and also that it is not always certain what even counts as licit or otherwise. But the point is that the different kinds of money from different sources are all thoroughly intermingled in the global financial system. The outcome is that the system lends itself to the forms of exploitation indicated. It follows that if one wishes to think about global justice in terms of redistributive taxes of some kind, one should not imagine that any fiscal policy enacted for the purposes of global justice would simply be able to take control of monetary assets and direct them to achieve its goals as if these were somehow neutral and objectively self-subsistent things. The specific way in which a monetary system is operated affects what can be achieved through it. Given this, an obvious response is to consider whether steps might be taken to prevent the mingling of different kinds of money, for instance, by means of some appropriate regulation or modest reform of the financial system. Such consideration, however, needs to take cognizance of the fact that once mingled, money cannot be unmingled, so the challenge is to ensure the system does not allow their mingling in the first place. The underlying problem, though, is that the drivers of mingling are inherent in the dynamic logic of the capitalist economic system.[10] The purposes of

[10] As was shown in Chapter 3, the problematic processes of financialization can be seen as rational responses to problems attendant on trying to ensure continued functioning of that system even as it starts to undermine its own material preconditions.

monetary governance as operative today prioritize ensuring the continuance of that system, which is not under real public control or constrained to serve the greater public interest. So before it can be feasible to think about financing fiscal schemes aimed at greater justice, there are fundamental questions to attend to about how the monetary system works and who controls it. Normative corollaries then are questions about who *should* control the monetary system and how.

This section has shown that the problem of illicit flows is intractable because the financial instruments carrying them are intermingled with licit money. Underlying that problem, as Section 9.3 will show, is the fact that the intermingling is a result of the inherent dynamics of the profit-driven economic system that generated them. It cannot therefore realistically be undone without transforming the system.

9.3 The Need for Political Control over the Monetary System

A question that has hardly been broached in relation to proposals of fiscal or other redistributive measures for global justice concerns the sort of monetary governance arrangements required to make their operation possible. Yet what has been shown in this book is that aside from—and, in some important ways, prior to—questions of how money might in principle be redistributed, there are questions about how the value of any given sum, or money form, or currency can in practice remain stable enough to function as required. Appropriately stable values cannot simply be taken for granted. What it takes to maintain stable money is the central problem for monetary policy; but the policy-making itself—even when carried out by 'technocrats'—presupposes certain parameters of action. What the guiding constraints should be and who sets them are matters involving political understandings of economic priorities. The most general constraint on monetary policy-makers operating within the global system today is to preserve the conditions for the functioning of the existing economic system. Hence we encounter again the general question of whether that imperative can be respected at the same time as a serious attempt is made to achieve global justice. The more specific question here is how money can be made to work for the ends of global justice in a system set up to maintain the monetary conditions needed for capitalism.

One cannot assume that money functions as a purely technical means of transferring value from one party or place to another. Insofar as money serves its functions, it has a distinct value in itself that arises from its capacity to do so, and the achievement involved in bringing such a system into existence is considerable, for it involves a vast practical infrastructure integrated with a complex normative order. Operations to transfer money from one tax jurisdiction to another presuppose further practical and normative arrangements. The maintenance of such a vast and complex system is demanding, and accordingly comes at a significant price.

The use of money for different sorts of purpose has a number of distinct kinds of price, and these, jointly and severally, are subject to a variety of market fluctuations. A fundamental problem with the global financial system today is that it can render unstable the value of money in all its dimensions. All major prices of money—as indicated by inflation rates, interest rates, and foreign exchange rates—can be affected, and the unpredictable fluctuations occurring in markets subsequently affect people's lives and livelihoods. Instability of any one of the money prices, moreover, can bring about uncertainty and the volatility of the others. This fact and its consequences were spelled out clearly some time ago by Susan Strange, particularly in her seminal book *Casino Capitalism*, originally published in 1986 and recently re-published (Strange 2016). It constitutes the basic problem that she starts from, namely, that remote dealings on financial markets have effects that wreak havoc for lives and livelihoods.

> A currency change can halve the value of a farmer's crop before he harvests it, or drive an exporter out of business. A rise in interest rates can fatally inflate the cost of holding stocks for the shop-keeper. A takeover dictated by financial considerations can rob the factory worker of his job. From school-leavers to pensioners, what goes on in the… big financial centres is apt to have sudden, unpredictable and unavoidable consequences for individual lives. (Strange 2016: 2)

Strange draws out the ethical and social consequences of 'casino capitalism', as she calls it, arguing that when 'skill, effort, initiative, determination and hard work count for less and less, then inevitably faith and confidence in the social and political system quickly fades. Respect for ethical values—on which in the end a free democratic society relies—suffers a dangerous decline' (Strange 2016: 2). In fact, even the capacities of governments are affected.

> Political leaders, and their opponents, like to pretend that they are still in control of their national economies, that their policies have the power to relieve unemployment, revive economic growth, restore prosperity and encourage investment in the future. But recent years have shown again and again how the politicians' plans have been upset by changes that they could not have foreseen in the world outside the state. The dollar has weakened—or become too strong. Interest rates have made the burden of servicing a foreign debt too heavy to sustain. The banks have suddenly decided to lend the country no more money. Oil prices have suddenly risen—or fallen. Other commodity prices, on which export earnings may depend, fall, because the major economies of major consuming countries are going through a recession. The uncertainty that rules in the financial world spills over not only into individual lives but into the fortunes of governments and of countries—and sooner or later into the relations between states. (Strange 2016: 3)

The degree of a state's political autonomy in relation to any money prices is constrained by factors in the financial system that are beyond the control of a government. Constraints related to exchange rates, especially, affect the performance of national economies to such an extent that 'they are arguably the world economy's most important prices' (Lyons 2001: 221).

Exchange rate volatility can be especially detrimental to poor countries in need of development (see also e.g. Essers 2013; Jérôme Héricourt and Sandra Poncet 2013). It can cause soaring inflation and dramatic declines in national output, 'which in many emerging market nations means higher unemployment in already distressed labour markets' (LiPuma and Koelble 2009: 222). In light of vulnerabilities to exchange rate movements, a country with a developing capitalist economy can face a quandary. It has reasons to seek to hold a strong international currency in its reserves, so as to protect the country's own currency against speculators attempting to short it (LiPuma and Koelble 2009). Yet to do so means such currency has to be held rather than used, and this in turn means forgoing needed investments: 'if the government is holding money in reserve, it is not using it to underwrite roads, hospitals, schools and whatever else is needed to improve the economy and people's standard of living' (LiPuma and Koelble 2009: 223). In other words, because of the risk of predation made possible by global finance, a country may find that it has to forgo measures to address poverty in its own land. A particular problem, argue LiPuma and Koelble, to which the mainstream political economy literature has paid insufficient attention, concerns 'the limits and constraints placed upon these newly emerging democracies by the new financial architecture, particularly the derivatives market, which now determines the value and price of emerging market currencies' (Koelble and LiPuma 2006: 605).

It is thus the financial architecture itself that generates situations of injustice, and the point to emphasize is the particular *dynamic* involved. Derivatives are significant because of how their use can amplify market movements. Insofar as people engaged in the business of finance seek a profit, this can only come from successfully exploiting differentials in the price of money, which essentially involves placing bets on future market movements: 'Generically, a derivative is a contractual wager on the volatility of the relationship between two assets over a specified time period. It is called a derivative because it focuses on the relationship between assets, rather than the assets themselves' (LiPuma and Koelble 2009: 206). Derivatives dealers need currencies to move—and the more dramatically, the better—to make their profits. A systemic problem, then, is that speculative capital thrives on currency volatility, since price movements are its sole source of profit, and so the holders of that capital accordingly have an incentive to stimulate it. The outcome is that the Euro-American banks and hedge funds do well from the dynamics of the system, while the losers are typically emerging market countries. The currency derivatives market is huge,[11] but its workings are opaque, since 'most principals are under no regulatory obligation to disclose their transactions' (LiPuma and Koelble 2009: 206). What has emerged in this massive market, then, is difficult to see or comprehend at the level of particular transactions, and yet its effects are all too evident. These are harmful socially, ecologically, and even economically.

The asset base of the system increasingly consists of people's future obligations: viewed in terms of social relations, its dominant characteristic is that of *debt bondage*. A corollary for a growing number of states is the imposition of *austerity* measures.[12] An ever-growing amount of debt apportioned to ordinary members of publics across the world is balanced against an ever-growing amount of claims to it held by a tiny global elite. Today, according to Oxfam's estimate, as was noted in Chapter 1, the eight richest individuals in the world hold as much wealth as the more than 3.5 billion poorest.

In short, extraordinary opportunities for speculators to profit have arisen in consequence of the liberalization of financial markets. These financial freedoms can thus undermine monetary policy formulated with the greater economic good in mind.

One obvious response to this situation is to recommend reining in those financial freedoms, particularly as so many aspects of financial governance appear to be rather weak. Yet improved regulation may not suffice to achieve the turnaround in financial incentives that the social and economic objectives require—especially if it is the case that a group of geeks and lawyers can readily devise a workaround for any new regulation.

In order to achieve a more significant effect, some political economists argue that structural reform of the financial system's architecture is required. According to Thiemann (2014), for instance, the current global governance mechanisms undermine the capacity of national banking regulators to deal with the disruptive innovativeness of their banks. He highlights the need to address structural constraints on attempts to regulate financial innovation that evades global rules. 'If no changes to the global financial architecture occur, these structural conditions at the margins of banking regulation will persist' (Thiemann 2014: 1231). Furthermore,

[11] 'To give some idea of the magnitude of the numbers in question, from 2004 through 2006 the outstanding currency derivative contracts of one firm, JPMorgan Chase, fluctuated between 4 and 5 trillion US dollars (US Treasury Department 2006). Speculative capital counts on momentum trading, meaning, as a given currency spirals downward (or upwards), more and more speculative capital wagers on its further fall. More than simply discounting future cross-currency rates, more than simply adding liquidity to the currency markets, inflows of speculative capital are increasingly enormous enough to become self-fulfilling prophecies in that they cause the volatility or directional price movements that they are presumably discounting' (LiPuma and Koelble 2009: 214).

[12] For a critical overview of the practical meaning of *austerity* for the moral economy of a society see e.g. Clarke and Newman (2012).

it is not just the resourcefulness of geeks and lawyers that challenges regulators, he emphasizes, because measures aimed at regulating finance 'generate mobilization not only from banks, but also from non-target groups such as industrial lobbies, crafts associations and the insurance industry' (Pagliari and Young 2014: 599). As Pagliari and Young emphasize, studies of the influence of financial industry groups on regulatory policy-making tend to neglect how the particular financial industry groups being regulated 'are often able to tie in their interests with those of other private sector groups affected indirectly by the regulation in question' (Pagliari and Young 2014: 576). This brings us back to Strange's central point that banks and other specialized financial institutions are not entirely separate from other sectors of the economy but are essential to the functioning of the system of production and exchange. This means that even structural reform, which aims to be more thoroughgoing than tightened regulation, may still fall short of the objective if it focuses on finance as isolated from the wider political economic system.

In thinking about this bigger picture, it is worth keeping in mind, as noted in Chapter 3, that the reasons for the liberalization of finance, in the first place, had to do with wider macroeconomic issues. Seen from a historical perspective, it appears that the period during which states maintained controls on capital movements—lasting from the financial crisis of 1931 through the era of Bretton Woods institutions until the late 1950s, in the midst of which was World War II—is something of an *exception* to a longer historical rule of liberalized international finance (Helleiner 1995). By the time of the 1970s experience of stagnant growth, with negative real interests and poor returns on capital, the affluent classes felt change was needed. UK Prime Minister Margaret Thatcher, for instance, convinced that Keynesianism had to be abandoned and that monetarist 'supply-side' solutions were necessary to cure the stagflation, recognized that this meant nothing short of a revolution in fiscal and social policies. The implications of this shift amounted to a programme for dismantling the social democratic state that had been consolidated in Britain after 1945. The era of Thatcher and Reagan thereby saw the consolidation of neoliberalism as a new economic orthodoxy.

It would therefore seem unrealistic to think that the financial sector could be significantly transformed without considerable effects on the functioning of the productive economy. Serious financial change has to be accompanied by quite decisive preparedness to tackle the more fundamental economic issues at the same time. If neoliberalism has come from a 'revolution in fiscal and social policies', then transforming it can be expected to require changes that are no less revolutionary. Some economists may have expectations or hopes for a pendulum swing back towards a new Keynesianism. Yet today we face circumstances that are quite different from those that gave birth to social democracy in the leading capitalist countries and to the Bretton Woods institutions those states used to govern international economic relations. The power of corporations has in many ways overtaken that of states; the ecological conditions of the planet place constraints on the extent to which further economic growth is even possible, let alone desirable. If financial innovation is out of control, and if the drivers for this are deeply rooted in the global capitalist economic system, then the answer has to involve asserting public political—democratic and accountable—control over it.

This points to a conclusion that appropriate governance of the monetary system is a pre-requisite for the possibility of any meaningful fiscal approach to justice. Fiscal policy needs to be supported by management of money. Questions about money are not just about formulating the 'right' monetary policy; a prior question is about who gets to decide and where lies the right to enforce it. At present, the answer by default is that it is the global financial elite. A primary political issue for those concerned with this aspect of global justice, therefore, should be how control in the name of the global public can and should be asserted.

9.4 Conclusion: *Mad Money* vs Global Justice

This chapter started out from a hypothetical question about whether reactions in financial markets might offset the beneficial effects intended for fiscal transfers as proposed by global justice theorists. As originally posited, the question was whether success in fiscal programmes for global justice would provoke adverse financial reactions. What we have since come to understand is that there is a more thoroughgoing problem: adverse financial events are liable to occur with or without progress being made towards relieving poverty, inequality, and injustice. Finance, which could in principle serve as a means to achieve the public good, has, under the existing global system, instead become an instrument of injustice. Tax proposals that aim to redistribute a portion of the proceeds generated by this system may be less likely to achieve the goals of justice than their advocates suppose.

The problem has to do with the very *nature* of money. A fundamental part of the challenge for global justice today is that the world has been overrun by *mad money*. Much of the money as it is now created cannot function as both an effective medium of exchange and a stable store of value. With the liberalization of financial markets and the untethering of the global monetary system from tangible assets, money as produced by financial innovation has the character of *securitized futurity*. Expectations of future profits are marketed as present values, and consequently greater expectations are loaded onto the future. This means ever-increasing levels of *debt*. Lenders' freedom from reserves constraints, or from any other constraints linking loans to materially productive capabilities, means that money can be created *ad libitum*. There is no ontological limit to the amount of debt-claims on people's future commitments that can be created. Yet the indebtedness that is enforced by law and social obligation has real ontological effects on the people bound by those obligations to strive to redeem it.

There is a severe vicious circle here: more and more money becomes concentrated in the hands of the financial elite, not only relative to the amount accessible by the poor majority of the global population, but also in relation to genuinely profitable investment opportunities. Hence the increasing securitization of futurity, where promises and aspirations of future growth are allowed to count towards present profits, not only sets up pernicious relations of indebtedness that drive social destitution; it also stokes the drive for ever-increasing economic growth without regard to the consequences for the planet's finite capacities. Due to this superabundance of money as securitized futurity there is far more capital available than sound and productive opportunities to invest in. Its holders will seek a return wherever they can, even if no net social good comes from it. If capital is allowed to grow on the basis of a securitized future, and thus have an increasingly indiscriminate approach to profit-making opportunities, there is a clear recipe for disaster.

This fact alone should be of concern to theorists of global justice. It has critical implications for any assumption that the present system of global finance can simply be lightly taxed in one way or another to make the world tolerably just. The challenge of global justice has to be understood as not just about redistributing some of the positive rewards of economic activity, nor about simply reforming some of the clearly inadequate regulatory mechanisms. It is about understanding how the conditions of production of any economic benefits are strongly governed by these arrangements that support the worldwide currency of *mad money.*

It is therefore arguable that not just structural reform, but structural *transformation* would be required to make possible the development of a global financial system that served the ends of justice rather than those of private interests. There is a crucial question here of a fundamental constitutional kind: who should control the institutions and what should their core mandate be. In a nutshell, public service or private interest?

10

Constituting Finance as a Global Public Good: the Scope of the Challenge

A question posed at the start of the book was whether it is necessary or possible to conceive of a systematic alternative to the 'universalization of Western liberal democracy as the final form of human government'. The intervening chapters have provided reasons to suggest that it is necessary. I have argued that the international institutional framework supporting Western liberal democracy entrenches economic incentives that work to the immediate detriment both of the more disadvantaged sections of the global population and the global environment. From a perspective of a concern with global justice, there are good reasons to doubt that minor reforms to Western liberal democracy will suffice as a basis for a sustainable and just world order. So if we can appreciate the *necessity* of conceiving of a systematic alternative to the universalization of Western liberal democracy, then what about the *possibility* of doing so? The aim of this chapter is to clarify some parameters for constructive thought about an alternative. For the claim is that a new research agenda is taking shape that merits the attention of political philosophers, so we can provisionally anticipate some basic questions at the heart of it.

A more just world order would depend on the creation of institutions. There are very practical questions about how exactly those institutions might be brought into existence and by whom that cannot be settled simply by means of philosophical thought; there are also questions of institutional design that require attention to numerous and momentous contingencies, and most of these would not be appropriately addressed as questions for a political philosopher, either. Where political philosophy has a distinct contribution to offer is in seeking to make clear and explicit the most fundamental constitutional principles that a just world order would depend on. In terms of substantive values, this book is premised on the thought that these principles fundamentally aim at achieving social justice and ecological sustainability; the objectives to these ends can nowadays be regarded as codified in the language of *human rights* as it has developed these past seventy years to refer to the basic norms of conduct human beings have affirmed in international treaties and other agreements. If human rights norms are currently honoured as much in the breach as in the observance, and even sometimes cynically instrumentalized—by states and other actors internationally—we can still endorse in good faith the goal of implementing their humane normative substance.

A recurrent problem for the protection of human rights under the existing order is the fact that it can come up against incursions pursued on the basis of private property rights. Certainly, the problems that can be attributed to the global financial system arise because that system gives overriding protection to property over humanity, wherever the two come into conflict. The fact is, as we shall see in Section 10.1, there is at present a deeply entrenched set of institutional arrangements internationally, that have real power in regard to the institutions of nation-states, and can be regarded as so systematic as to amount to an implicit, informal constitution for the global governance of finance. The effects of this systematic control can then be felt in all the other realms of life affected by finance, which ultimately leaves few, if any, untouched. From the standpoint of a concern with the political legitimacy of constitutional claims to our compliance, that implicit informal constitution can only be regarded, at least presumptively, as lacking legitimacy. One of the most egregious problems with the system is that it utilizes the power of nation-states to serve interests at odds with those very states and peoples themselves: it allows a few elite players to use legitimately constituted states to extract benefits from their domestic law enforcement capabilities while escaping any burdens of support for those states. This helps to account for how there can be a one-way street of aggregate financial flows and such an extreme polarization of wealth occurring today.

Accordingly, it may prove not to be realistic to think about how global justice can be achieved without first recovering some effective sovereignty on the part of states with regard to the financial conditions under which the people they serve live. Of course, cosmopolitan philosophers may not aim to be realists in a methodological sense. However, I maintain that to talk about global justice, specifically, where the epithet *global* really means justice as potentially applicable in the world as we know it and not in some idealized 'possible world', we need to maintain sufficient 'reflective equilibrium' to treat realistic propositions no less seriously than abstract idealizations. Thus, in practice, even those who regard themselves as morally cosmopolitan—and I would be one who does—have to be prepared to entertain such thoughts as that the path towards a *globally* just normative order might lie through an initial *strengthening* of sovereign states' powers rather than their further dissolution.[1] In principled terms, the challenge is to create constraints of a constitutional kind that respect the principle of ensuring that the powers exercised with regard to the control of money prices are proportionate to the responsibility for maintaining stability in those prices. In other words, integral to bringing about a globally just monetary order would be justice

[1] This proposition has been a topic of some critical debate. The first draft manuscript of this book was discussed at a panel of the 2018 Oxford Political Thought conference, and the commentators had reservations, some of which, with my response, have since been published: Wiedenbrüg, Hayward & O'Neill (2020).

in the workings of its constituent institutions and processes. The achievement of global justice cannot be assumed to depend on globalizing an inherently unjust set of arrangements. There are good reasons to assume the contrary.

The particular sorts of constitutional question these concerns imply include the appropriate relationship that should hold between a central bank and the political government of a state. This has not been a prominent topic for discussion in political theory to date. Questions about exactly which monetary powers, if any, should be held independently of which branches of the state, and how, are matters that have not been given the kind of close attention that those of, say, the constitutional role of supreme courts has received. Yet the powers in question are no less momentous or significant. If the constitutional status of a central bank is already a somewhat under-theorized element of domestic political theory of modern nation-states, it is a seriously neglected question in the context of globalizing finance. In opening up this question for the consideration of political philosophers, in Section 10.2, I also show that the role of the central banks' own central bank, the Bank for International Settlements, needs to be more openly and fully discussed as a constitutional issue of fundamental importance for questions of justice.

10.1 The Governance of Finance: a Privatized Global Constitution?

We are accustomed to think of finance as a monetary phenomenon and of its governance, accordingly, as largely a matter of monetary policy. But we need to appreciate the extent to which finance is inherently a *legal* phenomenon and also how money is inherently a *political* phenomenon. It then becomes evident why the governance of finance should be regarded not only as a policy issue, but as a *constitutional* matter. If both laws and politics need to have the legitimating force of authority, then the source and nature of that authority—in other words, its constitution as such—matters.

Law plays an indispensible role in finance because virtually any form of finance at all involves a contract of some kind. In contracting, two or more parties agree to abide by norms that have an authoritative status they similarly recognize. All deals, all trades, all loans, are inherently arrangements of a normative kind that 'exist' as they do because parties to them recognize and accept the normative rules implicitly governing them. This is conspicuous in a developed economy with explicit—and often minutely detailed—legal contracts. It is dominant in the world of high finance where trade in derivatives consists of nothing other than the creation of ever more complex contracts. Remove law from its framing and practices, and the entirety of global finance would thereby be erased.

Laws do not create or enforce themselves. They come from somewhere, and there has to be some concrete basis of social practices and institutions that make it the case that people abide by the law and generally rely on others to abide by it too. So the governance of finance does not only concern the primary rules on which people rely when agreeing contracts; it has also to operate at a higher level where laws for implementing and framing those rules are agreed; and, at a higher level still, questions must be settled concerning who gets to decide on what basis who makes those laws.

Katharina Pistor develops an understanding of how the very existence of finance has the form of a set of legal contracts underwritten by a system of legal norms and institutionalized means of enforcing them. Her legal theory of finance offers important insights for our purposes, and she emphasizes, in particular, four stylized facts of contemporary finance that apply in both national and global contexts, namely:

> first, that financial assets are legally constructed; second, that law contributes to finance's instability; third, that there is a pecking order of the means of pay, which implies that finance is inherently hierarchical; and fourth, that the binding nature of legal and contractual commitments tends to be inversely related to the hierarchy of finance: Law tends to be binding on the periphery and relatively more elastic at the apex of the financial system. (Pistor 2013: 317)

The first point is the one already outlined. But what about the second: how exactly does law contribute to finance's instability? Part of the answer lies in the fact that although the social purpose of finance is to support future projects, the actual outcome of any project, and thus also of its return to finance, is inherently *uncertain*. But why should the fact that a given business might do worse than expected mean the whole system becomes less stable? If one business seeks to liquidate some assets, this need not be a particular problem. Yet, as shown in Chapter 9, when many parties seek to liquidate assets at the same time, the availability of liquidity declines and its price rises. For, as Pistor emphasizes, liquidity is a function of money that comes at a price, and it cannot be regarded as a free good. A rise in the price of liquidity can lead to a vicious deflationary spiral and thus a crisis. A reason people could be seeking liquidity at the same time is that adjustments to expectations are quite likely to be prompted by developments in underlying economic realities and market conditions that affect a variety of actors in a similar way. The underlying causes of an unexpected development in markets are liable to apply widely to holders of relevantly affected assets. The question, though, is why does Pistor say that *law* contributes to the instability? If the law codifies a contract whose terms do not get fulfilled, in what way does it *contribute* to that failure? The problem, as Pistor describes it, is that the ever more complex contracts devised to trade various kinds of debt and derivatives require a very firm legal structure holding all the different obligations in place. However, the rigidity of these legal arrangements—intricately involving numerous parties around the world—can exacerbate the problem that arises when uncertainty meets liquidity shortage. For precisely when flexibility of response is most in need—in the interests of a wide range of parties and thus for the system as a whole—the legal fixity of the private contracts compounds the problem. The rigidly legal system has pervasive 'brittleness', we might say, whereas what people require of it is some elasticity.[2]

Pistor's third point concerns finance being 'inherently hierarchical'. Here she follows Perry Mehrling (2013) in seeing a hierarchical differentiation of forms of money in terms of the quality that distinguishes the general idea of money from the general idea of credit.[3] To illustrate: if gold is the 'ultimate money' in a system, then currency is a lower form, since it consists of promises to pay gold (and, of course, among currencies there can be a hierarchy too); bank deposits are lower again, because they are held as promises to pay currency; the various securities that represent promises of deposits, lie further down the hierarchy, with derivatives lying lower still.[4] A given sum of money held in any of these forms, nonetheless, has identical nominal value.

> In normal times most financial instruments appear as close substitutes to official or state money in the sense that they can easily be bought and sold for one another or for cash. However, when too many investors seek to change their portfolio of assets at the same time, some assets will no longer find takers as investors flee to safety: They buy cash or close cash substitutes, such as reputable corporate or government bonds. This implies that finance is not flat, but hierarchical'. (Pistor 2013: 319)

Accordingly, one would expect that when a crisis of confidence hits the financial system, those holding the instruments furthest from convertibility into the ultimate money form will be most vulnerable to suffering the consequences of defaults on the concatenated promises that constitute their assets. Yet this is not necessarily what happens. One might think that holders of bank deposits should be more secure at times of contraction than are holders of securities or, especially, of

[2] A simple illustration of this point is a mortgage: when a direct loan is made to a borrower, it is possible, in times of repayment difficulty, to renegotiate the terms of repayment, since this is at the borrower's discretion; when a mortgage consists of a package of derivatives, however, it can be next to impossible to 'unpick' the contractual obligations embedded in it, even in principle, let alone as a matter of practical negotiation.

[3] As Mehrling explains: 'what counts as money at one level in the system is merely credit for the level above. This means that higher levels of the system can generally solve the crisis of levels below them. Small crises can be solved by monetary expansion at the immediately higher level; large crises however may require involvement of the very highest levels. Just so, in the recent 2007–9 U.S. debt crisis, the banking system initially tried to absorb the brunt of the crisis, but when the crisis proved too big the central banking system had to get involved' (Mehrling 2013: 401).

[4] 'In financial markets, participants trade different forms of money, some of which is state-issued and some privately issued. A form of money is closer to the "apex" of the system the closer it is to entities that can issue liquid means or determine acceptable forms of payment, such as central banks and governments. During financial crises, market participants close to the "apex" are systematically advantaged' (Pistor 2017: 185).

the various derivatives. However, under a system of fractional reserve banking, only a small percentage of depositors will be able to recover currency from their account before the bank runs out. At that point, depositors are faced with the stark fact that they are creditors of the bank and have to 'stand in line' to see what return they can get. In the event of a severe crisis, they may find that their place in the hierarchy is not where they had thought, and, in an extreme situation, they may find themselves involved in a 'bail-in' of their bank (Zhou et al. 2012). That situation can arise for these reasons: if a bank is to make any repayments at all, it has to remain solvent; in order to remain solvent, it needs to get value from the loans it has made; if those loans have gone out into complex derivative contracts, then it will need those contracts to be respected. The upshot is that the banks may place priority on meeting claims of holders of derivatives over those of depositors. From the standpoint of depositors, of course, this will be experienced as a case of theft, but it is not a crime if the legal rules governing the financial system permit it. The hierarchy of moneys, as Pistor argues, is largely a function of law. 'Law enhances predictability and the credibility of commitments and thereby helps scale up financial markets, because those who have been able to shift risk to others are willing to take on even more risks' (Pistor 2017: 186). Viewed from the standpoint of ordinary depositors, of course, it appears that those taking the big risks do so with other people's money and reap the profits therefrom, while losses are returned to those who had contributed the soundest money in the first place.

In the light of these observations, one can readily see how Pistor comes to affirm her fourth point, namely, that precisely those with most power over the financial system are the least firmly bound by any socially or politically mandated norms. For the system as it has developed 'tolerates, perhaps even promotes, a structural mismatch between those who control the rules of the game and those who bear the inevitable costs condones injustice' (Pistor 2017: 186). This structural injustice, furthermore, could quite possibly become more extreme in the future. For finance is part of a *dynamic* system in which the priority of achieving 'shareholder value' entails an unending quest for profits on capital. A further foreseeable insecurity for ordinary people who do not even have savings is possible attrition of the value of what limited spending power they do have if it becomes available exclusively in 'cashless' form and thus liable to the kind of digital chiselling mentioned in Chapter 5. Under these circumstances, those who have a little saved would also become vulnerable to being 'bailed in' to help the banks whenever their big investments take a dive, or even, potentially, just whenever the rules allow for an imposition of negative interest or other kinds of deduction. Regarding the rules, these are not what the wider population of a democracy would ever willingly and knowingly mandate. But they are complicated and hard to understand—except by those who devise them, who themselves are paid by the financial institutions. As the financial institutions continue to thrive, these individuals are well placed to influence the legislation that governs their operation.

There is thus a problem today of a global 'rule of law' relating to finance that is determined by a kind of political order that itself has no constitutional oversight of the kind that could truly be said to represent the concerns of the people. We are becoming aware of an essentially private constitution created and imposed by a global economic elite that circumvents and subverts the politics of states. It is therefore arguable that finance is already part of a global constitutional order, but an order that has not been ratified by the people or peoples of the world. Gunther Teubner (2011), for instance, argues that since the 1980s, and under the influence of the Washington Consensus, the neoliberal world order has seen the development of 'fundamental principles of economic constitutionalism'. These 'aimed at providing worldwide operating corporations with unlimited latitude for action'. He indicates illustrations of this:

> the International Monetary Fund and the World Bank have developed regime constitutions whose guiding principle is to open national capital markets. The constitutions of the World Trade Organization (WTO), the European Union (EU), the North American Free Trade Agreement (NAFTA), the Mercado Común del Cono Sur (MERCOSUR), and the Asia Pacific Economic Cooperation (APEC) all aim toward the constitutional protection of the freedom of world trade and the promotion of direct investments. (Teubner 2011: 21–2)

Teubner argues that over and above ensuring due respect for the rules of contractual law, the *lex mercatoria* has developed a stratum of constitutional norms that centrally concern the corporate governance of multinational corporations. The constitutive function of this 'neoliberal constitutionalization' is to provide transnational corporations with a high degree of autonomy: 'It is fixated on the problem that the worldwide extension of corporate activities is hampered by the segmentary differentiation of the world into nation-states' (Teubner 2011: 22).

It becomes apparent that something like a global constitution is already in the process of formation, and this has two core immanent goals: 'free TNCs from nation-state regulation and establish the rule of law globally to provide legal security for their transactions' (Teubner 2011: 22). What is being constitutionalized, then, is a set of norms that work so as to positively incentivize the kinds of activity that seem most problematic and unconducive to dealing with the global challenges we face today.

A crucial problem at the current time is that private investors are running amok in the global economy. They are treating real productive enterprises as sources of financial value for extraction. This only serves to cast the financial sector further adrift from concerns of qualitative productivity, from interests of labour, from social value, and from ecological protection. The problem involves a lack of appropriate political authority in determining normative priorities. Very basic elements of a 'social contract' are absent from this informal global 'constitution'.

The problem has been analysed by Turkuler Isiksel (2016). She highlights the need to counter the ongoing de facto global constitutionalizing of private corporations' investors' rights, and, in particular, their tendency to colonize human rights regimes. She argues that, just as corporations were able to win recognition as legal persons in American and other courts a century ago, so today a similar process is allowing corporations to be treated as right-bearing agents on an international scale and even to avail themselves of provisions designed to secure *human* rights. She highlights how there are 'contemporary developments by which international economic agreements and dispute settlement mechanisms equip private economic actors with the legal means to constrain the regulatory capacity of states and challenge national obstacles to market access by asserting their status as bearers of rights under international law' (Isiksel 2016: 301).

This usurpation of the normative force of human rights to corporate ends could scarcely be further removed from reflecting the interests of those vulnerable human beings the rights ought to protect. It is something that clearly needs to be understood and addressed.

What would be the rationale and justification for extending to corporations the constitutional protection intended for natural persons? Part of the original rationale was to give corporations 'the status of private economic actors as legitimate (and valued) subjects of the polity in their own right' (Isiksel 2016: 303). This was justified by reference to the greater social goal of expanding commerce and generating more wealth for society as a whole.[5] Looking at the comparable process in the global context today we can see that the unquestioned objective of 'Economic Growth' is the corresponding 'great object'. Yet it is not even clear that this is being achieved, let alone that social and ecological goods are being protected.

At the time of writing there are more than three thousand international investment agreements in effect around the world, and many of these enable private corporations to sue signatory states in order to protect or reclaim assets invested in those states' territories. These disputes are heard in legal venues above the jurisdictional authority of states, mostly under the auspices of the International Center for the Settlement of Investment Disputes (ICSID).[6] This has meant that not only are corporations strongly empowered to defend their interests against any perceived unfavorable treatment by host states but also that the scope of states' obligations to corporations has, in the process of clarifying, refining, and interpreting them, expanded. This process has its own momentum:

[5] 'Although states were entitled to regulate their respective economic spaces, the Court reasoned that gratuitous interference with the activities of foreign corporations would stymie the "great object" of commercial expansion' (Isiksel 2016: 304).

[6] For a useful recent overview of developments and controversies relating to such investment agreements as the Trans-Pacific Partnership (TPP) and the Transatlantic Trade and Investment Partnership (TTIP) see Sornarajah (2017).

> The progressive elaboration of investment law creates more opportunities for private actors to bring claims against sovereign states, gradually establishing a feedback loop that promotes further development of the regime, often in directions not envisaged by the signatories. Litigation by private parties thereby helps to 'legalize,' entrench, and extend international norms to a greater extent than when this procedure is reserved to states. Furthermore, private litigation can prompt more rigid application of international law than states intend.
>
> (Isiksel 2016: 307)

Again we see that rigidity of private legal arrangements exacerbates their deleterious effects on public goods. As the 'investment' dimension of 'trade and investment' agreements comes to involve ever more egregious shifts of power from democratically legitimate state authorities to private corporate actors, private rights are effectively able to trump human rights. This happens, if only by default, because 'while international human rights treaties provide sparse procedural remedies and enforcement mechanisms and tend to lack direct effect within domestic systems, the rights of investors can be invoked against states before international arbitral tribunals' (Isiksel 2016: 308). Thanks to investor–state arbitration, 'investors' rights to legitimate expectations in their property may be the most effectively protected 'human' right that there is, at least at the global level' (Isiksel 2016: 309). 'Thus, the expansion of the rights of corporations under international law is likely to weaken the ability of sovereign states to protect the public interest at the domestic level, without a federal authority to compensate for the pernicious regulatory race to the bottom among states' (Isiksel 2016: 310).

It appears, therefore, that we are witnessing the ongoing de facto global constitutionalizing of private corporations' investors' rights. To counter this, there need to be clear and robust legal norms to constrain and reverse the increasing encroachment of private interests.

10.2 The Privatized Constitution: Central Banks and the Bank for International Settlements

The problem identified in Section 10.1 is the development of a privatized global constitution, which is implicated in the finance-driven problems discussed in this book. The overarching concern here, accordingly, is about bringing the informal private financial constitution under public accountability and control. This section highlights two crucial 'nodes' in the current arrangements: the central banks of individual countries and the Bank for International Settlements (BIS) which stands at the global apex of the financial system as, so to speak, the central banks' central bank.

Thinking about constitutional principles of governance for global money and finance inescapably brings us to thinking about the role of countries' central banks in the financial order. There is a functional necessity for these institutions under the existing system of global finance, and any reform or radical transformation of that system has to involve considering how that need itself might be transformed or else how it might be fulfilled in different ways. Central banks are institutions that dispose of decisive powers in the financial system, and yet whether those powers are exercised decisively in the public interest depends on whether their control is so constituted as to ensure that it is. Critical attention therefore needs to be directed to questions about what role they play in the financial system, about who controls them, to what purpose, and to whose benefit. For the crucial concern is with how they could be made more accountable to the public.

The role of central banks today, viewed from a constitutional perspective, is, in fact, a matter of some uncertainty. There is a quite general and inherent kind of tension, between the banking and political systems, that is in interesting ways akin to that between the political and judicial systems. A central bank, like a supreme court, exists in principle to do the will of the political state, but in order to discharge its functions it has to operate independently of the direct political will of government. Paul Poast (2014)indicates the kind of reason why central banks should play a superordinate role in relation to government:

> By being the sole direct purchaser of government debt, the central bank increases the effective punishment that can be imposed on the government for defaulting on the marginal lender. This increases lenders' confidence that the government will be punished in case of default, making lenders willing to purchase the debt at a lower rate of interest. The sovereign, dependent on the low borrowing costs offered by the central bank, has an incentive to retain the bank. (Poast 2014: 63)

The general point is that if the bank could not discipline government, it could not do the job that government needs it to do. In this respect, underexplored parallels with the role of a supreme court are evident.

If the question of principle can be stated quite succinctly in terms of a general immanent tension between finance and politics, the particular form of its practical appearance will always have complex historial specificity. Among developed economies, the period prior to the financial crisis of 2007–08 has sometimes been referred to as the 'great moderation'. Bowman et al. (2013) describe how, in the 1990s, central bank independence became the ideal, the IMF having promoted the model since the 1980s as part of structural adjustment programmes in the developing world. In support and justification of that model, the central bank role was seen as 'technocratic'. Thus by the 1990s, the typical central banker was a professionally qualified economist, and in this period central banking became increasingly scientized and autonomous in relation to democratic political actors. Since the crisis, however, the world has changed in ways that shake confidence in the old assumptions of political economy and how these bear on our understanding of the role of central banks. Their central task had previously been conceived of as controlling inflation, primarily by means of interest rate controls; after the crisis, 'the instrument of interest rate changes was redundant because interest rates were everywhere cut toward zero without either restoring the financial system or generating an economic upturn' (Bowman et al. 2013: 464). With interest rates at a historic low, new and 'unconventional' forms of central bank intervention had to be tried. Central bank balance-sheet policies—'quantitative easing', or, in lay terms 'printing more money'—thereby came to be seen as '*the only practically available tool of intervention*' (Bowman et al. 2013: 465). Thus central bankers had 'acquired a new (and never explicit) superordinate policy objective of keeping the banks and markets going and avoiding collapse of business lending and the disruption of everyday life that would ensue from bank failure' even though this involved 'experimentation with unconventional monetary policies' (Bowman et al. 2013: 465). This, according to Bowman et al., has generated a situation 'of *fundamental uncertainty*, in which central bank actions have diminished impact, with less experience to draw upon, less ability to predict impacts, less intellectual credibility, and less political legitimacy' (Bowman et al 2013: 467).

What has nevertheless also become more apparent, amidst that uncertainty, is how central banking is inherently political, in the sense of being concerned with mediating conflict over resources. Indeed, 'central banks have historically been *distributive* in the sense that their policies have differential social effects, *political* in the sense that they have used their platform to promote particular interests and ideologies, and *allocative* in that their policies can affect access to credit among different types of industries' (Bowman et al. 2013: 481). The limits of their supposed political neutrality become more evident as the allocative and distributive impacts of their actions become more explicit. In the governance of money, inflation is not the only problem to address, and measures taken to fight inflation can, from other points of view, have worse effects than the problem itself. The financial elite recognized this general point, in their response to the financial crisis, by switching their monetary policy from control of interest rates towards quantitative easing. We should note, though, that they thereby made a choice of a particular distributive outcome for society.[7] Bowman et al. accordingly argue that discussion of central bank policy should be related to broader and more radical

[7] Mario Seccareccia makes an interesting observation in this connection, by reference to some words of Lord Rothschild: 'There's an old saying that in difficult times the return *of* capital takes precedence over the return *on* capital' (Rothschild (2015: 3). Seccareccia suggests that this captures the rationale for the difference in monetary policy before and after the global financial crisis. There was an abrupt shift, from 'sustaining high return on financial capital to largely preserving the value of financial capital', which was thus a shift from 'supporting rentier income to, first and foremost, protecting rentier wealth, regardless of its impact on the former' (Seccareccia 2017: 342).

social debates about debt. They emphasize the need to understand the connections between the 'expensive system of bank welfare', which serves the private interest of bankers, and the cutbacks on social welfare that are exacted from increasingly debt-burdened countries. For while the ordinary people in such countries have had to endure the consequences of 'austerity' measures, and the flow of credit into the nonfinancial economy has scarcely improved, the new monetary policy has nevertheless meant business as usual with continued high earnings for investment bankers. The nonstandard central bank policies have thus had regressive distributive effects. This can be taken as evidence that no matter how 'technocratic' the business of central banking might be, the goals and constraints defining its purpose should be brought under democratic political control. Thus Bowman et al. argue that finance should be placed more decisively at the service of what they call the *foundational economy* (and see also Bentham et al. 2013). This, in broad strokes, captures the valuable social goal that has been ascribed to finance as a normative benchmark for critical discussion throughout this book. Yet the current system of central banking is a long way from fulfilling this function.

The tendencies we have identified of the financial system to be working contrary to its normative mission are facilitated by the system of central banks. They have therefore to be seen as part of the problem. Bringing them under public control therefore seems at least a prudent objective and perhaps an indispensible one. That could prove to be a very hard task, however, given the sheer extent of their power and the fact that central banks in the globalized system are not simply organs or servants of the state whose name they bear. It is not obvious how might it be achieved, or by whom. Central banks are not entirely controlled by their respective states, and, as part of a wider international system, they are significantly independent of state control altogether. The supra-national integration of a global elite into a global system is, to a great extent, politically uncontrolled and unaccountable.

Particularly to consider in this connection is the role of the relatively little discussed Bank for International Settlements (BIS). This organization at the apex of the global financial system is privately controlled and even somewhat secretive in its operation, yet in practice it has powers of an order that could meaningfully be described as features of a privatized global constitution. We noted in Chapter 3 that, as the economy globalized, the distinct central banks became increasingly integrated, and a role of the BIS is to serve, in effect, as the clearers' clearer. It is wholly owned and controlled by them acting in concert. If the central banks themselves are in certain important respects constitutionally anomalous, the BIS is truly exceptional. Its ways and aims transcend those of any political state. For if the central bankers have amongst themselves a kind of private compact, whereby the various instruments they issue are mutually honoured, that mutual understanding is itself underpinned and underwritten by their own central clearing facility. This global hierarchy of financial institutions has come to stand aside from, and, in many material ways, above, the law and politics of even the most powerful states. A fundamental question, therefore, is how well and in what ways, if it does at all, this organization serves the public interest. It certainly appears not to be *accountable* to the public in any way, as it is not evidently subject to any national or even international law.[8]

At the time of BIS's creation, John Fischer Williams (1930) offered some interesting reflections on its status in relation to legal and political institutions. He began with a contextual observation that 'the exclusive possession of the field of international law by States . . . is being broken down by the invasion of bodies which are neither States, nor individuals, nor combinations of States or individuals, but right-and-duty-bearing international creations, to which for want of a better name the title of "international body corporate," "personne juridique internationale" may perhaps be accorded' (Williams 1930). Yet alongside examples of international cooperation, including the League of Nations, that have evident political purposes, the proposal for the BIS set it apart. An essential feature that distinguished this institution from all others, and also made it *sui generis* among banks, Williams noted, was that it was to have 'no single fiscal allegiance'. This would imply, he pointed out, that it was not to be subject to the revenue laws of any country. It would thus be a financial institution that was not subject to any municipal financial legislation and thus 'would surely come near to possessing something not wholly remote from international independence (the word "sovereignty" would, of course, be out of place)' (Williams 1930: 667).

BIS is indeed an extraterritorial entity and appears to be subject to no international laws, even though established by international treaties. It has a sort of diplomatic status despite being a private profit-making entity. It is the world's only commercial bank protected by international treaty. It cannot be sued.

During the 1930s, the BIS was the central meeting place for central bankers, and during World War II, the BIS accepted looted Nazi gold and foreign exchange deals for Nazi Germany. In June 1939, the BIS 'handed over the Czech gold deposits to the German Reich, as protector of the Republic which it had occupied in defiance of international law' (Glazer 1957: 1105–6n92). Governments in Washington and London were aware of this, and yet it was not something they had constitutional or legal means to prevent. Nor did the British Government intervene when the gold was then deposited with the Bank of England. The arrangements of mutual obligation amongst the bankers evidently took precedence over any national loyalties, as well as being untrammelled by any constraints of international public law.

[8] 'The Bank for International Settlement was established under the law of Switzerland. It also has legal capacity pursuant to the municipal law of each of its member states, but it lacks international legal capacity. It was denied a specific international personality. The bank is, therefore, solely in the control of its members' West's Encyclopedia of American Law, edition 2. S.v. 'Bank for International Settlements'. https://legal-dictionary.thefreedictionary.com/Bank±for+International±Settlements Accessed 14 February 2018.

This noteworthy spirit of cooperation at the apex of the world's banking elite has proven resilient over time. BIS has so far survived 'the first global depression, the end of reparations payments and the gold standard (two of its main reasons for existence), the rise of Nazism, the Second World War, the Bretton Woods Accord, the Cold War, the financial crises of the 1980s and 1990s, the birth of the IMF and World Bank, and the end of Communism' (LeBor 2013: xxii).

There are clearly questions of constitutional interest concerning this unique and extraordinarily important institution. One kind of question is how satisfactory it is, from the perspective of public interest relating to global justice, for the handful of individuals with ultimate control over the world's financial system to be unaccountable to anyone other than each other. A related concern is whether the strong commitment of BIS to promoting the independence of its constituent central banks from any national political control is in the public interest of each polity and globally. These questions, I believe, are worthy of the attention of political philosophers of global justice.

10.3 Conclusion

The chapter started with the aim of clarifying parameters for constructive thought about the nature of a global constitution oriented to serving the public interest. In ideal terms, such a constitutional order would ensure institutional support for basic normative principles requiring all humans to be treated equally and decently, with all due freedoms as well as access to opportunities and goods on a just basis. In more political terms, there would be scope for debate about the organization and design of institutions. This would include consideration of appropriate ways to integrate broad unity of purpose with reasonable autonomy of action across various levels and locations of governance. Such consideration would include reflection on principles for distributing elements of political authority that in modern times have been aggregated together as the sovereignty of the several states in the world.

However, although such matters are quite appropriate for debate by political philosophers, a critical question is how much *purchase* such debate may have on the circumstances of reality today. For what the considerations of this chapter tend to suggest is that with the development of the privatized global constitution, and in view of the crucial role in it of the financial sector, the situation faced is significantly different from what would be needed as a basis for building progressive programmes of determinate institutional change. Certainly, any discussion of different ways of distributing powers in a more cosmopolitan global order would appear somewhat premature. For the people and peoples of the world would need to be in a position to influence the creation and development of such programmes. Yet at present they are not. In fact, the developments sketched above tend to suggest that such a prospect may even diminish if the current trajectory of development in the global order continues.

The matters discussed in this chapter have led to the raising of an unexpected question. It is prompted by an observation made, in closing, in Section 10.2. If bankers can get along with each other so well, and rise above the tensions between nations, even in time of war, why cannot everyone else? Why, in other words, do there even need to be wars at all? Lest this question seem something of a *non sequitur*, as well as hopelessly simple-minded, I think it is well to consider—especially given the devastating human harm wars inflict so needlessly on so many people—certain reasons why some people take the view that *all wars are bankers' wars.* Certainly, the response cannot simply be that warmaking is a matter for the politicians of nations, rather than for financial 'technocrats' who can be attributed no responsibility for the formers' decisions. For given that the powers to control finance can set the most fundamental constraints on the world's economic activity, then if any wars at all are driven by intense struggles over geopolitical control of economic resources, then the exercise of those powers can contribute very substantially to the incentivization of war.

The critical question here is whether war can be seen as an incidental kind of failure of a more rational system of globalizing political economy or whether the view of Hardt and Negri is nearer to the truth. They argue that the contemporary global order has to be understood in terms of an organization of power that is imperial, in which perpetual war functions as an instrument of rule. In their view, the possibility of people and peoples—or as they say 'the multitude'—achieving a world democracy 'is obscured and threatened by the seemingly permanent state of conflict across the world' (Hardt and Negri 2004: xi).

The question is thus by no means a *non sequitur* for an inquiry seeking to understand the necessary preconditions for seeking to achieve greater justice in the world. For one thing, there has to be something worth learning from the demonstrable ability of a worldwide institution to rise so far above the affairs of ordinary people that it can even be impervious to the effects of world wars. The banking system stands as an indication of a strength and resilience that could be a remarkable asset to humankind if it were put in the service of transcending conflict and injustice. And yet, that strength and resilience under the actual arrangements appears to support the opposite. Certainly, if there is indeed a connection between the imperatives of this system and the phenomenon of perpetual war, then this would be a particularly extreme form of a general tendency, as already noted in other contexts, of the privatization of benefits—in this case peaceful coexistence—being accompanied by the socialization of costs. The costs here would be counted in the death, destruction, mutilation, rape, torture, displacement, trafficking, maiming, bereavement, anguish, and ruined lives and livelihoods of millions of people.

11
Finance, War, and 'Humanitarian Intervention'

A premise of this book is that the world faces serious problems. The problems emphasized have been those of social injustice, economic counter-productivity, and ecological damage. Another fundamental and all-encompassing problem, however, is the one we shall close by considering: *War*. Nothing is socially more unjust, economically more counter-productive, or ecologically more damaging than modern warfare. Humanity has developed the capacity to annihilate our own and many other species, irreparably damage the biosphere, and destroy all modern industry with the weapons of mass destruction that exist today. Already, warfare by more 'conventional' means wreaks untold death and destruction around the world. If a global constitution is to have any purpose at all, it has to underpin *peaceful* relations around the world.

The *privatized* global constitution has taken shape in a period of intense and protracted warfare in many places around the world. As we have noted, the international banking system demonstrated remarkable resilience throughout World War II and has continued to do so during the many further conflicts in the time since. The fact that the banking system is *compatible* with intense and persistent warfare can be regarded, I think, as demonstrated. A further observation, though, is that the privatized financial constitution has not only *survived* but seems possibly even to have *flourished* in these circumstances. This is something we should be concerned about because it could suggest a lack of incentive on the part of the financial elite to support measures to prevent or contain wars. Once we acknowledge that concern, we are brought to posit a hypothesis that is more disturbing still: *it could be that those who have assumed responsibility for the global banking system are themselves under incentives that include an active interest in the perpetuation of warfare*. Reasons for taking this hypothesis to be one meriting further research are provided in Section 11.1. The question considered in Section 11.2 is whether the work of some political philosophers has not also shown a tendency to be too ready to acquiesce in allowing justification to wars, particularly when these have a purportedly humanitarian purpose. This leads, in Section 11.3, to consideration of the need to be particularly scrupulous, when making recommendations in applied ethics, about the epistemic warrant for the assumptions made about the facts at the locus of prospective intervention.

The argument of the chapter has critical purchase in relation to any suggestion that a just global world order might be achieved or even conceived as the universalization of a scheme of values that supports military intervention as a means to reaching it. The chapter closes by reflecting on some interesting similarities and connections between ideas of using military means to just ends and ideas about money in the global financial system being serviceable to such ends.

11.1 The Synergies of Finance and War

Finance and war are interrelated in three quite general respects: finance needs to be raised in order to fund war; war can be used for the pillage that replenishes collateral to support finance; war can serve as an outlet for the capital on which finance can draw profits, in particular through arms manufacture and its associated businesses. Those functions can be mutually reinforcing. Fighting may have predated finance in the history of human development, but organized warfare has required the organization of finance to sustain it, while prospects of financial rewards can motivate it. So an interest in amassing wealth is not simply a consequence of bellicose needs but can also be a driver of them. In our time, a global capitalist economy stands ever in need of investment opportunities, and if these cannot be found in productive enterprise, they can be found in destructive enterprise. This has several advantages from a business point of view: the turnover of products is inherently quick when they are used for destructive purposes, and when countries perceive themselves to be facing existential threats they do not spare the expense of placing large and regular orders for more armaments. The profits are therefore potentially immense, and that is before counting any potential shares in the spoils of war or returns on reconstruction work in the aftermath. But the sustainability of such a business model depends on the constant perpetuation of war.

As well as the general and familiar connections between finance and warfare it is worth asking about the possibility of some quite specific connections between the way the global financial architecture is governed and the particular wars of the present epoch. Financial interests, as we have already noted, do not necessarily align with those of states: the Germans, British, and Americans, for instance, maintained banking cooperation even throughout World War II. On the other hand, it is states that are not well integrated into the dominant system of global financial governance under the Bank for International Settlements (BIS) that seem particularly liable to find themselves embroiled in wars that are not of their choosing. This correlation applies to a number of states upon which war has been visited in recent years, including Afghanistan, Iraq, Libya, Syria, and Yemen; the correlation also holds for other countries that have been subject to economic sanctions by the United States, such as Iran, Venezuela, North Korea, and

Cuba. A further distinguishing feature of those named countries is resistance to accepting the continuance of the dollar as the world's reserve currency.

Correlation is not causation, of course, but if we are thinking about the potential threats that a global constitutional order in the public interest would need to guard against, it is as well to be alert to conflicts of interest between those seeking to integrate the states of the world more completely into a global financial system geared to supporting private profit taking and those states that might be holding out for greater international economic equity or more sovereign power to secure domestic public goods. It is certainly worth seeking to understand whether arrangements under the BIS have any inherently problematic features from the point of view of the public interest. Accordingly, if it should transpire that plausible hypotheses could account for how financial interests may play a contributing motivational or incentivizing role in causing wars where wars might not otherwise be, that would be just the kind of scenario that prudent constitutional design would be concerned to provide checks and balances to preclude.

To illustrate reasons for at least treating such hypotheses seriously, let us briefly consider some cases. Regarding, first, the 2003 war on Iraq, it is now well understood that this was not genuinely motivated by concerns about weapons of mass destruction or terrorism (Robinson 2017). While many critics have argued that corporate oil interests in the territory were prominent among the motives, some have added the suggestion that it could also have been an oil *currency* war (e.g. Clark 2005; Shipley 2007).[1] In the year 2000, Saddam Hussein had switched Iraq's oil sales from the dollar to the euro under the UN Food for Oil programme. Although the oil sales permitted under that programme were relatively small, the imminent lifting of UN sanctions would mean that all sales one of the world's largest reserves could then move from the dollar to the euro. This would have consequences for confidence in the dollar, and threaten the status it has in virtue of critical commodities, and especially oil, being denominated in dollars: everyone is willing to trade in dollars because they can buy oil (Liu 2002a). The dollar's hegemonic status plays an important part in sustaining the deficits, the consumption and the growth of the US political economy. The 'structural privilege' of the dollar's status has allowed the United States to 'build up debt for a protracted period on a scale that would wreck any other country's currency' (Hensman and Correggia 2005: 1091). The downside, however, was that as fiscal and trade deficits were allowed to climb, the productive economy was allowed to decline unnoticed: 'Only its pre-eminence in the global financial services industry remains intact. And this is underpinned by US dollar hegemony' (Hensman and Correggia 2005: 1091).

[1] Although available evidence is only circumstantial, some scholars find the suggestion credible (Hopkins 2007: 111n54; Patomäki 2008: 169), and the fact is that President Bush's Executive order 13303 of 22 May 2003 made 'certain that the future sale of Iraqi oil will be in dollars, the international currency for oil transactions, once the UN lifts the anti-Saddam sanctions' (Scott 2007: 364n52).

If the dollar were to lose its world reserve status, then, the consequences could be very significant. The multiple business advantages of maintaining high military spending thus include the direct curtailing of attempts by resistant nations to undermine the status of the dollar.

The point here is not to privilege one factor amongst a number that could contribute to explaining the decision to invade Iraq. It is rather to highlight the relevance of seeking to understand the extent to which the businesses benefiting from such actions—notably the oil and arms industries, but not only them—are linked at a fundamental level by their integration into a global market economy that is secured by financial arrangements.[2] So while different economic sectors may sometimes have competing interests in a given situation, they are aligned in this fundamental dependence on a certain kind of monetary discipline.

Not only with Iraq, but with Libya too, there are concerns that control of the monetary system may have been among the factors motivating the war (Brown 2011; Campbell 2013). This would certainly help account for a remarkable event. It so transpired that, in early 2011, when the opposition forces in Libya appeared to be in a state of some desperation and disarray (McGreal 2011), there came the incongruous report that rebels in Benghazi had established a new central bank. Commentators at the time noted that it was historically unprecedented for a revolutionary group, in the midst of fighting the entrenched political power, to take time out from an ongoing life-and-death battle to create such an institution (Carney 2011; Newman 2011). The rebels also announced that they had created a new national oil company to replace the corporation controlled by leader Muammar Qaddafi whose assets were frozen by the United Nations Security Council. To informed observers it was thus 'abundantly clear that Libya's rebels are not some unknown quantity, nor lacking independence from the coalition forces' (Cotterill 2011). It is noteworthy that the rebels' two institutional initiatives—creating the oil company and the central bank—exactly matched the conditions laid down in precedence by the United States for unfreezing Libyan assets (Cotterill 2011). The rebels had thus done what was needed to take a significant degree of control over the country's oil and money supplies (Davidson 2017).

The case of Libya thus not only suggests some international coordination and planning, but also provides an indication of what passes for legitimacy in this world of interventionism.[3] The rebels had literally broken into the Benghazi bank

[2] According to Horace Campbell, there was 'fierce competition between French and other Western forces for control over the future of Libyan oil', with 'varying Western powers compet[ing] for political influence, strategic positions, and profits' (Campbell 2013: 82). However, it was not only about oil: 'for Britain military intervention is mainly about arms; Italy, natural gas; France, water; and for the U.S. counter-terrorism and reconstruction contracts' (Campbell 2013: 81; see also the analysis in Davidson 2017).

[3] For critical discussion of the background manoeuvres, involving especially Qatar along with France, the UK, and the United States, see McKinney (2012), Boyle (2013), Campbell (2013), and Davidson (2017).

in March 2011,[4] and, when interviewed about it, their US-educated oil and finance minister, Ali Tarhouni, said that 'the bank heist serves as an illustration of the rebels' ingenuity, wherewithal and organizational skills. It's proof, he said, that they are ready to run the nation' (Raghavan and Grimaldi 2011). It appears, then, that, with the support of the United States, favoured rebel leaders can treat entire nations as if existing in a state of nature. The justification offered in the case of Libya, as in others, was supposedly 'humanitarian', and directed against a 'brutal dictator';[5] yet it is hard to accept that a genuine humanitarian motivation is manifest in bombing entire countries to destruction, or in supporting the overthrow of existing state institutions without having any clear plan for establishing either a better constitutional order or potential political leadership.[6] And that criticism does not even touch on basic questions about the criteria for legitimate external intervention at all in a sovereign state's affairs or the seizure of its assets.

We have noted the congruence of incentives regarding dollar hegemony and control of oil markets, but the case of Libya alerts us to a further possible dimension of financial interests in war. The rebels may have established the central bank in order to get control of Libya's oil and wealth, but how might that be of benefit to the global financial elite? Some observers believe that while establishing the central bank served the particular interests of the rebels, it also served a purpose for their backers. Horace Campbell, for instance, finds it significant that the Central Bank of Libya had taken the controlling position

[4] 'The rebel movement brought in a professional safe cracker from the United Arab Emirates who successfully opened the cash vault safe. The rebels had their hands on 900 million in Libyan dinars and $ 500.5 million in U.S. dollars' (Madsen 2012: 35).

[5] Even before the uprising, and guided by the CIA via 'soft' intervention organs such as the National Endowment for Democracy (Snow 2012: 228), the media were central to the preparation of the public for the planned operation. 'The "reliable" information outlets, such as the BBC, CNN, Voice of America, Radio France International, and Al Jazeera, carried the line that Gaddafi was a "threat to his own people" as well as to the peace and security of Western interests' (Campbell 2013: 143). Mahdi Nazemroaya notes that a main source of allegations against Gaddafi was the Libyan League for Human Rights (LLHR), an organization 'tied to the International Federation for Human Rights (FIDH), which is based in France and has ties to the National Endowment for Democracy (NED)' (Nazemroaya 2012: 131). 'Not once did the UN Security Council and the member states pushing for war bother to even investigate the allegations' (Nazemroaya 2012: 132).

[6] For all his flaws, and notwithstanding the genuine scope for domestic political reforms, it is hard to sustain the case for removing Gaddafi on humanitarian grounds, in good faith, in light of what is known publicly now and was known at the time by those with the power of decision-making (for a succinct summary of the 'myths' that were invoked to justify the intervention see Forte 2011.) Not only was the quality of life for many ordinary people in Libya very good in some important respects, but with the most effective potential opposition being Islamist, for many Libyans Gadaffi's leadership was 'the least worst alternative when faced with the prospect of a rebel-led government' (Davidson 2017: 103). This was especially the case for the black third of the population, for evidence suggests 'that the targeting of black Libyans as well as black immigrants was as critical to the insurrectionists and mutineers as was the goal of killing Muammar Qaddafi in breaking the will of the Libyan people to fight' (T-West 2012: 67). Davidson suggests that 'the "real genocides" of the Libyan uprising were, in fact, the bloody and largely ignored reprisals and revenge attacks perpetrated by rebels against populations of black Libyans and African expatriates accused of fighting for the regime' (Davidson 2017: 102).

in the Arab Banking Corporation based in Bahrain: 'Any move for making independent decisions in the Arab Banking Corporation threatened the web of speculators in the derivatives industry that depended on the recycling of petro-dollars from the oil-rich nations of Kuwait, Libya, and the Emirates. Libya had gone for the jugular, by seeking to capture the base of the Intercontinental Exchange' (Campbell 2013: 113). Thus Campbell also finds that 'writers and analysts from Wall Street with links to the think tanks that Wall Street financed were front and center in the call for war' (Campbell 2013: 115). Although not mentioned much by western politicians or media, it can thus appear significant that the Central Bank of Libya was 100 per cent state owned. The same is true of the other countries designated by President George W. Bush as the *Axis of Evil*. Among the commonalities of these countries was an independent central bank, a stance of resistance in the face of what they regarded as US imperialism, and an active interest in finding ways of avoiding being bound under dollar hegemony and the globalized financial order.[7]

Iran, for instance, has been actively exploring alternatives to the dollar since at least 2002 and has taken various significant steps to that end, including establishing its own oil bourse that trades in non-dollar currencies (Shipley 2007: 23). Meanwhile, it has remained committed to the principle that the Central Bank of Iran should not fall under private control. The United States has responded with further economic sanctions, and commentators have suggested that their unstated aims specifically include 'shutting down Iran's central bank' (Agence France Presse 2012). At the time of writing, Iran has not become the subject of a war, but it does not seem to be a possibility that can confidently be ruled out.

Then there is Syria. The country's Central Bank is state-owned and state-controlled with a mission to serve the national economy and the Syrian people. It is not beholden to the international banking class nor therefore subject to the loan conditions that have been imposed on other nations.[8] Certainly striking is the fact that, despite (at time of writing) more than seven years of warfare and economic sanctions, the country's administration and army retain the practical

[7] A 2012 report from the World Bank shows geostrategic targets of Libya, Iraq, Iran, Syria, and Yemen to be among the countries that are least integrated into IMF/World Bank debt structures. In fact, the MENA region stands out as registering an actual decrease in debt. 'The Middle East and North Africa was the only developing region where net inflows declined in 2010 with increased bond issuance not enough to offset a halving of net debt inflows from official creditors…' (World Bank 2012, 3–4). For a discussion of the report see Robicheau (2014).

[8] Robicheau notes that 'two years before the 2011 outbreak of internal conflict, it was admitted by the IMF that Syria's lack of integration into the global economy meant that levels of debt affecting other countries of the world would not affect Syria's "infant banks," with Syria's growth rate predicted in 2009 to be 6.5%' (Robicheau 2014: 203). Not being linked to large, international, consortium banking systems, he adds, meant that 'like other countries in the region, Syria maintained subsidization policies, which provided low cost food items and transportation petrol, along with subsidized fuel for heating and cooking, and free or low cost university education, health care, and public transportation' (Robicheau 2014: 202).

cooperation of the wider population; and although the country's finances and infrastructure are under massive strain, full provision of public services is as far as possible maintained, including salaries in opposition-held areas (al-Hourani and Clark 2016; Enab Baladi 2017). To be noted, moreover, is that no part of the domestic political opposition—secular or sectarian—has been arguing for a more capitalist or globalist constitution; nor have they been ideologically committed to integrating Syria into the privatized constitutional arrangements of the foreign powers that have been pressing their regime change agenda (Gowans 2017).

It is not only in the Middle East and North Africa that we find countries that are resistant to global finance and are also in the crosshairs of bellicose intentions. North Korea, for instance, in shifting towards the euro for the pricing of its oil may not have the same material impact as Iraq and Iran, but it does have symbolic significance. Venezuela, with its vast oil reserves, presents both a symbolic and material challenge with its moves to detach its trade in oil from the dollar (Shipley 2007). With several nations starting to look at euros to replace the dollar, and Russia and China looking at alternatives too, the threat to the dollar's status is evidently becoming increasingly serious. It is not only independence of the dollar but resistance to the forces of globalized finance more generally that appears to be in play here.[9] Looking ahead, change coming to the geopolitical order is likely to be just a matter of time, with a greater role for China to be realistically anticipated in a world economy that is more multipolar.[10]

Without being drawn into speculation about possible geopolitical futures, I do think it is as well for political philosophers to reflect on the historical specificity of the period in which the current framings of questions about justice have been formed. In particular, I think we should be aware that the post-World War II period, in which Rawlsian assumptions had some purchase on the social, economic, and political realities of liberal democracies in the West, had a quite different character from what can be expected in future. We should perhaps also reflect critically on what has been assumed about the period too. In particular, although liberal political theorists and international relations scholars have tended to think of the period as a peaceful one, it is as well to be aware of the limits of this perspective. The 'liberal peace' thesis that has been much discussed in international relations theory applies as between countries that have embraced liberal, even

[9] It may be surmised that the BIS, while having no nationalist allegiance to the United States—and having Russian and Chinese central banks among its members—can still have an interest in there being effective political guarantees for the financial system it controls, and a hegemon can provide this. An orderly shift of hegemonic currency need not be a problem, but resistance and disruption would be unwelcome.

[10] There is considerable uncertainty as to what kind of global order will succeed the current unipolar period. For instance, despite 'dissatisfaction in China with the nature of the current global order, it is hard to find a clear and coherent Chinese vision of what an alternative world might look like' (Breslin 2013: 615); China certainly 'does not yet have a fixed blueprint for a new world order' (Schweller and Pu 2011: 41). Furthermore, Breslin notes, 'the existing order has in fact served China quite well in its transition towards becoming a global power' (Breslin 2013: 615).

neoliberal, institutions, and are called 'liberal states' (Doyle 2005). From the perspective of concern about global justice, one also needs to think about how peacefully other peoples on the planet have lived, and, indeed, how peaceable the liberal states have been in their dealings with them. For while the countries that have fully embraced the global banking regime have indeed, by and large, been allowed to live at peace, the list of countries that have been on the receiving end of military attentions since World War II consists of others that have not. The following—while possibly not exhaustive—is a list of countries where 'liberal states' have intervened militarily and which also do not have a central bank that is a member of the BIS system: Korea, Guatemala, Cuba, Congo, Dominican Republic, Laos, Vietnam, Cambodia, Lebanon, Grenada, Libya, El Salvador, Nicaragua, Iran, Panama, Iraq, Kuwait, Somalia, Sudan, Afghanistan, Syria, and Yemen.[11] A longer list would additionally include those non-member countries in which the United States actively supported regime change by more indirect or covert means. Certainly, to speak of this recent period of history as *the post-war period*, as we in the West have tended to, is to take a quite specific stance as to what counts as war. An event significant enough to count, it seems, is what we call a 'world war', one in which liberal states with banking cooperation get directly involved on opposing sides.

Resistance on the part of independent nations to the privatization or denationalization of their central banks evidently appears to have some possible correlation with being vulnerable to sanctions, intervention, coup, or invasion. This observation is consistent with there being a conflict between the interests of peoples, which it is the duty of a decent state to serve, including through its domestic banking arrangements, and of the elite at the apex of global finance. While national banks can in principle aim to support the valuable social purposes associated with finance, in line with the policy goals and practical objectives of society, the global financial system under the BIS constrains national banking systems 'to serve the needs of highly sophisticated global financial markets, regardless of the developmental needs of their national economies' (Liu 2002b). According to Henry Liu, the globalized private banking system 'puts institutional creditworthiness and profitability as prerequisites, serving the needs of the global financial system to preserve the security and value of global private capital. National policies suddenly are subjected to profit incentives of private financial institutions' (Liu 2002b). As Liu puts it, the 'BIS does to national banking systems what the IMF has done to national monetary regimes'. In fact, he observes:

> The IMF and the international banks regulated by the BIS are a team: the international banks lend recklessly to borrowers in emerging economies to create

[11] Also to note are some countries which have been bombed and whose central banks subsequently became BIS members (with date of joining): China (1996), Indonesia (2003), Peru (2011).

> a foreign currency debt crisis, the IMF arrives as a carrier of monetary virus in the name of sound monetary policy, then the international banks come as vulture investors in the name of financial rescue to acquire national banks deemed capital inadequate and insolvent by the BIS. (Liu 2002b)

In reality, Liu argues, large segments of many national economies have no intrinsic need for foreign investment, and they are certainly not helped when its effect is to drive them into 'unbalanced development toward export, merely to make dollar-denominated interest payments to FDI, with little net benefit to the domestic economies' (Liu 2002b).

The point to be taken from this is not that state-owned central banking should necessarily be regarded as an ultimate normative objective, but only that it is something the loss of which can foreseeably do more harm than good in the absence of a properly worked out alternative. To the extent that cosmopolitan philosophers do not address this issue, and instead rest content with assumptions that 'moderate reforms' will suffice to achieve a globally more just institutional order, there is a risk of being misled about the nature of the tasks—theoretical and practical—that face us.

11.2 The Epistemological Deficit of Liberal Interventionism

It is easy to be misled. Arguably, nothing demonstrates this more starkly than how readily people can be convinced war is a justified means of dealing with problems that could be dealt with in more cooperative ways, or that need never arise in the first place, or that, indeed, are not real problems at all but constructed pretexts. Since a fundamental purpose of philosophy is to evaluate truth claims, it is especially incumbent on political philosophers to be careful in the handling of claims that may be asserted in justification for war. The need for scrupulous examination of the *normative* principles involved is well established in the literature on the ethics of war. Such discussions of principles necessarily make reference to abstract and stylized situations, however, and so, when it comes to applying the principles and advising on policy, questions arise about how well the abstract stylizations capture the real circumstances. These are questions of *applied epistemology*, in that they involve establishing not only what knowledge is claimed of a situation but also how reliable are the claims. Meriting especial attention of this kind are policies that involve using coercive, even military, means to achieve a given normative objective. Proposals justifying military intervention for humanitarian ends are a major class of example.

The idea of using bombs to achieve humanitarian ends, or to secure conditions of freedom and democracy, or to make the target nation and the wider world order more just, is, on the face of it, a perplexing one. To be sure, if military action is claimed to be what it takes to achieve a humanitarian end, then there is an onus of proof on the claimant at least to show that such a damaging course of action is all-things-considered better than refraining. One thing that showing this necessarily depends on is the quality of information appealed to concerning the situation where intervention is proposed. Of course, there also has to be an ethical argument that explains the justification, but, in the abstract, all manner of arcane and even extreme ideas can be explored philosophically. When it comes to considering the ethics of a determinate situation where people's lives are actually at stake, any action-guiding advice has to be anchored more firmly in a sense of real responsibility. In the case of a recommendation of humanitarian intervention, this implies a justification in terms of acting responsibly on behalf of humankind. To seek to establish any such justification, not only must deliberations of applied ethics be supported by the due diligence of applied epistemology, but there is also the further requirement of accounting for how such a momentous responsibility is assigned or assumed in the world. So that will be the starting point for the argument here.

In the early years of the new century, an idea began to crystallize, among nations represented at the United Nations, of a 'responsibility to protect' grounded in shared principles aimed at the *defence of common humanity.*

> This responsibility lies, first and foremost, with each individual State, whose primary raison d'être and duty is to protect its population. But if national authorities are unable or unwilling to protect their citizens, then the responsibility shifts to the international community to use diplomatic, humanitarian and other methods to help protect the human rights and well-being of civilian populations. When such methods appear insufficient, the Security Council may out of necessity decide to take action under the Charter of the United Nations, including enforcement action, if so required. (UN General Assembly 2005: 35)

However, if the UN provides an ethical reference point in international relations, the responsibilities it theoretically adumbrates have to be assumed in practice by particular states or coalitions. In reality, the United States has been the major protagonist, and its interpretation of the ethical question has been shaped by its own interpretation of what the principle entails. So the idea of *humanitarian* intervention has in practice come to be assimilated to that of *liberal* interventionism, or 'liberal internationalism', as its advocates have tended to call it post-Iraq.

Michael C. Desch has reflected critically on the logic of purportedly benign interventionism in the case of US foreign policy insofar as the guiding idea is that 'virtue and self-interest can be reconciled in altruistic imperialism . . . which can bring the benefits of progress to benighted regions of the world' (Desch 2008: 16). He points out that this is in line with a long tradition of foreign policy thinking in the United States that runs deeper than party differences, with continuities in its core elements being traceable from Woodrow Wilson through to George W. Bush. Desch thus endorses the view that any difference between interventionist Liberals and interventionist neoconservatives is a matter of degree rather than principle,[12] and he argues that 'it is precisely American Liberalism that makes the United States so illiberal today' (Desch 2008: 8). Thus in response to the prospect of intervention in Iraq, for instance, we would find, 'support in the United States for the war was bipartisan, largely because it was justified within the Liberal tradition' (Desch 2008: 29).

One might have expected the Iraq experience to dampen the enthusiasm of thinking people for foreign interventions—on epistemological as well as ethical grounds, given the humanitarian catastrophe caused on a pretext that was so quickly and publicly exposed as false. In some quarters, however, it seems instead to have stimulated more creative thinking. In light of the reputational harm endured by the United States in consequence of the Iraq war, leading thinkers of the liberal establishment in America set about disavowing the position that had supported the invasion. For it was now understood that by 'invoking the rhetoric of human rights and democracy to further the aggressive projection of unilateral military power, conservatives have tainted liberal internationalist ideals and the United States' role in promoting them' (Nossel 2004: 134). Across that influential section of American society it became established wisdom that a line must be drawn under the Bush era and the Iraq invasion. With the 'neocon moment', as it was now called, pronounced as having passed into history (Ikenberry 2004), even its former celebrant Fukuyama speaks of a need for a 'recalibration of American foreign policy' of 'democratic globalism' (Fukuyama 2004: 68). In this period we see the formation of policy transition involving a considerable coordination of American intellectual talent.[13] This envisages the use of 'soft power' (Nye 2004) to be backed up with force, as needed, in a strategy involving 'smart power' (Nossel 2004). As Suzanne Nossel explains, in order to restore the trust of citizens and allies in the principles of *liberal internationalism*, and support for 'the spread of

[12] Parmar discerns the 'development since the late 1980s of a robust, crusading and theoretically confident liberal interventionism, built around a belief in the efficacy of 'democratic peace' and 'democratic transition' theory' (Parmar 2009: 178). Right and Left may have differences in domestic policy, but they 'have forged an "organic ideology", an historically effective ideology of global intervention' (Parmar 2009: 178). He says the 'liberals' "muscular multilateralism" for global human rights, dovetailed with the conservatives' and neocons' unilateralism' (Parmar 2009: 180). See also Pan and Turner (2016) and Vaïsse (2010).

[13] At the intellectual heart of this transition is the Princeton Project on National Security (PPNS), which Inderjeet Parmar argues captures the thinking among centrists—liberal and conservative alike. The Project culminated in a 90-page Final Report *Forging a World of Liberty Under Law* (PPNS 2006). In Parmar's judgement its scholarly claims of social-scientific rigour and thorough analyses of history are compromised by its 'more or less completely uncritical overt and covert belief in the United States as the "good", peace-loving, freedom-promoting, "well-intentioned" but "misunderstood" or "envied" nation' (Parmar 2009: 181). Certainly, the projection of a 'world of liberty' as the fulfilment of US *national security* goals is open to criticism of that kind. It advocates that 'the United States should work with its friends and allies to develop a global "Concert of Democracies"—a new institution designed to strengthen security cooperation among the world's liberal democracies' (PPNS 2006: 7). Independent of the United Nations, 'the Concert would provide an alternative forum for liberal democracies to authorize collective action, including the use of force' (PPNS 2006: 7).

American values', the strategy of smart power 'recognizes that military power and humanitarian endeavors can be mutually reinforcing' (Nossel 2004: 138). To achieve this, however, there is a problem of perception to deal with, since '[a] superpower that is not perceived as liberal will not be trusted as a purveyor of liberalism' (Nossel 2004: 134). Given the suspicions abroad about America's humanitarian motivations and intent, she understands, it is important to have credible reassurance about them from organizations that are perceived to be independent. In view of this, it is noteworthy that Nossel's own subsequent career involves moves between government and leading positions at Human Rights Watch (2007–09), Amnesty International (2012–13), and PEN America (since 2013). And perhaps more so is the fact that such organizations are ready to appoint avowed hawks to leadership positions.[14] What I want to reflect on here, though, is the nature of the ethical argument that serves to support an ethos among the intellectual elite that normalizes such arrangements.

Creativity in academic thinking is important and necessary; attaining relevance for policy-makers also has its own kind of importance in helping to realize some of the latent value of creative thinking. Another aspect of academic thinking, however, and a fundamental one, is the exercise of due diligence with regard to the reliability of evidence accepted and the soundness of arguments advanced when making recommendations of policy. The importance of this becomes very clear when abstractly developed ideas of principle are applied in the advocacy of practical proposals. The creative thinking that we have just been considering led to an increasing tacit acceptance, in influential circles, not only of a presumptive case for military intervention as a means to humanitarian ends, but even of the idea that the circumstances of the new century feature a 'type of conflict that can be won only by employing illiberal tactics' (Desch 2008: 8).

A tactic that is strikingly illiberal—as well as inhumane—is the use of torture. Even 'before the September 2001 attacks, some liberals had begun to argue that under certain circumstances torture was acceptable' (Desch 2008: 33), and the question was now revived, with liberal thinkers taking seriously, and in some cases even granting, a case for justifying torture.[15] The nature of the moral issue here has certain parallels with that regarding military intervention, insofar as killing people

[14] As it happens, the grassroots membership of AIUSA pressured the organization following the appointment of Nossel, leading to her early resignation. The concerns were articulated by Human Rights Investigations (HRI 2012). Individual cases aside, it is salutary to heed the more general reflections on 'sixteen years of experience having dealt with AI/London and AIUSA at the highest levels' that have been shared by Francis Boyle: 'There are many people of good will and good faith working at the grassroots level of Amnesty International and AIUSA who genuinely believe that they are doing meaningful and effective work to protect human rights around the world. But at the top of these two organizations you will find a self-perpetuating clique of co-opted Elites who deliberately shape and direct the work of AI and AIUSA so as to either affirmatively support, or else not seriously undercut, the imperial, colonial, and genocidal policies of the United States, Britain, and Israel' (Boyle 2012: 3).

[15] See, e.g., the collection of papers in Levinson (2006).

is no less wrong than torturing people. In each case, a conceivable justification for an exception to the moral proscription is that the alternative would effectively be to permit a still more egregious human rights violation. It might therefore quite reasonably be maintained that given that these are genuine moral questions, it is entirely appropriate for philosophers to investigate them. However, it has also to be recognized that a defining feature of any exceptional situation is that it has particular features not generally present in unexceptional situations. If appropriate moral judgements are to be made in relation to any exceptional situation, then, the nature of the particularities of the case need to be sufficiently well understood. This is where the application of philosophical thinking to concrete moral questions demonstrably requires epistemic diligence as well as ethical reasoning. In developing this point, in what follows I shall draw on Henry Shue's discussion of torture.

Shue is mindful that with an artfully enough constructed scenario, an argument might be developed, in the abstract, to yield an exception to an otherwise firm moral norm. He thus emphasizes that ethical policy decisions have to address the real context of their application. On this basis he has challenged the admissibility of attempted justifications for the use of torture, particularly insofar as they are developed in relation to an imagined scenario of application that would not typically, or perhaps ever, be met in the reality that the practical thinking is ostensibly concerned with. His thinking on this makes an important methodological point of more general relevance.

Shue makes the point in relation to the archetypical circumstance depicted in influential arguments concerning torture. This is the 'ticking bomb' scenario, the gist of which is that you have captured a terrorist who has planted a device that will kill a vast number of people and if you can extract the information from him quickly enough you will be able to save those people: the question then is 'should you torture him in order to get the information to save those people?' While some, notably Alan Dershowitz (2002), have been ready to arrive at an affirmative answer on the basis of that scenario, Shue has challenged its premise. He rejects the 'ticking bomb' thought experiment on the grounds that it is misleading and inapplicable with respect to the circumstances in which torture is practised in the world. Torture is an institutionalized practice, he emphasizes, and as such involves 'a culture, expert teachers, innovative students, equipment testing, technique improvement, international communication, plus corrupt medical doctors who collaborate and corrupt lawyers (like those around Bush and Cheney) who cover-up and deny' (Shue 2009: 314). All of that is abstracted from in the contrivance of the ticking bomb scenario, which, by contrast, involves 'a sociological fantasy'. To think that all the complex specificity of the facts involved can be set aside, Shue argues, 'is to think that one can make wise moral assessments of practices without knowing how the practices work—indeed, without really knowing what the practices are. This is intellectually and morally irresponsible' (Shue 2009: 314).

A similar point might be made in relation to humanitarian intervention. Shue himself relates his argument to *preventive* intervention,[16] and although the different rationales raise some distinct issues, the general point about the need for awareness of epistemic constraints holds for both. The crucial question regarding the possible justification for any kind of intervention is whether intelligence 'can be sufficiently reliable that it is not irresponsible to take human lives on the basis of it' (Shue 2009: 316). Shue maintains that 'intelligence agencies are notoriously unsuccessful' and so one must be cautious about relying on them for the purposes of such momentous decisions as embarking on war (Shue 2009: 315). In a related paper he picks up this point noting that decisions should be 'based on well-verified, solid intelligence collected by a highly competent agency (unlike CIA)' (Shue 2007). However, although this proposal seems sensible in principle, I would question how well it might fare if subjected to the test of sociological credibility that Shue applies to putative justifications for torture. Shue thinks it would fare better: he presents the 'ideal spy' as a more credible sociological posit than the hypothetical torturer in the ticking bomb scenario. He thinks that what is entailed in running the ideal spy may involve considerable organization and resource, but in principle could be achieved. In his judgement, 'the ideal torturer sounds like fantasy, but the ideal spy mainly sounds fabulously expensive' (Shue 2009: 316). However, it might be asked how an intelligence body that is 'unlike CIA' is going to be constituted and how it will have access to needed information without inside access to intelligence gathered by bodies like CIA. Even if investigators independent of the CIA could be set up, could it be assured that the CIA—and other intelligence agencies too—would not be able to influence the information that reaches them anyway? (You cannot just write the CIA out of the picture without any idea of how that could be made to happen, I think, on pain of indulging in sociological fantasy.) My point is that an intelligence service involves no less complex arrangements than does the institutionalized practice of torture. Of its nature, moreover, it may be even more resistant to independent monitoring. Since the world of espionage is inherently about maintaining deceptions, the ideal spy could be someone you would not know whether to trust.

The inescapable question, more generally, is how one can ever be sure that intelligence, or what is made available of it to public or academic researchers, is reliable. This question has not always been regarded as falling within the remit of normative theorists, and yet any attempt to arrive at all-things-considered judgements in relation to determinate cases clearly depends on an adequate understanding of the salient features of the case. How is that to be assured? Where is the

[16] He thinks 'some of the most powerful considerations against preventive military attacks, even attacks against terrorists with weapons of mass destruction, parallel the argument above against torture' (Shue 2009: 315). He nonetheless sees the moral prohibition as less absolute in the intervention case. Against this latter suggestion, Vittorio Buffachi (2009) has urged considerations that would reinforce the argument I make in the text.

information in question to be sourced? If timeliness as well as accuracy is a requirement—which may often be the case with real situations requiring action-guiding decisions—then prior academically reviewed research is unlikely to be available. Regarding matters in which governments and corporations have an interest, as is the case when an international intervention is on the agenda, one might think it the job of investigative journalists to seek out the truth so that those in power may be held to account. However, in circumstances where most of the media outlets are owned and/or controlled by governments and corporations, it is not always possible for journalists to exercise that role.[17] This situation serves to heighten appreciation of a duty that is anyway incumbent on academics, namely, to do due diligence regarding the information that they accept and thereby implicitly validate in their own publications. This certainly means being alert to the potential distorting effects of strategic forms of communication, or propaganda. The need for caution and provisional scepticism with regard to corporate and governmental narratives is reinforced by the fact that, since the seminal theoretical and practical contribution of Bernays (2004 [1928]), those responsible for communicating corporate or political messages have understood that propaganda is most effective when it is not recognized as such.

11.3 Applied Epistemology in Conditions of Conflict

Verifying evidence relating to situations of war is always difficult (Wood 2006; Sacco and Bossio 2015). From an academic perspective, due scrupulousness means recognizing that much of what can be understood about events unfolding in the build up of a conflict is provisional and somewhat uncertain. Key information can be unavailable; available information, including from witnesses, can be unreliable. When a particular potential case for military intervention arises, however, decision-makers need timely and reliable information. Academics in general, and philosophers in particular, are not necessarily well placed to advise in such situations, for their professional vocation involves prioritizing accuracy and reliability of knowledge over timeliness of its attainment.[18]

[17] Many individual journalists are honourable and honest in their work, but across the corporate and state media as a whole there appear to be editorial constraints that are quite restrictive according to critical commentators on politics, journalism, and the media (Dinan and Miller 2007; Miller and Dinan 2008). The underlying structure of the problem has been analysed by Herman and Chomsky (1988) in terms of the 'propaganda model' of news, according to which deeply institutionalized and internalized filters on information flows prevent disruptive knowledge from being disseminated. Chomsky's model is generally regarded as a key starting point for social scientific analysis of the role of the media as a part of a broader propaganda apparatus today: for an overview of the literature, see Zollmann (2017b), who builds on the refined conceptual framework of Bakir et al. (2018).

[18] This, I take it, is what distinguishes the social role of an academic from that of a journalist. A journalist can offer reports on a provisional basis, in good faith, in order that *some* public understanding may be arrived at in timely manner. A journalist may also be privy to informed sources

When academics are called upon to give advice relating to policy decisions, there can be a tension between making a clear recommendation and acknowledging the full range of limiting assumptions on which it depends.[19] Indeed, when scholars discuss applied normative questions, their arguments are typically hedged by caveats, qualifications, and *ceteris paribus* clauses. This makes contributing to policy debate, where straightforward demands to recommend this or that course of action are at issue, difficult if not impossible. It is not surprising then that many philosophers take the firm position that their part in the division of intellectual labour is to examine the quality of arguments, and not to provide explicit normative prescriptions or policy recommendations. However, applied ethics—and under this generic heading one may include the kind of political philosophy that aims to contribute more directly to making the world a better or more just place—relinquishes that self-denying ordinance. An implication of this is a need to reckon with the fact that although any recommendation may come only with major caveats and qualifications, it is the recommendation that 'goes out into the world'. The academic thus has a professional and social responsibility to ensure that the recommendation does reflect the all-things-considered best judgement attainable at the time of making it. This responsibility also has important ethical dimensions that are especially evident when the policy debate is about the justifiability of a war.

There is a responsibility to ensure that the grounds of the recommendation are firm enough to meet an appropriate standard of assurance, which, with regard to a case for military action, should be a high standard. If the only admissible basis for embarking on or entering a war on foreign territory is that some egregious crime is being committed—crimes against humanity or war crimes—then the evidence should in principle be compelling enough to meet the standard of proof usually required for the determination of the commission of a crime. In the nature of the case, however, there is unlikely to be an opportunity for a timely legal testing of the evidence. Where there are reasonable doubts with serious practical implications, these cannot simply be ignored. Knowingly to gloss over them would be indefensible. Thus what can be expected from academics is to make plain where there are reasonable doubts and to refrain from explicitly endorsing any course of

not in the public domain, but privileged information may not always and necessarily be more accurate and reliable than information that has been publicly checked, and may sometimes even be misleading. In short, journalism can involve taking epistemic risks that academics have a professional and vocational duty to avoid. Intelligence services, by contrast with both journalists and academics, are expected to use their enhanced investigative powers to produce information that is both timely and accurate. A problem, however, is that their social role is not necessarily understood as one of providing public information, and in practice their modus operandi can be such that the public might be left uninformed or even misinformed about matters of public interest. This means that the public understanding of the circumstances pertaining at a time when military intervention is being considered might be insufficient to support an informed evaluation of the case for it.

[19] This was illustrated in Chapter 7, by reference to the recommendations of the Stern Review.

action whose justification depends on ignoring or overriding them.[20] A specific temptation to avoid arises in a situation where there appears to be overwhelming evidence supporting a particular course of action because a consensus in the news media gives the impression there is. For it is the social role of academics rigorously to test knowledge claims rather than simply acquiesce in them. If it would be wrong to influence public opinion or policy-makers in a direction that runs contrary to what justice requires, and I assume it would, then it would be culpably negligent to exercise such influence for want of epistemic due diligence.

It cannot necessarily be expected that an applied philosopher engaged in normative theory can fully test the descriptive and explanatory claims appealed to in an ongoing debate about a potential intervention. What can be expected is that if a contribution to such a debate is made, the empirical assumptions it depends on should be clear, as should their epistemological basis and any explanatory hypotheses they imply. A responsible contribution would also seek to ensure that the material features of the situation at hand do correspond appropriately to those assumed when framing the theoretical model that generates the normative principles to be applied. Moreover, one should take some responsibility for ensuring that any description or theory relied upon is robust. Certainly, any account about which there is known to be reasonable doubt should not be relied on when it is also reasonably foreseeable that an argument mistakenly relying on it could support a harmful course of action.

Any proposal for a military intervention has a heavy burden of proof which includes meeting all the criteria established for justifying a war of defence as well as the additional onus that comes from the fact that intervening in another state is not the same as defending one's own and even shares features of a war of aggression. All the key criteria—of just cause, right intention, prospects of success, legitimate authority, proportionality—are rendered more complex and uncertain in such situations. There is also a nexus of questions concerning what standing and interests prospective intervening parties have in the matter, along with attendant concerns about guaranteeing the good faith of their involvement. This good faith requirement is additional to that of right intention: for, prospectively, which is when these questions of *jus ad bellum* are addressed, it is possible to articulate a right intention that turns out not to be the intention manifest in the actual conduct of the war.[21]

[20] If a lower standard of proof comes in practice to be accepted by decision-makers, and if academic experts are thereupon asked to provide *balance of probabilities* assessments, then their responsibility is to ensure that any calculation and assessment of probabilities advised is methodologically coherent and epistemologically defensible (see e.g. McKeigue 2017).

[21] As James Pattison noted regarding Libya, 'in the early stages of the intervention regime change did appear to be an intention, but only a secondary one' (Pattison 2011: 273). He does not explain the basis of his assessment of the original intention, however, and that is where due diligence about good faith is important. Pattison acknowledges 'that as the intervention progresses, the primary objective may become regime change rather than the protection of civilians' (Pattison 2011: 273–4), and he

In a context where one state is proposing to intervene, uninvited, in the affairs of another, good faith should generally not simply be assumed. With regard to proposed interventions by *liberal states*, particular reasons for caution have been adduced in the first two sections of this chapter. The hypothesis made explicit in Section 11.1 is that structural incentives favouring recourse to war are inherent in the dynamic system of global financialized capitalism that liberal states now uphold. Unless or until that hypothesis can reliably be excluded from a credible explanation of the intervener's interests and intentions, it points to concerns that an advocate of humanitarian intervention should be especially alert to. Given what was then noted in Section 11.2, about a readiness on the part of some to articulate an account of justice in the world that is premised on and even defined in terms of promoting US national security, there is a specific concern that cannot be neglected.

These reasons for concern are exemplified in relation to debates about humanitarian intervention in recent years that have focused on countries in the Middle East and North Africa (MENA) region. Guided by the first hypothesis, direct connections can be traced between incentives in the privatized global system of profit extraction and potential motives on the part of key players to promote regime change operations in countries that are resistant to joining it. Guided by the second hypothesis—the tendency of the United States and allied states to see the good of the international community as aligned with their own national security interests—one can readily explain why the pursuit of *regime change* has been such a persistent theme of Western activities in the MENA region since World War II.[22] The vast oil wealth of the region is a vital economic resource and control of it a matter of significant geopolitical contestation.[23] The possibility of

contemplates the problem of 'the morality of an intervention that was permissible when it was launched but that later becomes morally problematic' (Pattison 2011: 274). In apparently giving the benefit of the doubt regarding the intervener's initial motivation, Pattison assesses the case for intervention on the basis of a predicted outcome that is rather optimistic both epistemically and substantively: 'It is a mistake to think that we are completely in the dark when it comes to judging the likely consequences of an intervention. On the contrary, there is in most cases sufficient information available to make a reasonable judgment about the long-term consequences of intervention' (Pattison 2011: 275). Thus he affirms: 'The intervention in Libya (as long as it remains about the protection of civilians) appears sound according to these requirements, and for that reason can be expected to be successful in the long term' (Pattison 2011: 275). Looking at Libya in 2018, such optimism appears tragically misplaced. Disregard of the good faith requirement cannot, in my view, be justified by blaming 'mission creep' on unforeseen developments. Scholars, I believe, would be wise not to suppose that their most sceptical powers outmatch the potential cynicism of war-minded actors in the real world.

[22] For critical overviews see e.g. Noam Chomsky (1991), Mark Curtis (2003, 2018), Christopher Davidson (2016). For the context as it related more specifically to Syria, see Gowans (2017). The lack of sufficient thought about or insight into the nature of the countries intervened in, or thus the potential outcomes, is foregrounded by Jonathan Steele (2008).

[23] As Davidson summarizes: 'by 1950 the United States was importing a million barrels per day, and by the 1960s more than a third of U.S. energy demands were being met by such imports, mostly from the shah's Iran and the Gulf monarchies, but also from the Kingdom of Libya, which had become the region's third-biggest oil producer. With Britain's oil needs also growing, its interests and relations in

the nations of the region joining together in an independent bloc in relation to the globalized system, in particular, runs counter to Western aspirations and interests. The fact that within that group of nations there could be strong Arab socialist—Ba'athist—influences would make the possibility still more problematic from the West's perspective: this influence could make them less amenable to integration than those states that, even if more autocratic domestically, were ready to embrace global capitalism. So a reason for seeking regime change in these countries would be to get them integrated into the private profit economy and the financial system that both supports and depends on it.

None of this in itself can be taken to imply that there could never be a genuinely humanitarian case for an intervention in such countries. It does show, however, that in making such a case the standing duty of academic due diligence is of special importance. For in discussing any such circumstance when it is still live—in 'real time', so to speak—academics cannot scrutinize knowledge claims with the thoroughness that depends on studying a prior literature and building on it with work that undergoes processes of review. If they are to contribute to debate in a timely way, they must instead largely rely on less well-tested sources. Opting to do so, then, carries epistemic risks that do not loom so large in normal kinds of academic work where processes of peer review and general presumptions of good faith give greater assurance of its soundness. It is an open question whether academics should accept to run such risks, but it is certainly incumbent on them to be duly aware of them.

This point is amply demonstrated by reference to literature debating the case for Western military intervention in Syria since 2011. Particular reasons for caution about the bona fides of humanitarian intentions in relation to Syria stem from the observation that the installation of a pro-Western regime in Damascus had been an objective of dominant Western powers at least since the end of World War II.[24] An additional reason for caution is the lack of independent

the region fell increasingly in the U.S. shadow, with Whitehall planners admitting that Middle Eastern oil was "a vital prize for any power interested in world influence or domination"' (Davidson 2017: 93). Thus we find that the United States and Britain 'repeatedly sought to undermine or overthrow several Arab and other Middle Eastern governments in the 1950s and the 1960s that threatened to nationalize industries or chart new foreign policies' (Davidson 2017: 93).

[24] The CIA was already attempting to influence elections in 1947–48, and as these attempts failed, the CIA next 'tested its influence by sponsoring three coups in Syria within two years' (Lucas and Morey 2000: 97). By 1956, following yet another abortive coup, the United States and the UK agreed that change 'would be better to appear to come spontaneously from within, and not from outside intervention' (Gorst and Lucas 1989: 581). Operation Straggle was to involve an 'indigenous conspiracy' and an 'internal subversion program', led by an expert in psychological warfare and the use of 'gray propaganda' (Lucas and Morey 2000: 113). The plan failed on that occasion, but was not definitively abandoned. A CIA briefing from 1983 reveals continuity of thinking, advising now on 'bringing real muscle to bear' against Syria's hammerlock on US interests in the region by covertly stimulating military threats from neighbouring countries [https://www.cia.gov/library/readingroom/document/cia-rdp#32#88b00443r001404090133-0]. In 1986 a further, now partially declassified, CIA memo

witnesses on the ground, particularly the absence of Western journalists.[25] Lack of appropriate caution, however, is noticeable when academics have taken evidence supporting the case to be more compelling than even governments, guided by sophisticated intelligence services, have apparently judged it to be.[26] This means that a lot of confidence has been placed in other sources.[27] Much of the

develops 'a number of possible scenarios that could lead to the ouster of President Assad' [https://www.cia.gov/library/readingroom/docs/CIA-RDP86T01017R000100770001-5.pdf]. Definite plans were afoot even before the Iraq invasion, according to General Wesley Clark, former Supreme Allied Commander of NATO. He related that a Pentagon contact had advised him at the time of 'a memo that describes how we're going to take out seven countries in five years, starting with Iraq, and then Syria, Lebanon, Libya, Somalia, Sudan and, finishing off, Iran' (Clark 2007). Indeed, British Prime Minister Tony Blair was already corresponding by the end of 2001 with US President Bush on strategies concerning regime change in a number of countries including Syria (Blair 2001a, 2001b) under the rubric of the post-9/11 'War On Terror'. By 2005 it was such public knowledge that a CNN interviewer openly stated to Bashar al Assad: 'Mr President, the rhetoric of regime change is headed towards you from the United States. They are actively looking for a new Syrian leader. They are granting visas and visits to Syrian opposition politicians. They are talking about isolating you diplomatically and perhaps a coup d'état or your regime crumbling' (CNN recording: https://edition.cnn.com/videos/international/2012/07/11/exp-amanpour-assad-2005.cnn) In fact, a leaked CIA briefing from 2006 reveals quite starkly the planning for a systematic weakening of the Syrian president, who is clearly perceived as the key figure preventing an otherwise rather corrupt and unpopular elite quite readily being displaced by a pro-West regime. The cynicism of the US approach to Syria is on full view in this briefing. 'As the end of 2006 approaches, Bashar appears in some ways stronger than he has in two years. The country is economically stable (at least for the short term), internal opposition the regime faces is weak and intimidated, and regional issues seem to be going Syria's way.... Nonetheless, there are some long-standing vulnerabilities and looming issues that may provide opportunities to up the pressure on Bashar.' (CIA memo https://wikileaks.org/plusd/cables/06DAMASCUS5399_a.html) By 2009 concrete plans were underway to exploit those vulnerabilities and exacerbate the issues, as attested by the former French foreign minister, Roland Dumas, who recounted that almost two years before the start of hostilities in Syria British officials told him that 'Britain was preparing gunmen to invade Syria' (Ahmed 2013). Much of the strategic thinking is set out in detail in Pernin et al. (2008), a report prepared by the Rand Corporation on behalf of the US Army. In short, by 2011, a great deal of groundwork had been laid for various psychological and military operations that could lead to war on the country's territory.

---

[25] The reason there were few independent observers on the ground in opposition areas was well known from the testimony of those reporters who had tried it. Channel 4's Alex Thomson narrowly escaped death in a trap aimed at framing the Syrian government: 'I'm quite clear the rebels deliberately set us up to be shot by the Syrian Army', and he warned 'do not for one moment believe that my experience with the rebels in al Qusair was a one-off' (Thomson 2012).

[26] For instance, an allegation—potentially significant enough to trigger military intervention by the United States—that was treated as fact by some commentators, such as Thomas G. Weiss, was of 'the regime's use of chemical weapons in August 2013' (Weiss 2014: 16). This disregards the widely reported concern of officials, even at the time, that 'intelligence tying Syrian President Bashar Assad or his top lieutenants to an alleged chemical weapons attack last week is no "slam dunk"' (Crabtree 2013; see also Hersh 2014). In fact, politicians in neither the United States nor the UK found the evidence robust enough to act on. Subsequent research has yielded further and troubling reasons for doubt about where to attribute responsibility for the deaths in this and other alleged cases involving chemicals throughout the war (see e.g. O'Brien 2014; McKeigue et al. 2018; and, for a copious collection of critical studies on evidence relating to these and other incidents throughout the war in Syria, the wiki http://acloserlookonsyria.shoutwiki.com/wiki/Main_Page).

[27] For instance, a source for what Weiss (2014) calls 'Nuremberg-like evidence of war crimes' alleged against the Syrian government was an anonymous defector codenamed Caesar. Said to have been a Syrian police photographer, his Qatari handlers arranged for his 'gruesome trove of 55,000 photographs' to be made public on the eve, as Weiss points out, of the important *Geneva II* negotiations. Yet, while an FBI statement affirms that the photos 'appear to depict real people and real events' (Rapp

information reaching Western audiences has come—translated and interpreted—via videos, analysis, and commentary circulated through social networks whose compositions and identities were often unverifiable. Syria's has been 'the most socially mediated civil conflict in history', according to Marc Lynch and colleagues, who note that 'there were few international observers on the ground to offer external validity checks of claimed protests or massacres' (Lynch et al. 2014: 5). Thus they highlight critical questions: 'how credible was such information? How was it produced? Why did some gain attention and others, equally intriguing, fade into obscurity? And how did such information actually flow through the rapidly changing online social media?' (Lynch et al. 2014: 5). The news reported from crucial areas has tended to rely on information supplied by 'civil society actors' or 'citizen journalists'[28] whose identities, affiliations, and bona fides have not necessarily been verified.[29] Certain NGOs have also supplied reports, but their sources have often remained beyond the reach of meaningful verification,[30] and among the most influential NGOs are those like Amnesty International and Human Rights Watch that also play a role in the exercise of US 'soft power'. Even an organization

2015: 163), questions of who was responsible for which exact events that led to those undisputed deaths still require proper examination; and claims about them still require corroboration, particularly in the light of serious questions that critical researchers have raised (Larson 2014; Murphy 2014; Human Rights Investigations 2015; Sterling 2016).

[28] It is worth noting, for instance, that Hillary Clinton, as US Secretary of State, 'pledged increased support for civilian opposition groups, including satellite-linked computers, telephones, cameras, and training for more than a thousand activists, students, and independent journalists' (Clinton 2014: 464).

[29] The use of anonymity to conceal witnesses' identities is sometimes understandable and sometimes less so. Notably, in the case of the witness codenamed 'Caesar', for instance, the rationale for his anonymity appears to depend on supposing that the Syrian government is incapable of identifying a photographer apparently in its own employ for thirteen years (Larson 2014). Not only anonymous witnesses, though, but even fictitious characters have been encountered. Notoriously, the *Guardian* ran numerous articles reporting on the so-called 'Gay Girl of Damascus' who turned out to be a fiction created from an IP address used by an American couple in Edinburgh (for a critical overview of the story see Mansour Robaey 2011). Worse, the *Guardian* journalist supposedly based in Damascus who introduced the character wrote under a pseudonym—Katherine Marsh—had filed at least one other, and much more damaging, false report. The allegation in Marsh's article 'Syrian soldiers shot for refusing to fire on protesters' (*Guardian* 12 April 2011) attracted considerable public attention at a critical time of public opinion formation about events in Syria and yet was afterwards revealed to be false (Landis 2011).

[30] As Hiroyuki and Shingo (2015) note, a routinely cited source of data from Syria is the so-called Syrian Observatory For Human Rights, and they warn that 'the political bias that lurks in the data supplied by the Syrian Observatory... is hampering correct understanding of the Syrian situations' (Hiroyuki and Shingo 2015: 8). The Observatory, it might be mentioned, particularly in view of its impressive name, is actually run by one man who left Syria a decade before the war started and is based in Coventry, England (Macfarquhar 2013); he has received substantial funding from UK FCO (Hitchens 2018). Sources relaying accounts of ongoing events from Syria, meanwhile, have otherwise tended to be routed via media centres located in neighbouring countries and sponsored by European countries. For instance, the Aleppo Media Centre—which had a virtual monopoly on coverage from Aleppo when the eastern part of the city was under opposition control—was established in Turkey by France (CFI 2015) and received its reports largely from Western-funded information operations such as that administered by the British-led Mayday Rescue, registered in the Netherlands. Concerns that this operation was inextricably bound up with extremist militants on the ground led to the Netherlands Government eventually withdrawing support from it (van Es 2018).

with such a worldwide reputation as *Médicins Sans Frontières* (MSF) has admitted to publicizing 'secondhand testimony' from opposition-held areas in Syria without attaining independent verification of it.[31] Meanwhile, some verified sources of information are liable to be ignored by journalists, for reasons that themselves would merit investigation.[32] In short, as careful scholars have noted, but for 'a small handful of scientific papers, the critical eye of academic research over reportage is lost', and, instead, 'there is an unhealthy overlap between the two' (Sen et al. 2016: 4L).

The nature of the relationship between the media and academia, and the degree of autonomy of either with respect to corporate and state influence, are arguably matters of wider and more general concern. While it is easy to talk about 'speaking truth to power', the reality is that power does not necessarily tolerate truth being spoken. We know this from many historical precedents of censorship and suppression of dissidence; we have no reason to be complacent here and now.[33]

[31] Having written a blog post about this problem (Hayward 2016b), it transpired that within MSF itself there was already concern, with internal tensions about the issue becoming publicly evident in the reflective article published a couple of months later (MSF 2017). MSF invited me to their annual research meeting in Brussels that year to speak at a plenary panel addressing the dilemmas associated with 'secondhand testimony'. That experience further enhanced my respect for the volunteer medics while reinforcing my sense that the MSF press office is part of a relatively autonomous operation. Representing the latter was the Creative Content and Special Projects Manager, whose approach to storytelling is outlined in al-Saadi (2014). His approach to evidence, as outlined in al-Saadi (2018) includes accepting as 'independently verified' reports like that of Bellingcat (2018) on an alleged chemical attack in Douma in April 2018. For an academic critique of that and related reports see the contrasting approach to evidence in McKeigue et al. (2018).

[32] For instance, at the critical early stages of opinion formation about the nature of the uprisings in Syria, when Al Jazeera was the primary international broadcaster, it is said to have suppressed reports on—and footage showing—how armed Islamist elements, which had infiltrated via Jordan, were already active at the first demonstrations in Da'ara in March 2011, thereby concealing the extent to which the character of those demonstrations was sectarian and anti-democratic, even though this was attested by the Qatar-owned station's own journalists (Suliman 2012).

[33] This was evident when a group of academics announced the formation of a Working Group on Syria, Propaganda and Media (http://syriapropagandamedia.org/) in order to do exactly the sort of due diligence being recommended here. Within weeks of the announcement, and before even having published any research, the group was the subject of three critical articles by former *Guardian* journalist Brian Whitaker (he being one of the journalists who had previously promoted the 'Gay Girl of Damascus' story that was revealed to be a hoax). These were shortly afterwards followed by a front-page attack in *The Times* on 'Apologists for Assad in Our Universities', with a further inside spread amplifying the accusations; in that same week, the *Huffington Post* prominently accused the group of 'Whitewashing War Crimes'; and the attacks were echoed in other UK papers such as the *Sun*, *Express*, and *Mail*. All this was still before the group had published anything on Syria beyond an open letter about a problematic article in the *Guardian*! As a founder member of the group, I declare an interest here, and that interest is entirely consonant, and not in conflict, with, the purposes of academic research undertaken in independence and good faith. I would further refer to the statement of the group's remit at http://syriapropagandamedia.org/about, and to the more than thirty published responses linked from Hayward (2018) that critically analyse the pre-emptive attacks on the group. International criminal lawyer Christopher Black is in no doubt about the real issue here, which is about the exposure of inconvenient truths: 'these attacks are meant to intimidate, and not only the targets, the Haywards, the Fisks, the Robinsons, the Beeleys, but to intimidate the rest of us too' (Black 2018). The tactic is familiar to critical investigative journalists and well understood by scholars, including the co-author (with Noam Chomsky) of the landmark work *Manufacturing Consent*, Edward S. Herman. In 'The Oliver Kamm School of Falsification: Imperial Truth-Enforcement, British Branch', Herman

Academics should certainly be no less careful about which claims to reject than they are about which to accept as verified knowledge about the world. In the age of social media it has become possible as never before for ordinary citizens to be aware of propaganda in the informational environment. Critical counter-narratives have flourished under these conditions—to the point that governments and the corporate-controlled media have become concerned that the public may be *misled* by what they brand as *conspiracy theories*. The influential liberal thinker Cass Sunstein gave voice to this concern, during his time as adviser to President Obama, in a leading political philosophy journal.[34] Sunstein claimed that people engaged in what he designated 'conspiracy theory' tend to suffer from a 'crippled epistemology'. This he diagnoses as a problem that is hard to escape from due to its 'self-sealing' quality whereby contrary evidence is taken by the sufferer to be just a further sign of a plot to deceive.[35] However, the presumption that anyone who asks critical questions about official narratives manifests an epistemological and/or psychological failing is not one that should be granted without question, even on principle.

Sunstein, of course, is aware that conspiracy theories sometimes prove to be true, but he argues that this should not cause us to let down our guard in relation to *dangerous* conspiracy theories. He avows a concern that where available information 'justifies conspiracy theories and (therefore) extremism, and (therefore?) violence, then terrorism is more likely to arise' (Sunstein and Vermeule

along with David Peterson reveals how an 'important and perhaps growing feature of official and strong-interest-group propaganda is the resort to personal attacks and flak to keep dissidents at bay and inconvenient thoughts out of sight and mind' (Peterson and Herman 2010). Relatedly, see Brian Leiter (2005) on the smearing of Noam Chomsky, and Sharyl Attkisson (2017) on the smearing of independent British journalist Neil Clark. Louis Allday (2016) has revealed how this tactic has been conducted specifically in connection with Syria reporting, and several independent journalists have recounted first hand experiences with identifiable 'narrative correctors' who use it (Blumenthal 2017; Gosztola 2017; Norton 2017).

[34] The specific paper referred to was co-authored with Adrian Vermeule, but because Sunstein has written and spoken about conspiracy theory in numerous places, and has had the opportunity to refer to his ideas on the subject in his role as adviser to President Obama, I am following the precedent of other commentators (e.g. Griffin 2011; Hagen 2011) in focusing on Sunstein as the influential author and disseminator of the central ideas under discussion.

[35] This characterization keys into a strand of thinking in American public life since the 1960s that associates conspiracy theory with the *paranoid style*. Early ideas of a '*conspiracist mindset*' were developed in the work of Harold Lasswell and Franz Neumann. These informed Richard Hofstadter's seminal study of the political pathologies of the 'paranoid style' in the 1960s (Hofstadter 1965). This association of conspiracy suspicions with irrationality and paranoia was then actively promoted in the United States. Lance deHaven Smith notes that 'the conspiracy-theory label was popularized as a pejorative term by the Central Intelligence Agency (CIA) in a propaganda program initiated in 1967' (deHaven Smith 2013: 21). The programme was created as a response to critical citizens' questions about the assassination of J. F. Kennedy. It 'called on media corporations and journalists to criticize "conspiracy theorists" and raise questions about their motives and judgments'. Its reach has extended greatly since. Knight takes to be a now generally accepted fact that 'some of the labelling of particular views as "conspiracy theories" is a technique of governmentality' (Knight, P 2014: 348).

2009: 212). Although this set of vague associations appears tenuous and unclear,[36] it is invoked to support his commitment to defend the government's epistemic authority. So while sometimes the government may be mistaken, he believes, it is still better to protect its authority than risk societal disintegration.[37] In thus offering an argument that runs so directly counter to John Stuart Mill's on freedom of thought and expression, Sunstein provides a stark illustration of Desch's point about Liberal illiberalism. For whereas Mill, in his seminal essay *On Liberty*, speaks of *the peculiar evil of silencing the expression of an opinion*, no matter how convinced one is of one's own truth and cause, Sunstein advocates precisely this, and even proposes strategies for achieving it. Thus he envisages that 'government efforts might succeed in weakening or even breaking up the epistemological complexes that constitute these networks and groups' (Sunstein and Vermeule 2009: 224). Among the means recommended are that governments should 'hire credible private parties to engage in counterspeech', or 'government officials would participate anonymously or even with false identities', if they judge that compared to less inherently dishonest tactics, it 'potentially brings higher returns' (Sunstein and Vermeule 2009: 225). Although Sunstein's proposals have been subject to severe criticism by applied epistemologists,[38] the fact is that the stigmatizing of 'conspiracy theorists' and the practices of cognitive infiltration are quite standardly encountered throughout the mainstream and social media (Greenwald 2014; Greenwald and Fishman 2015; Bradshaw and Howard 2017). Meanwhile, even some academics have joined in the quest to 'diagnose' conspiracy theorists as subjects for psychological study rather than as potentially interesting participants in debate.[39]

[36] Sunstein's thinking appears to be that conspiracy theories are likely to be implicated in terrorist acts because they somehow connect together in *'extremist' groups.* He thinks that Russell Hardin's analysis of the so-called 'crippled epistemology of extremism' (Hardin 2002) can usefully be applied to groups of people who share beliefs arising from conspiracy theories. Yet critical hypotheses about possible conspiracies need not be 'extreme' in any pernicious sense, and even if an inquirer may be *extremely* persistent and inquisitive, any such *extreme* intensity of concern might be well directed to *extremely* benign objectives, such as challenging false pretexts for a humanly devastating war. The kind of extremists people have to fear are those that engage in extremely violent acts. The two sorts of groups are quite distinct, conceptually and sociologically. In order to connect them at all, the idea of a conspiracy theorist is conflated with that of a bearer of 'conspiratorial dispositions' or 'conspiracy beliefs', as by Uscinski and Parent (2014). Even then, the link is unclear: 'Maybe conspiratorial beliefs drive violence. Or maybe conspiracy theories are only symbols exploited by actors who would commit violence anyway. Only with careful study can we begin to untangle the connections' (Uscinski and Parent (2014: 8). Meanwhile, the fact is, as they point out, that a large proportion of the American population holds some conspiracy beliefs.

[37] Lee Basham (2018) analyses the logic manifest in this kind of reasoning, and discusses the idea that some conspiracies are just too damaging to reveal and so should not be revealed. To keep people in the dark about truths too toxic to tell, he argues, is actually to pose a threat to democracy.

[38] Something of a philosophical school of thought is emerging around the question of critically evaluating 'conspiracy theory' as a rational form of intellectual inquiry. This has developed in quite conscious and often explicit response to Sunstein's position. (See e.g. Hagen 2010, 2018; Basham 2016, 2018; Dentith 2016a, 2016b, 2017; Pigden 2016 ; Coady 2018).

[39] For instance, one finds asserted that 'in the main conspiracy theories are unproven, often rather fanciful alternatives to mainstream accounts' (Douglas and Sutton 2011: 544) and argued that

Aside from the wrongs of pre-emptively stigmatizing people whose beliefs may run counter to those of a majority population, let alone to an 'authoritative' view imposed by a government, it should be clear that academics must always be prepared to evaluate a theory on its merits, without fear, favour, or prejudice. Spurious and mistaken theories will not survive much scrutiny but even so-called 'conspiracy theories' can sometimes be importantly enlightening. That is especially so when it comes to matters relating to war.

Of primary concern when debating the rights and wrongs of a possible military intervention should be the quality of argument and not the identity of subscribers to it. This should go without saying, and yet when a matter involves all-things-considered judgement, as such questions generally do, then one should aim to be duly reflexive about the various influences that may affect one's judgement, even in unnoticed ways. Certainly, when there is clear contestation between identifiable communities of interest, an individual academic's membership of one rather than the other needs to be duly reflected upon. Academics, as members of their own communities, are not necessarily immune from becoming orientated by reference to received wisdom that holds within their own community.

This point has a quite specific salience with regard to the ethics of intervention, since an alternative to the liberal theory, as discussed in Section 11.2, has been advanced from a Russian perspective. Russia has tended to be recalcitrant in the face of Western proposals for humanitarian war. Western scholars are often at pains to point out that the Russian position is grounded in strategic political interests and to be cautious about whether it manifests a deep moral commitment. If such caution is quite appropriate, it is no less appropriate with regard to the Western position, as I have already argued. But having established that the existence of ulterior motives does not suffice to deny that intervention can *ever* be justified, so the existence of contrary motives cannot simply be assumed to invalidate every argument against intervention. The salient point is, as Averre and Davies (2015) show, the normative interpretation defended by Russia offers a cogent alternative to the theory and practice of liberal interventionism. It accepts the normative idea of a responsibility to protect populations from genocide, war crimes, ethnic cleansing, and crimes against humanity. The primary focus of this responsibility, however, and consistent with UN provisions, is on providing support for states to fulfil their own responsibility to protect populations rather than on how to trigger a

conspiracy theorists are likely to believe conspiracy theories because they are more likely to sympathize with conspirators. From such a perspective, '[t]he specifics of a conspiracy theory are less important than its identity as a conspiracy and its opposition to the official explanation' (Wood and Douglas 2013: 2). Alessandro Bessi et al. (2015: 2) characterize conspiracy theories as narratives that 'tend to reduce the complexity of reality and are able to contain the uncertainty they generate'. Several philosophers, including David Coady (2007) and those cited in footnote 38, have commented critically on these kinds of characterization. Dentith (2017) has particularly criticized the failure of such approaches to consider the possibility of finding merits in conspiracy theories.

justification for coercive intervention.[40] While this principled stand may also quite conveniently support more pragmatic political objectives, Averre and Davies argue that Russia's foreign policy philosophy nonetheless amounts to 'a normative challenge to the values-based intervention inspired by western liberalism' (Averre and Davies 2015: 827; see also Charap 2013).

In fact, the idea of *humanitarian intervention* as a just exercise of military force has come to acquire a degree of presumptive legitimacy in philosophical debate that could appear remarkable from other perspectives on what humanitarianism entails. It is interesting to note that between the different ethical framings of Russia and the West one may discern a contrast of a kind similar to that discussed in the literature on the ethics of care.[41] That debate was sparked by the observation of two distinct trajectories of moral thinking that are revealed by two different ways of hearing the same question. In the original case, the moral question was whether Heinz, to save his wife's life, should steal the drug he cannot afford to buy from a druggist that won't lower his price.[42] Adapting the example to the present case, one trajectory of ethical thinking pursues the question as heard to be '*should* there be military intervention?' whereas the other treats the question as asking 'should there be *military* intervention?' Had that second line of inquiry been more resolutely pursued, then the nature of the debate in the West could have been different, the actions of those in power might have been different, and the consequences for the people of countries where intervention took place might have been different.

[40] By reference to the principles affirmed in UN Security Council Resolutions 1674 (2006) and 63/308 (2009), Russia has criticized the way in which the UN mandate has sometimes been applied by the Western powers. For instance, with regard to the 2011 intervention in Libya, Moscow believes NATO's air strikes 'went beyond the protection of civilians and amounted to support for one side in a civil war' and the justificatory appeal to the responsibility to protect 'was ultimately an elaborate cover for regime change, perceived by Moscow as illegitimate' (Averre and Davies 2015: 818).

[41] While this view does not seem to be widely shared in the literature, it has been articulated by Virginia Held: 'The ethics of care encourages states to take responsibility for protecting vulnerable populations and for promoting peaceful resolutions of conflicts. Negotiating disputes noncoercively and addressing the problems of those politically disenfranchised or exploited can clearly become practices of care. Properly developed, they should reduce the need for military intervention, for forces to keep the peace between warring groups, and for enforcement of the reasonable restraints of law to which all can become accustomed. Instead of focusing on rules to be followed and violations to be punished, the ethics of care would attend to the political and social and economic problems that make the rules so often inadequate in their protection of actual persons and groups. And instead of relying on military intervention to punish violators of the norms of international law, the ethics of care would counsel preventive engagements and measures aimed at deflecting violations and undercutting the need for punishments' (Held 2008: 14).

[42] The developmental psychologist Lawrence Kohlberg (1981) had introduced this moral dilemma as a test of advancement of moral reasoning in children. The reasoning assumed by Kohlberg prioritizes ideas of rights and justice and focuses on whether or not it can sometimes be morally right to break the law. That reasoning is deployed by a test subject called Jake, who scores more highly for Kohlberg than does Amy. Amy seems to Kohlberg to prevaricate by asking whether there might be other ways to solve the problem, such as, for instance, reasoning with the druggist or appealing to his better nature. The seminal move of Carol Gilligan (1982) was to argue that Amy manifests a whole other way of looking at ethics, and thus that moral reasoning can develop in more than one direction. Thereafter, this 'ethics of care' has been regarded as a distinct alternative to the ethics of justice and rights.

11.4 Conclusion

In an imperfect world, where various manifestations of greed and grievance can lead to serious conflicts between peoples, war may sometimes be hard to avoid, and wars of *defence* against aggressors may have some justification. But as we human beings on this planet deliberate ethically together about how the world might become more just, it is critical to consider how to make war more avoidable. In fact, we ought to reflect carefully on how it is that people can be brought to believe that something so horrifyingly inhumane as war could ever really be unavoidable.

This chapter began by broaching the question of how the drivers of war might relate to those of finance. It was noted that although connections between war and finance have existed throughout history, there are particular incentive structures embedded in the institutions governing international economic and financial arrangements today, in supporting a system of relentless profit seeking, that are not well suited to pre-empting recourse to war. They could even make war appear an attractive option to those with the power to engineer it and to persuade the public of its unavoidability. While it would have been beyond the scope of this book to examine exactly how a vast apparatus of 'organized persuasive communication' can be created and deployed, I maintain in principle that the role of political philosophers in relation to it ought to be critically alert to its possible effects. Hence Section 11.2 emphasized the need not only to think carefully about the justification for any given proposal of a military intervention but also to ask more fundamentally critical questions about how that question ever came to be on the table. Most basically, *why ask the question is military intervention justified, at all, without first exhausting every alternative to military intervention?* War is an extreme form of damage, and the idea that it can be used to serve humanitarian ends needs to be treated with particular caution by political thinkers.

The need for due diligence, emphasized throughout the book with respect to assumptions about the nature of money and finance, applies no less to the assumptions that are brought to bear on arguments justifying war. Given the egregious affront to justice that war presents, it is very much worth being alert to how deep may run the connections between war and finance, not only in terms of the interests that drive them, but also in terms of how the practical norms of a given society make both possible. Such connections of several kinds may be discerned in the light of what has been shown, and so in now drawing them out, this concluding section will be a little more expansive than those of previous chapters.

A first point of comparison is that a belief in the value of a currency and a belief in the necessity of a war have a similar kind of epistemic status. A widespread perception of the necessity of a given war, like the validity of a given currency, is something that can only exist in the mind of human beings in society. In a certain ontological sense, it has the nature of a collective illusion. Collective illusions, though, have their own kind of reality, the kind had by all the conventions, norms, laws, and moral precepts that people generally abide by. They have that reality, though, only on condition that people treat them as having it: acquiescence in a norm on the part of each depends on a belief that others will generally abide by it too.

A second point of comparison is that both finance and war, in depending on beliefs of people whose activities make them possible, require a similarly extensive kind of social infrastructure. Sustaining a monetary system requires extensive institutional arrangements, and confidence in that system is maintained as long as it functions as it is supposed to. Sustaining a widespread social belief that wars are from time to time necessary also depends on the support of a vast material infrastructure. In both cases, the workings—and even existence—of these systems of belief maintenance are scarcely noticed by most people most of the time. But throughout the book it has been emphasized what a massive accomplishment is the maintenance of a monetary system, and this chapter has outlined reasons to think that persuading people to kill, be killed, or even just approve of others getting killed—and on a potentially enormous scale, even aware that innocent men, women, and children will suffer unspeakably in the process—requires some formidable infrastructure of ideological persuasion. Moreover, just as the value of money ultimately depends on the organization of the productive forces of societies, perceptions of the necessity of war depend on the capacity of a society actually to engage in it. For the possibility of embarking on a particular war depends on having armed forces in place, and such forces are likely to be most effective if they can draw on institutional learning from real experience of war; it also requires armaments, and these must have been developed and produced, which will have required a massive investment over an extended period. From the point of view of a well-trained military force, accordingly, any given war may appear as but one of a series that they must, at some time or other, prosecute. So, in fact, one momentous moral question—whether something as horrific as war can ever be justified—has already in effect been presumptively settled in precedence for any people that maintains an army. But the terms of the justification as traditionally set out—in just war theory, for instance—focus on the need and right of a people to defend itself against external aggression. So the fact of war-readiness alone is not sufficient to explain a readiness of a people to accept a need to support a war of intervention, but it does make such a course of action an option. Wars of intervention are, in fact, often referred to as optional wars—wars that are morally permissible but not necessarily obligatory to undertake.[43]

[43] Whether for any war to be permissible means meeting a standard of justification so strong that it would also be obligatory is a proposition that has not been considered as much as it might be in the literature, but see the argument of Oberman (2015b) in support of it.

A third point of comparison that follows from this concerns the illusion that the determinate means of war can be pressed into the service of any freely chosen ends. The existence of a military apparatus might be thought of, by a philosopher doing thought experiments, as simply a technical means of achieving an end if that end were ever to be aimed at; the mere fact of its existence as a means could not count as a principled reason to deploy it to that end. This way of thinking is analogous to the idea that money is simply a technical means to achieving whatever ends might be proposed on philosophical grounds. Earlier chapters examined reasons to question whether existing instruments of global finance can be pressed into the service of just any ends that might be politically desired. For the instruments available do not exist as isolated tools but as functional nodes in a system that inherently constrains the scope and purpose of their deployment. It is salutary to add now that a similar point applies with regard to attitudes and assumptions about the nature of war. In normative deliberations about the general conditions under which war should or should not be engaged in, it may heuristically be assumed that there are armed forces in existence that can in principle be pressed into the service of whatever ends might be ethically decided. Thus applied philosophers in the West, for instance, may assume that the forces of the United States, NATO, and their allies could in principle be sent anywhere on any kind of mission. In reality, though, they will normally be sent where those with the power decide.[44] For the creation of an army, and its direction, are under the control of an integrated nexus of power often referred to as the *military industrial complex*.[45] At the controlling heights of that complex is a clear understanding that the power of persuasion is of indispensible and even primary importance.[46]

The very fact of maintaining an army entails a commitment to the maintenance of an arms industry that will be developing ever more effective weapons systems. If

[44] 'Global NATO evolved as an umbrella for the protection of Wall Street and the international economic system dominated by the U.S. oligarchy' (Campbell 2013: 41).

[45] Horace Campbell suggests this might now be regarded as a *financial–military complex* given 'the financialization of energy markets and the close alliance between the banks and the oil companies' (Campbell 2013: 107).

[46] As evidence, one may note, for instance, that in the era of George W. Bush, Vice President Cheney and US Secretary of Defense Rumsfeld, the Pentagon rolled out a programme under the rubric of Total Information Awareness (TIA) that would treat information operations as a core military competency, and aim, *inter alia*, at 'gaining uninhibited support for the prosecution of wars around the globe' (Campbell 2013: 145). Some of the activities undertaken were such as have since been pursued by tech giants like Facebook and Google (DiResta 2018). Under Secretary of State Clinton, the Pentagon's doctrine of 'Full-Spectrum Dominance' was taken up into the 'Whole-of-Government' approach as the military footprint becomes smaller and the persuasive communications side expands (Sottile 2014). The 'liberal internationalist' idea of 'smart power' meant fully integrating military and ideological forces, Clinton emphasized, since 'the power to project values' involves 'shifting from mostly direct exercise and application of power to a more sophisticated and difficult mix of indirect power and influence' (Clinton 2010: 7). Integrating 'defence' with 'diplomacy' and 'development' is 'just a smarter way to get the resources we desperately need' (Clinton 2010: 33). Meanwhile, in Britain, the army's 77th Brigade has developed the use of psychological operations and social media to help fight enemies in the 'information age'. The 1,500 strong unit is intended to 'help the military shape and control the narrative in conflicts and areas of interest' (Defence IQ 2015).

that has always been true to an extent, it has become especially significant in a situation where the needs of an army are met by a system of production that is premised on the competitive pursuit of profit, for the logic of an arms race is built into it. The military industrial complex is a dynamic system kept in motion by the same profit-seeking drive that underpins the financial destruction of real productivity, social justice, and ecological sustainability. If the case of war differs at all, it is in being more directly and swiftly destructive.

In a democratic, free, and open society, the question of whether to maintain an expansionary arms industry would be a matter for critical public debate, since people would be aware of alternative uses for the labour and resources involved—alternatives could more clearly, directly, and peaceably serve real human interests. If people in all societies could decide these matters democratically, the arms race would likely be wound down and the chances of wars diminish. It is therefore clear that insofar as interests are vested in the military–industrial complex, these are opposed to a more pacific public interest. It is rational for agents whose job is to promote or serve those particular interests to find ways to alter the perceptions of what is in the public interest. The construction of an ever-present threat—even if from time to time shifting as regards its exact source or nature—would be a way to inculcate deeply and widely enough the needed perceptions. If this threat were to be communicated to the public only by those who have a demonstrable interest in having it believed, it would not be credible. So more subtle ways of persuading the public would be sought. Public relations firms could be employed for the purpose; politicians could be offered inducements; inquisitive journalists could be dissuaded, by various means, from undermining it; the public could be assured that only crazy conspiracists would question it. As for academics, some could be made aware of the peaceful uses of military technology and help develop it; some could be mindful of a public's need for technology that is up to the job of serving the military that protect the public. And political philosophers concerned with global justice, how might they be brought to be acquiescent? This chapter has given some indication of how they might—and also of how we need not.

12
Conclusion

We humans, as inhabitants of this planet, and insofar as we want to live at peace with one another, on civilized terms, are under an imperative to deal with the dual challenge of radical inequality and ecological overshoot. A major reason why we are failing to do so is that our political organization—domestically and internationally—is in thrall to the interests of financialized capitalism.

Practically speaking, humanity is a *disorganized* collectivity. The institutions that shape and constrain the decision-making that most profoundly affects humanity at a global level did not come into being on the basis of any constitutional process such as might have oriented them to the tasks that are now becoming imperative. We humans can conceive of the idea of *humanity* as a moral collectivity, but to date it is the many different individuals, families, tribes, nations, classes, and states that actually form political organizations and institutions in the world. Hence, while one can readily conceive ideas of *moral* cosmopolitanism, it is much more difficult to agree clear ideas about what *political* cosmopolitanism might entail. Meanwhile, to the extent that globalizing processes have given rise to a particular kind of transnational organization, the effects of its institutionalized norms have become increasingly problematic for a great part of the human collectivity. The institutional arrangements as described in Chapter 10 make for an irresponsible and humanly unresponsive form of organization that is not directed to achieving what is good for people or planet. In fact, as was argued in Chapter 11, they tend to support the imposition of a further grave threat, namely, war.

In light of the magnitude and interlocking nature of the potentially existential threats faced, humanity is a collectivity in the sense, at least, of sharing a dependence on certain conditions of life as a terrestrial species. We have ample reason to be cautious about supposing that proposals of modest reform of the emerging global institutional order will provide a basis for meeting the imperatives of our age. Proposals put forward as steps towards global justice are often framed in terms inherited from the modern liberal tradition of political thought. This was largely developed on the basis of socio-economic assumptions about the world that could reasonably be taken to have purchase within the context of a modern developed nation-state with a broadly liberal economy and government. The world does not consist only of affluent liberal democratic states, however, and even the part that does is changing as a result of the globalizing dynamics that are bringing the challenges we now all face, albeit from different positions. In order to deal adequately with these challenges, new research agendas need to be recognized, and the methods and assumptions brought to the task of dealing with them need to be appropriate.

This book has critically questioned assumptions about how money in the existing system of global finance might be pressed into the service of justice. In doing so it has highlighted reasons for thinking that the valuable social functions that finance could in principle fulfil can only now be fulfilled in practice by setting out in a direction that goes against the current trajectory of global finance. The financial system globally as it has come to exist today is, in critical respects, the antithesis of what humanity requires for the achievement of justice, sustainability, and peace. This means radically questioning not only the economic system that underpins it but also the intellectual system that accommodates it.

A foundational belief for defenders of the existing system against more egalitarian alternatives is that allowing private profit is the key to incentivizing creativity, innovation, and industry. Notwithstanding concerns about how private profit-taking from large businesses can *subtract* from the value that an enterprise has for those materially engaged in and dependent on it, some thinkers still support the idea that it provides a necessary stimulus for needed economic development. This view was defended by one of the most significant economists of the twentieth century, whose ideas are still influential for those who favour social democratic reform of free market capitalism:

> For at least another hundred years we must pretend to ourselves and to every one that fair is foul and foul is fair; for foul is useful and fair is not. Avarice and usury and precaution must be our gods for a little longer still. (Keynes 1930: 372)

Yet a system in which such traits are positively incentivized is likely to be dominated by them. Is there no alternative to acquiescing in the idolatry of that dominant system?

A firm ethical principle, assumed throughout this book, is that human beings are under a collective imperative to find a way of organizing globally so as to fulfil the demands of social justice, ecological sustainability, and peace. Political philosophers already deliberate about how exactly these demands should be understood and interpreted, with such matters being standing items on the agenda of research. What has been foregrounded here is the need to identify, at a certain level of determinacy, the factors in the world that militate against fulfilment of the principles, on any reasonable interpretation of what more exactly they entail. Thus the criticisms of liberalism found in this book have not been directed against the humanistic moral principles that some of its adherents emphasize.[1] In fact,

[1] There is an established tradition of thought that sees continuity between liberal values and socialism, whose representatives include Brian Barry, Norberto Bobbio, G. A. Cohen, Norman Daniels, and C. B. Macpherson; in fact, both John Rawls and John Stuart Mill were accommodating of socialist perspectives in their liberal theories.

those principles are by no means tied to an understanding of the world framed in terms of liberal political economy or liberal international relations theory.

If ethical principles require a certain firmness of conviction and a corresponding readiness to engage in thorough criticism of institutional arrangements that compromise them, reflecting on how they might be actualized requires a certain epistemic caution. In particular, one should recognize not only the potential limits of particular proposals to do good but also the ways in which such proposals might unintentionally promote harm.

Regarding the limits to the good that political philosophers can hope to do, due intellectual humility commends recognition of the likelihood that the impetus and momentum necessary for change might come not from the affluent West but from the Global South. Real transformation towards global justice might depend on mass mobilization, internationally, *from below*. That is not in the gift of a political philosopher to deliver, and insofar as one can aim to frame theory in the service of those who organize for change, it could be useful to think in terms of how movements around the world can coalesce into a critical mass. Given that there may be limits to what those of us who live in the affluent West can even understand about the nature and extent of the needed transformation, we also need to be aware of the risks of misdirected help. For example, as noted in Chapters 5 and 6, proposals based on a supposition that those in a globally advantageous position can leverage a little effort to achieve a great deal for the mass of the worst off depend on asymmetries in circumstances and life chances that global justice depends on eliminating rather than utilizing. As for the risks of misdirected humanitarian help, these are especially acute when assistance is proposed for delivery by means of military intervention. In this matter, Chapter 11 showed very serious reasons for scrupulous caution rather than precipitate action.

Potential unintended harms to be aware of include those that could be attendant on a premature dissolution of powers of political states. This is where the difference between cosmopolitanism, moral and political, becomes critical. From an anticipatory perspective of global justice, it is conceivable that the organizing of political agents within a state, on a genuinely progressive basis, could be a step towards building wider coalitions internationally. Certainly, while progress towards global justice may ultimately imply transcending the constraints of nation-states, their dissolution can only be part of a cosmopolitan process if it is accompanied by the creation of a new institutional order. It may be morally progressive for individuals to see themselves as 'global citizens', but in political reality it misses a fundamental pre-requisite of actual global citizenship, namely, membership of a global collectivity that is organized as such.[2] There is particular

[2] Wolfgang Streeck captures part of the thought here:'Socialist politics requires and is possible only in collectivities that have a capacity to make effective demands on their members. In the modern world, such collectivities are organized as states that draw their moral authority from being democratic. While socialists must be, and are, willing to find a place in society for communities other than states, socialism has been and continues to be intricately bound up with statehood...' (Streeck 2017: 149).

reason for caution about acquiescence in the dissolution of state sovereignty when the result risks allowing a further concentration of power in the hands of an unaccountable globalist elite. This is not to imply an exalted view of the state as an ideal or to foster any illusions about the reality of how states can be repressive apparatuses that serve the interests of the elite over the people. It is simply to recognize that if the state would need to be a site of *struggle* against elite domination, it at least may be the *possible* site of one.[3] In fact, what is meant by 'the state', and what new forms of organization may be possible, are questions open for debate. Certainly, 'liberal states' should not be regarded as a definitive or morally exemplary form of government, especially given what follows from being premised on de facto acceptance of the workings of liberal political economy and liberal international relations. States can only play a progressive role under conditions prevailing now insofar as they are *not* beholden to transnational capital, and that is why I have cited examples of *resistant*, and especially *socialist*, states as being potentially progressive. John O'Neill (*forthcoming*) has rightly cautioned against exaggerating the promise of the 'peoples of resistance', particularly given that their domestic politics and economic policies may not be exemplary or progressive in other respects. But their example does serve to demonstrate the immensity of the challenge involved in resisting the powerful and hostile forces that appear to underpin the normative arrangements of the privatized global constitution—for they have been targets of wars, sanctions, interventions, and coups. Thus the cosmopolitan impulse to support steps towards the dissolution of borders would prudently be tempered by awareness that the primary beneficiaries of such a process, under the current global system, are likely to be those whose economic position is based on the most mobile factors of production—that is, those who command capital rather than the classes of those who depend for their livelihood on their labour or *a fortiori* on land. Unless and until there is a clear alternative in prospect, the risk is of a dissolution of state powers into a privatized globalist monopoly dominated by the interests of capital, and especially financial capital, whose mobility in time and space knows no meaningful limits.

Having thus established a need for due awareness of the harms one can risk being complicit in, as well as of the limits to the extent or directness of the contribution of good one may do, one can then consider possible avenues of constructive thought. There may be lessons to learn not only from distant others

[3] See also Lea Ypi on the conception of a 'statist cosmopolitanism' that is intended to avoid the pitfalls of both a 'civil society' model (with its abstract unrooted universalism) and a 'nationalist' model (with is excessive cultural particularism) of how political obligations are generated: 'When enforcing political obligations, citizens can legitimately constrain the activities of fellow-members and act collectively to reform particular political institutions so as to align them with cosmopolitan goals. Where this kind of political action has been successful, it is possible to continuously support cosmopolitanism and maintain a stable political association by relying on historical and cultural practices developed among community members. There is no guarantee that political agents will succeed in establishing a cosmopolitan order globally promoting justice. But by identifying in the political community the most relevant associative context for the allocation of cosmopolitan obligations they will at least have set the parameters for such a struggle' (Ypi 2008: 71).

who are our contemporaries, but also from those who have gone before, as well as from those who are already starting to shape the world of the future.

In thinking about more just ways in which finance might be organized, some insights are to be found in earlier debates. The general question of how finance can work in the service of society as a whole has been considered in various contexts in the past. John O'Neill points out that some salient themes—including concerns about the spatial and temporal mobility of finance—were already being debated in the seventeenth and eighteenth centuries.[4] More specific investigations of radical alternatives to a capitalist economy are to be found in the socialist calculation debates between the first two World Wars.[5] Otto Neurath, for instance, put forward ideas for a socialist economy which, oriented only to the use value of goods, 'would be a non-market economy, an *in natura* "economy in kind" lacking monetary units to compare the different uses of productive goods. Indeed a socialized economy would have no need for a single unit of comparison' (O'Neill *forthcoming*). Related ideas formed the basis of the practical experimentation of Che Guevara as Minister of Finance in 1960s Cuba with his budgetary finance system (Yaffe 2009, 2012). Such ideas have of course met with objections in principle and problems in practice, and yet consideration of these could still lead to the development of new insights, particularly if in conjunction with awareness of how new technologies might make possible the organizing of finance in ways that track valued substantive goals rather than relying on market price signals as proxies.[6]

The technological possibilities for organizing finance in the future could be of a scope that is beyond our current imaginings, but it is readily conceivable that they might relieve certain constraints on non-monetary economies or create innovative forms of money more conducive than current prevalent forms to the pursuit of valuable social goals. For instance, if a major objection to socialist economics is that planning is more bureaucratic and less efficient than relying on price signals in markets, then an answer might be found in information technology; or if the objection to a more decentralized system is that it would lack the necessary coordination, this might also find some solution in forms of technological integration. Joseph Stiglitz has already proposed augmenting market price signals by 'information economics', but more radical proposals might draw on forms of coordination based on modern information technology for non-market socialism that involve economic planning in terms of physical units without any

[4] 'They are expressed in the memorable phrase of one of the defenders of the new financial order, Defoe, where he notes the complaint made of the new world of finance and public credit: "it has no Whereness, or Whenness, Scite, or Habit" (Defoe 1710)' (O'Neill, *forthcoming*). For further discussion see also Sherman (1996) and Mitchell (2008).

[5] For an overview from a particularly relevant perspective see O'Neill (2002) and O'Neill and Uebel (2018).

[6] Guevara, according to his companion Fidel Castro 'used to dream of using information technology to gauge economic efficiency under socialism and saw this as essential' (Habel 1991: 47).

reference to money or prices. Huckle and White (2016), for instance, have explored the possibilities of utilizing blockchain technology for purposes of socialist organization.[7] This and future kinds of technology, as they further develop, and assuming they can be made more energy efficient (Yli-Huumo et al. 2016), could potentially give practical purchase to a fundamental rethinking about the very social purpose of finance and investment. They could even support the possibility of thinking 'beyond money'.

So there is considerable scope for imaginative and innovative thinking, but it does need to be harnessed to the service of a clear ethical goal and informed by a robust empirical awareness of the forces that might annul potentially successful attempts to reach that goal. For the system that currently militates against global justice itself thrives on imaginative and innovative thinking. It has been emphasized in this book that social institutions and the technological forms of their operation are not neutral with respect to the possibility of pursuing alternative social goals, so that a system oriented to supporting private profit-making cannot necessarily be adapted to supporting the pursuit of public goods. This means that any innovation that can take hold within the system is usually likely to be functional for the system, even if it can be presented as oriented to other goals of a more publicly oriented ethic. Sometimes, however, a new technology can be sufficiently 'disruptive' that it threatens to be dysfunctional for the system and potentially supportive of an ethically attractive alternative. This, arguably, is the case with the internet and social media insofar as they have facilitated a dissemination of knowledge and ideas that can be radically challenging to the institutions that are invested in the status quo; it could be the case with crypto-currencies; and there are far more technological innovations than I am aware of that could potentially be harnessed to ethically attractive goals. If and when real challenges arise, however, a strong reactive response can be expected. Thus, at the time of writing one sees a marked reaction to the democratization of knowledge on social media in the form of a new programme of censorship and suppression that rivals the anti-democratic extremes of the McCarthy era. The 'chilling effect' of this is to encourage critical thinkers to 'rein in' their criticisms of the ruling order and internalize an understanding that to engage in a more than modest challenge is a risky business. The deep effect of this is to render increasingly *unthinkable* the possibility that the world's institutions could be radically different—or at least

[7] Blockchain, although initially developed as the architecture for the Bitcoin system, is essentially a database that serves as a public ledger that people can use to record transactions without reference to any money system. Decentralized public ledgers, collectively maintained by networks of participants, have conceivable applications with momentous implications. They can store all manner of diverse data, including property titles, contracts, shares, voting decisions, or even reputation scores (Scott 2016b: 11). They can support *smart contracts*, whereby the execution of a contract can be linked to data from some external source and used to build complex multi-stage contracts that handle a range of different agreements and contingencies (Swan 2015).

different in a better way, rather than in the very much worse way that can happen in consequence of military interventions.

Ultimately, what is vital in our age, as in any other, and even if it is not alone sufficient, is a clear ethical vision. Questions about what exact steps need to be taken to bring the world closer to its realization may be complex and uncertain; fine-grained proposals for fairer distributive arrangements globally may be somewhat premature: what can nonetheless be held fast to are the basic ethical ideals of global justice. These can be alluded to in a variety of idioms, but in the contemporary context it is the idiom of human rights—as this is interpreted in the terms of moral purpose as it is by Shue (1996), for instance—that stands as a touchstone for challenging any proposals for social organization that depend on allowing the rights of private property to take precedence (Hayward 2013). Holding fast to these ideals allows a critical perspective to be endowed with a clear ethical direction. This book has shown how the current order of institutions globally systematically tends to prioritize private property claims over the fulfilment—as opposed to the ideological proclamation—of basic human rights. It has developed a critical view of how the global financial system incorporates sophisticated arrangements for transforming the tangible assets of the world into financial representations that can then be appropriated by the market actors with greatest power and skills. With the liberalization of financial markets and the untethering of the global monetary system, money as produced by financial innovation has the character of *securitized futurity*. When expectations of future profits are marketed as present values, there is no real limit to the amount of debt-claims on people's future commitments that can be created. Yet the indebtedness that is enforced by law and social obligation has real effects on the people bound by it. This has been the experience of people in the Global South who have contested the imposition of what they describe as *odious* debt repayments by advancing the counterclaim that those pursuing the financial debt in fact owe a far greater *ecological debt*. The idea of an *ecological debt* of rich industrialized countries to the poorer countries from which they have extracted resources is a moral counterweight to the financial debt that the dominant institutions have contrived to impose. The idea of an *ecological* debt, as noted in Chapter 4, refers not only to a reversed moral polarity—who owes whom?—but also to a different kind of ontological consideration about *what* is owed and *why*. You cannot eat money, you cannot build homes or repair ecological damage with money, and you cannot truly compensate for death or injury with money. Yet those who control the production of money and the form it is supplied in, have extraordinary power over others. The point is to find ways for people to take back that power. This means not simply trying to get fairer shares in that problematic system—which is liable to become an increasingly forlorn undertaking for all of us if the current trajectory continues—it means getting a fairer system.

In a fairer system, access to the world's natural resources and the return on people's labour would be equitable globally; inequalities that meant some human beings had insufficient access to the necessities of a minimally decent life would be treated as unjust and unacceptable. At root, as members of the same species on the same planet, and given minimal assumptions about reasonableness and reciprocity characterizing our species being, each of us has the same presumptive right as every other to access at least that basic minimum. A way of thinking about humanity as a differentiated collectivity in relation to the material realities of our planet is in terms of access to ecological space. This general concept refers to the totality of the biophysical world that we all—individually and jointly—depend on and form part of. Human relationships with regard to ecological space can be described in terms of its use, occupation, and command (Hayward 2016a). In activities of production and consumption human beings *use* the ecological space from which the particular materials are drawn, and into which by-products are returned. Through the political assertion of territorial claims, groups of people—for example nations or corporations—are able to *occupy* vectors of ecological space, without necessarily using them, but with the power to exclude others from using them, or to charge a rent for their use. The *command* of ecological space is a higher order power to determine who is to be recognized as having the right to occupy any given vector, or, ultimately, any ecological space at all. That kind of power, I have argued in this book, is exercised globally at the highest levels of organized finance. This is something that those whose land and livelihoods are expropriated by international financial institutions and associated corporations see very clearly.

Hence global justice and finance, as finance is currently organized in the world today, stand in a worryingly antithetical relationship to each other. Questions of how ecological space gets used are of no inherent significance financially, and questions of tangible economic productivity are of relative indifference from the perspective of financial control, as has amply been noted in the course of this book. So fundamentally important matters regarding humans' relationship with the natural world are matters of indifference to the world of global finance. Still less is there a concern from that quarter about questions of distributive justice with respect to whether or how the benefits of economic use are equitably shared. Hence some of the most fundamental concerns of humans' social relations with each other are matters of indifference to the world of global finance. Add to this the worrying relationship of finance to war, and it is reasonable to conclude that the things that most directly and vitally matter to real human beings are matters of indifference from the perspective of the global financial system. Finance under the current system treats ecological and human realities as inconsequential while attaching value to concatenations of promises derived from promises that may in reality never be redeemed.

By adopting a perspective of collective humanity one can step back and see the bigger picture and how it could be different under conditions of more tangible human solidarity. From that perspective it appears quite evident how, under the present global regime, the forces of production—namely, the constituents of ecological space and the human bearers of labour power—are under a system of ownership and control that is harmful to them. The pursuit of profit answers to no real need, human or natural; it drives devastating harms. It needs to be excised. An orientation to ethical goals entails a sense of proportion as between real human concerns and the distribution of financial assets.

If we think in simple and quite tangible terms, it is clear how a shift in the balance of power could be brought about. What is required is a global upending of the situation in which eight individuals weigh in the financial balance against 3,500,000,000 people: the financial system needs to be constrained to track more realistically the sense of proportion to be discerned in the natural order of things. A rough equality of every human being is, after all, what talk of human rights presupposes. Since the financial system is essentially a concatenation of legal contracts, the terms of those contracts could be radically altered were a legal system so to be empowered by a political system with the will that it be done. The challenge, viewed as a normative objective of global justice, is to supplant the current implicit and private constitution that facilitates the rule of finance globally by arrangements whose immanent purpose is to support the achievement of justice, sustainability, and peace. Such arrangements are unlikely to come about from modest reform to existing institutions, but they could be forged through processes that support the constituting, as a self-ruling collectivity, of the people of this planet.

Bibliography

Abramsky, Joshua and Drew, Steve (2014) 'Changes to National Accounts: Inclusion of Illegal Drugs and Prostitution in the UK National Accounts', Office for National Statistics, 29 May 2014.

Acción Ecológica (2000) *Trade, climate change and the ecological debt*, Quito: Acción Ecológica.

Adrian, Tobias and Shin, Hyun Song (2010) 'Liquidity and Leverage', *Journal of Financial Intermediation*, 19: 418–37.

Agence France Presse (2012) 'U.S. wants to "close down the Central Bank of Iran" over nuclear concerns', National Post, 12 January 2012: https://nationalpost.com/news/u-s-wants-to-close-down-the-central-bank-of-iran-over-nuclear-concerns [accessed August 2018].

Ahmed, Nafeez (2013) 'Syria intervention plan fueled by oil interests, not chemical weapon concern', The Guardian, 30 August.

al-Hourani, Abdelrahman and Clark, Justin (2016) 'In rebel controlled Idlib regime schools continue to operate alongside opposition alternatives' *Syrian Voice* 23 October: http://syrianvoice.org/en/archives/1379 [accessed August 2018].

al-Saadi, Yazan (2014) 'Syria, storytelling, and all things between: a meta-commentary on "the Prisoner Series"', *openDemocracy*, 30 May: https://www.opendemocracy.net/north-africa-west-asia/yazan-alsaadi/syria-storytelling-and-all-things-between-metacommentary-on-%E2%80%98-prisoner- [accessed August 2018].

al-Saadi, Yazan (2018) 'Irony, irrelevance, paradox, and hypocrisy in arguing over Syria', *Muftah*, 6 May: https://muftah.org/irony-irrelevance-paradox-hypocrisy-in-arguing-over-syria/#.W-VfmHr7TIE [accessed August 2018].

Allday, Louis (2016) 'Controlling the Narrative', *MR Online*, 13 December: https://mronline.org/2016/12/13/allday131216-html/ [accessed 2 February 2019].

Ansar, Atif, Caldecott, Ben, and Tilbury, James (2013) 'Stranded assets and the fossil fuel divestment campaign: what does divestment mean for the valuation of fossil fuel assets?' Smith School of Enterprise and the Environment University of Oxford, Oxford.

Armstrong, Chris (2012) *Global Distributive Justice: An Introduction*, Cambridge: Cambridge University Press.

Armstrong, Chris (2015) 'Distributive Institutions', in Darrel Moellendorf and Heather Widdows (eds), *The Routledge Handbook of Global Ethics*, New York: Routledge.

Attkisson, Sharyl (2017) *The Smear: How Shady Political Operatives and Fake News Control What You See, What You Think, and How You Vote*, London: HarperCollins.

Averre, Derek and Davies, Lance (2015) 'Russia, Humanitarian Intervention and the Responsibility to Protect: the Case of Syria', *International Affairs*, 91(4): 813–34.

Baker, Raymond (2007) 'Illicit Financial Flows and their Impact on Development', Remarks delivered at a meeting convened by Norway at the UN, 23 October: https://www.gfintegrity.org/press-release/illicit-financial-flows-impact-development/ [accessed August 2018].

Bakir, V., Herring, E., Miller, D. and Robinson, P. (2018) 'Organized Persuasive Communication: A New Conceptual Framework for Research on Public Relations, Propaganda and Promotional Culture', *Critical Sociology*, OnlineFirst: https://doi.org/10.1177/0896920518764586.

Ballard, Richard (2013) 'Geographies of Development II: Cash Transfers and the Reinvention of Development for the Poor', *Progress in Human Geography*, 37(6): 811–21.

Barry, Brian (1982) 'Humanity and Justice in Global Perspective', *Nomos*, 24: 219–52.

Barry, Christian and Øverland, Gerhard (2009) 'Responding to Global Poverty: Review Essay of Peter Singer, *The Life you can Save*', *Bioethical Inquiry*, 6: 239–47.

Basham, Lee (2016) 'The Need for Accountable Witnesses: A Reply to Dentith', *Social Epistemology Review and Reply Collective*, 5(7): 6–13.

Basham, Lee (2018) 'Joining the Conspiracy', *Argumenta*, 3(2): 271–91.

Beitz, Charles R. (1979) *Political Theory and International Relations*, Cambridge: Cambridge University Press.

Bellingcat (2018) 'Open Source Survey of Alleged Chemical Attacks in Douma on 7th April 2018', Bellingcat blog 11 April: https://www.bellingcat.com/news/mena/2018/04/11/open-source-survey-alleged-chemical-attacks-douma-7th-april-2018/ [accessed August 2018].

Bentham, Justin et al. (2013) 'Manifesto For The Foundational Economy', CRESC Working Paper 131 Centre for Research on Socio-Cultural Change, University of Manchester and Open University.

Bernays, Edward (2004 [1928]) Propaganda, New York: Ig Books.

Bessi, A., Coletto, M., Davidescu, G. A., Scala, A., Caldarelli, G., and Quattrociocchi, W. (2015) 'Science vs Conspiracy: Collective Narratives in the Age of Misinformation', *PLoS ONE*, 10(2): 1–16.

Birner, Jack (2012) 'If Bad Money is a Collective Bad, Isn't Good Money a Collective Good? *Corvinus Journal of Sociology and Social Policy*, 3(2): 3–38.

Black, Christopher (2018) 'Operation Barbarossa II Update: The Battle Will be Everywhere', *New Eastern Outlook*, 27 April: https://journal-neo.org/2018/04/27/operation-barbarossa-ii-update-the-battle-will-be-everywhere/

Blair, Tony (2001a) 'Confidential and Personal for the President', memo from Downing Street 11 October: http://webarchive.nationalarchives.gov.uk/20171123122709/http://www.iraqinquiry.org.uk/media/243721/2001-10-11-letter-blair-to-bush-untitled.pdf [accessed August 2018].

Blair, Tony (2001b) 'The War Against Terrorism: The Second Phase', Top Secret and Personal, 4 December: http://news.bbc.co.uk/1/shared/bsp/hi/pdfs/06_07_2016_memo4dec01.pdf [accessed August 2018].

Blumenthal, Max (2017) 'The Murder of Seven White Helmets in Syria', *The Real News Network*, August 30: https://therealnews.com/stories/mblumenthal0824helmets

Bowman, Andrew et al. (2013) 'Central Bank-Led Capitalism?', *Seattle University Law Review*, 36: 455–87.

Boyle, Francis (2012) 'Amnesty International: Imperialist Tool', SSRN: https://ssrn.com/abstract=2324944 [accessed September 2018].

Boyle, Francis (2013) *Destroying Libya and World Order*, Atlanta, GA: Clarity Press.

Bradshaw, Samantha and Howard, Philip (2017) 'Troops, Trolls and Troublemakers: A Global Inventory of Organized Social Media Manipulation', Computational Propaganda Research Project Working Paper 2017/12, University of Oxford: https://ora.ox.ac.uk/objects/uuid:cef7e8d9-27bf-4ea5-9fd6-855209b3e1f6 [accessed August 2018].

Breslin, Shaun (2013) 'China and the Global Order: Signalling Threat or Friendship?' *International Affairs*, 89(3): 615–34.

Brock, Gillian (2008) 'Taxation and Global Justice: Closing the Gap between Theory and Practice', *Journal of Social Philosophy*, 39, 161–84.
Brock, Gillian (2015) 'What Burden Should Fiscal Policy Bear in Fighting Global Injustice?' in H. P. Gaisbauer, G. Schweiger, and C. Sedmak, (eds), *Philosophical Explorations of Justice and Taxation, Ius Gentium: Comparative Perspectives on Law and Justice*, Dordrecht: Springer International Publishing: 185–201.
Brock, Gillian and Pogge, Thomas (2014) 'Global Tax Justice and Global Justice', *Moral Philosophy and Politics*, 1(1): doi:10.1515/mopp-2014-0999.
Broome, John (2008) 'The Ethics of Climate Change'. *Scientific American*, 298: 96–102.
Brown, Ellen (2011) 'Libya all about Oil, or Central Banking?' Asia Times, 14 April.
Buffachi, Vittorio (2009) 'Not Making Exceptions: A Response to Shue', *Journal of Applied Philosophy*, 26(3): 329–35.
Campbell, Horace (2013) *Global NATO and the Catastrophic Failure in Libya*, New York: Monthly Review Press.
Caney, Simon (2005) *Justice Beyond Borders*, Oxford: Oxford University Press.
Caney, Simon (2006) 'Global Justice: From Theory to Practice', *Globalizations*, 3, 121–37.
Caney, Simon (2009) 'Climate Change and the Future: Discounting for Time, Wealth, and Risk', *Journal of Social Philosophy*, 40(2): 163–86.
Caney, Simon (2011) 'Justice and the Distribution of Greenhouse Gas Emissions', in H. Widdows, and N. J. Smith (eds), *Global Social Justice*, Abingdon: Taylor & Francis.
Cappelen, Alexander W. (2001) 'The moral rationale for international fiscal law', Ethics & International Affairs, 15: 97–110.
Carney, John (2011) 'Libyan Rebels Form Their Own Central Bank', *CNBC* 28 March: https://www.cnbc.com/id/42308613
Carney, Mark (2015) 'Breaking the Tragedy of the Horizon–climate change and financial stability', Speech at Lloyd's of London 29 September, London: Bank of England.
Casal, Paula (2011) 'Global Taxes on Natural Resources', *Journal of Moral Philosophy*, 8: 307–27.
CFI Media Development (2015) 'Aleppo Media Center set to launch its radio station in northern Syria': https://www.cfi.fr/en/news/aleppo-media-center-set-launch-its-radio-station-northern-syria [accessed September 2018].
Charap Samuel (2013) 'Russia, Syria and the Doctrine of Intervention', *Survival*, 55(1): 35–41.
Chomsky, Noam (1991) *Deterring Democracy*, London: Verso Books.
Chonghaile, Clár Ní (2016) '"A system of privilege and benefits": Is a Global Tax Body Needed?' The Guardian, 11 April: https://www.theguardian.com/global-development/2016/apr/11/system-privilege-benefits-global-tax-body-oecd.
Christophers, Brett (2017) 'Climate Change and Financial Instability: Risk Disclosure and the Problematics of Neoliberal Governance', *Annals of the American Association of Geographers*, 107(5): 1108–27.
Clark, Wesley (2007) Interviewed by Amy Goodman for *Democracy Now!*, video and transcript: https://www.democracynow.org/2007/3/2/gen_wesley_clark_weighs_presidential_bid [accessed September 2018].
Clark, William R. (2005) *Petrodollar Warfare: Oil, Iraq and the Future of the Dollar*, Gabriola Island: New Society Publishers.
Clarke, John and Newman, Janet (2012) 'The Alchemy of Austerity', Critical Social Policy, 32(3): 299–319.
Clinton, Hillary (2010) 'Previewing The Obama Administration's National Security Strategy: a conversation with Secretary of State Hillary Clinton', The Brookings Institution,

Washington, DC: https://www.brookings.edu/wp-content/uploads/2012/04/20100527_national_security_strategy.pdf [accessed August 2018].

Clinton, Hillary (2014) *Hard Choices*, New York: Simon & Shuster.

Coady, David (2007) 'Are Conspiracy Theorists Irrational?' *Episteme*, 4(2), 193–204.

Coady, David (2018) 'Cass Sunstein and Adrian Vermeule on Conspiracy Theories', *Argumenta*, 3(2): 291–302.

Coleman, Isobel (2014) 'Segovia: A New Player in Cash Transfers' Council on Foreign Relations https://www.cfr.org/blog/segovia-new-player-cash-transfers [accessed August 2018].

Commons, John R. (1931) 'Institutional Economics', *The American Economic Review*, 21: 648–57.

Costanza, Robert et al. (1997) 'The Value of the World's Ecosystem Services and Natural Capital', *Nature*, 387: 253–60.

Cotterill, Joseph (2011) 'The Central Bank of Benghazi', Financial Times, 23 March.

Crabtree, Susan (2013) 'US intel on Syria no "slam dunk"', *Washington Examiner*, 29 August: https://www.washingtonexaminer.com/report-us-intel-on-syria-no-slam-dunk/article/2534880 [accessed August 2018].

Curtis, Mark (2003) *Web of Deceit: Britain's Real Role in the World*, New York: Random House.

Curtis, Mark (2018) *Secret Affairs: Britain's Collusion with Radical Islam*, updated edition, London: Serpent's Tail.

Cutler, Kim-Mai (2015) 'With Reid Hoffman's Backing, Development Economists Build Segovia, A Startup That Tackles Poverty', TechCrunch: (http://techcrunch.com/2015/10/01/segovia/).

Das, Satyajit (2017) 'Negative Feelings', *Wilmott*, 89: 20–5.

Davidson, Christopher (2016) *Shadow Wars: The Secret Struggle for the Middle East*, London: Oneworld Publications.

Davidson, Christopher (2017) 'Why was Muannmar Qadhafi Really Removed?' *Middle East Policy*, 24(4): 91–116.

De Wispelaere, Jurgen and Stirton, Lindsay (2004) 'The Many Faces of Universal Basic Income', *The Political Quarterly*, 75(3): 266–74.

De Wispelaere, Jurgen and Stirton, Lindsay (2007) 'The Public Administration Case against Participation Income', *Social Service Review*, 81(3): 523–49.

De Wispelaere, Jurgen and Stirton, Lindsay (2012) 'A Disarmingly Simple Idea? Practical Bottlenecks in the Implementation of a Universal Basic Income', *International Social Security Review*, 65(2): 103-21.

Defence IQ Press (2015) 'The New Verbal Battlespace where "Weaponised Words" and Information Operations Meet', *Defence IQ*, 2 October: https://www.defenceiq.com/defence-technology/articles/the-new-verbal-battlespace-where-weaponised-words

Defoe Daniel (1710) 'An Essay upon Publick Credit'. Available at: http://quod.lib.umich.edu/e/ecco/004843879.0001.000/1:3?rgn=div1;view=fulltext

deHaven Smith, Lance (2013) *Conspiracy Theory in America*, Austin, TX: University of Texas Press.

Dentith, Matthew (2016a) 'When Inferring to a Conspiracy might be the Best Explanation', *Social Epistemology A Journal of Knowledge, Culture and Policy*, 30(5-6): 572–91.

Dentith, Matthew (2016b) 'Treating Conspiracy Theories Seriously: A Reply to Basham on Dentith', *Social Epistemology Review and Reply Collective*, 5(9): 1–5.

Dentith, Matthew (2017) 'The Problem of Conspiracism', *Argumenta*, 5: 1–17.

Dequech, David (2007) 'Neoclassical, Mainstream, Orthodox, and Heterodox Economics', *Journal of Post Keynesian Economics*, 30(2): 279–302.

Dershowitz, Alan (2002) *Why Terrorism Works: Understanding the Threat, Responding to the Challenge*, New Haven, CT: Yale University Press.

Desch, Michael C. (2008) 'America's Liberal Illiberalism', *International Security*, 32(3): 7–43.

Dietsch, Peter and Rixen, Thomas (2014a) 'Tax Competition and Global Background Justice', *The Journal of Political Philosophy*, 22(2): 150–77.

Dietsch, Peter and Rixen, Thomas (2014b) 'Redistribution, Globalisation, and Multi-level Governance', *Moral Philosophy and Politics*, 1: 61–81.

Dillard, Dudley (1987) 'Money as an Institution of Capitalism', *Journal of Economic Issues*, 21(4): 1623–47.

Dinan, W. and Miller, D. (eds) (2007) *Thinker, Faker, Spinner, Spy: Corporate PR and the Assault on Democracy*, London: Pluto Press.

DiResta, Renee (2018) 'How The Tech Giants Created What Darpa Couldn't', *Wired* 29 May: https://www.wired.com/story/darpa-total-informatio-awareness/ [accessed August 2018].

Douglas, Karen and Sutton, Robbie (2011) 'Does it Take One to Know One? Endorsement of Conspiracy Theories is Influenced by Personal Willingness to Conspire', *Psychology*, 50(3): 544–52.

Doyle, Michael W. (2005) 'Three Pillars of the Liberal Peace', *American Political Science Review*, 99(3): 463–6.

Dworkin, Ronald (1981) 'What is Equality? Part 2: Equality of Resources', *Philosophy & Public Affairs*, 10: 283–345.

Enab Baladi (2017) 'Idlib Electricity War: The Regime is Providing it and Hayat Tahrir Al-Sham and Ahrar Al-Sham are Cutting it off' *Enab Baladi* 20 June: https://english.enabbaladi.net/archives/2017/06/idlib-electricity-war-regime-providing-hayat-tahrir-al-sham-ahrar-al-sham-cutting-off/ [accessed August 2018].

Essers, Dennis (2013) 'Developing country vulnerability in light of the global financial crisis: Shock therapy?', *Review of Development Finance*, 3: 61–83.

Farrington, John and Slater, Rachel (2006) 'Introduction: Cash Transfers: Panacea for Poverty Reduction or Money Down the Drain?' *Development Policy Review*, 24: 499–511.

Faye, Michael and Niehaus, Paul (2015) 'Ending Poverty with Electronic Payments', Policy Brief for Blum Roundtable, Brookings Institution, Washington, DC: https://www.brookings.edu/research/brookings-blum-roundtable-policy-briefs/ [accessed August 2018].

Forstater, Maya (2015) 'Can Stopping "Tax Dodging"By Multinational Enterprises Close the Gap in Finance for Development?' CGD Policy Paper 69, Washington, DC: Center for Global Development.

Forte, Maximilian (2011) 'The Top Ten Myths in the War Against Libya', *Counterpunch* 31 August: https://www.counterpunch.org/2011/08/31/the-top-ten-myths-in-the-war-against-libya/ [accessed August 2018].

Fukuyama, Francis (1992) *The End of History and the Last Man*, New York: Free Press.

Fukuyama, Francis (2004) 'The Neoconservative Moment', *The National Interest*, 76: 57–68.

Galbraith, James K. (2012) *Inequality and Instability: A Study of the World Economy Just Before the Great Crisis*, Oxford: Oxford University Press.

Gelb, Alan and Decker, Caroline (2012) 'Cash at Your Fingertips: Biometric Technology for Transfers in Developing Countries', *Review of Policy Research*, 29(1): 91–117.

Gilligan, Carol (1982) *In A Different Voice*, Cambridge, MA: Harvard University Press.

Glazer, J. Henry (1957) 'A Functional Approach to the International Finance Corporation', *Columbia Law Review*, 57(8): 1089–112.

Goeminne, Gert and Paredis, Erik (2010) 'The Concept of Ecological Debt: Some Steps towards an Enriched Sustainability Paradigm', *Environment, Development and Sustainability*, 12: 691–712.

Goodhart, Charles and Meade, Ellen (2004) 'Central Banks and Supreme Courts', *Moneda y Crédito* 218: 11–59.

Gorst, Anthony and Lucas, W. Scott (1989) 'The Other Collusion: Operation Straggle and Anglo-American Intervention in Syria, 1955–56', *Intelligence and National Security*, 4(3): 576–95.

Gosztola, Kevin (2017) 'Advocates for Syrian Rebels Convince Student Group to Cancel Event with Journalist Rania Khalek', *Shadow Proof*, 27 February: https://shadowproof.com/2017/02/27/advocates-syrian-rebels-convince-student-group-cancel-event-journalist-rania-khalek/

Gowans, Stephen (2017) *Washington's Long War on Syria*, Quebec: Independent Publishers Group.

Greenwald, Glenn (2014) 'How Covert Agents Infiltrate the Internet to Manipulate, Deceive, and Destroy Reputations', *The Intercept*, 24 February: https://theintercept.com/2014/02/24/jtrig-manipulation/ [accessed August 2018].

Greenwald, Glenn and Fishman, Andrew (2015) 'Controversial GCHQ Unit Engaged in Domestic Law Enforcement', *The Intercept*, 22 June: https://theintercept.com/2015/06/22/controversial-gchq-unit-domestic-law-enforcement-propaganda/ [accessed August 2018].

Griffin, David Ray (2011) *Cognitive Infiltration: An Obama Appointee's Plan to Undermine the 9/11 Conspiracy Theory*, Northampton MA: Olive Branch Press.

Habel, Janette (1991) *Cuba: The Revolution in Peril*, London: Verso.

Hagen, Kurtis (2010) 'Is Infiltration of "Extremist Groups" Justified?', *International Journal of Applied Philosophy*, 24(2): 153–68.

Hagen, Kurtis (2011) 'Review of David Ray Griffin's *Cognitive Infiltration*', *Florida Philosophical Review*, 21(1): 66–8.

Hagen, Kurtis (2018) 'Conspiracy Theories and the Paranoid Style: Do Conspiracy Theories Posit Implausibly Vast and Evil Conspiracies?' *Social Epistemology*, 32(1): 24–40.

Hall, Anthony (2008) 'Brazil's Bolsa Família: A Double-Edged Sword?' *Development and Change*, 39: 799–822.

Hardin, Garrett (1968) 'The Tragedy of the Commons', *Science*, 162(3859): 1243–8.

Hardin, Russell (2002) 'The Crippled Epistemology of Extremism', in A. Breton, G. Galeotti, P. Salmon, and R. Wintrobe (eds), *Political Extremism and Rationality*, Cambridge: Cambridge University Press.

Hardt, Michael and Negri, Antonio (2004) *Multitude: War and Democracy in the Age of Empire*, New York: Penguin Books.

Harvey, David (2005) *A Brief History of Neoliberalism*, Oxford: Oxford University Press.

Hayek, F. A. (1990) *Denationalisation of Money—The Argument Refined*, 3rd edn, London: The Institute of Economic Affairs.

Hayward, Tim (1992) 'Ecology and Human Emancipation', *Radical Philosophy*, 62: 3–13.

Hayward, Tim (1995) *Ecological Thought: An Introduction*, Cambridge: Polity Press.

Hayward, Tim (1998) *Political Theory and Ecological Values*, Cambridge: Polity Press.

Hayward, Tim (2005) *Constitutional Environmental Rights*, Oxford: Oxford University Press.

Hayward, Tim (2008) 'On the Nature of Our Debt to the Global Poor', *Journal of Social Philosophy*, 39(1): 1–19.
Hayward, Tim (2009) 'International Political Theory and the Global Environment: Some Critical Questions for Liberal Cosmopolitans', *Journal of Social Philosophy*, 40(2): 276–95.
Hayward, Tim (2013) 'Human Rights vs Property Rights', Just World Institute Working Paper No. 2013/04. Available at SSRN: https://ssrn.com/abstract=2461207 or http://dx.doi.org/10.2139/ssrn.2461207
Hayward, Tim (2016a) 'Ecological Space: The Concept and its ethical significance', in Steve Gardiner and Allen Thompson (eds), *Oxford Handbook of Environmental Ethics*, Oxford: Oxford University Press.
Hayward, Tim (2016b) 'How We Were Misled about Syria: the Role of Médecins Sans Frontières (MSF)', Wordpress blog: https://timhayward.wordpress.com/2016/12/30/truth-a-casualty-neglected-by-medicins-sans-frontieres-msf-in-syria/
Hayward, Tim (2017) 'Introduction', in T. Hayward (ed.), *Human Rights and The Environment*, Vol. 1, London: Routledge.
Hayward, Tim (2018) 'How the Media Reveal Inconvenient Truth about Syria', Blog post 23 April: https://timhayward.wordpress.com/2018/04/23/how-the-media-reveal-inconvenient-truth-about-syria/ [accessed August 2018].
Hayward, Tim (*forthcoming*) 'Global Justice and Finance: A New Agenda for Political Theory', *Contemporary Political Theory*.
Held, Virginia (2008) 'Military Intervention and the Ethics of Care', *The Southern Journal of Philosophy*, 46: 1–20.
Helleiner, Eric (1995) 'Explaining the Globalization of Financial Markets: Bringing States Back In', *Review of International Political Economy*, 2(2): 315–41.
Hensman, Rohini and Correggia, Marinella (2005) 'US Dollar Hegemony: The Soft Underbelly of Empire', *Economic and Political Weekly*, 40(12): 1091–5.
Héricourt, Jérôme and Poncet, Sandra (2013) 'Exchange-rate volatility is a problem for trade… especially when financial development is low', Vox CEPR Policy Portal 19 January: https://voxeu.org/article/when-exchange-rate-volatility-affects-trade [accessed August 2018].
Herman, Edward S. and Chomsky, Noam (1988) *Manufacturing Consent: The Political Economy of the Mass Media*, New York: Pantheon.
Hersh, Seymour M. (2014) 'The Red Line and the Rat Line', *London Review of Books*, 36(8): 21–4.
Hiroyuki, A. and Shingo, H. (2015) 'Political Bias lurking in Fatality Statistics Published by the Syrian Observatory for Human Rights', *Contemporary Middle East Political Studies in Japan* (CMEP), ed. Japan: CMEP-J, 2015: 1–3. CMEPS-J Report no. 1.
Hitchens, Peter (2018) 'What Moral Standing Do We Have after this Outrage?', Peter Hitchens Blog, MailOnline, 13 May: https://hitchensblog.mailonsunday.co.uk/2018/05/what-moral-standing-do-we-have-after-this-outrage-and-are-we-about-to-join-another-idiotic-war-like-.html.
Hofstadter, Richard (1965) *The Paranoid Style in American Politics*, New York: Alfred A. Knopf.
Hopkins, A. G. (2007) 'Capitalism, Nationalism and the New American Empire', *The Journal of Imperial and Commonwealth History*, 35(1): 95–117.
HRI (2012) 'Suzanne Nossel Executive Director of Amnesty International USA', *Human Rights Investigations*, 30 September: https://humanrightsinvestigations.org/2012/09/30/suzanne-nossel-executive-director-of-amnesty-international-usa/ [accessed September 2018].

Huckle, Steve and White, Martin (2016) 'Socialism and the Blockchain', *Future Internet*, *8*(4), 49: doi:10.3390/fi8040049

Hughes, Nick and Lonie, Susie (2007) 'M-PESA: Mobile Money for the "Unbanked" Turning Cellphones into 24-Hour Tellers in Kenya' *Innovations: Technology, Governance, Globalization*, 2 (1–2): 63–81.

Human Rights Investigations (2015) 'New Human Rights Watch Report and the Caesar photos' 17 December: https://humanrightsinvestigations.org/2015/12/17/new-human-rights-watch-report-and-the-caesar-photos/ [accessed August 2018].

Hume, David ([1739] 1896) *A Treatise of Human Nature*, reprinted from the Original Edition in three volumes and edited by L.A. Selby-Bigge, Oxford: Clarendon Press.

Ikenberry, G. John (2004) 'The End of the Neo-Conservative Moment', *Survival*, 46(1): 7–22.

Ingham, Geoffrey (1998) 'On the Underdevelopment of the "Sociology of Money"', *Acta Sociologica*, 41(4): 3–18.

Isiksel, Turkuler (2016) 'The Rights of Man and the Rights of the Man-Made: Corporations and Human Rights', *Human Rights Quarterly*, 38(2): 294–349.

Jamieson, Dale (2005) 'Duties to the Distant: Aid, Assistance, and Intervention in the Developing World', *The Journal of Ethics*, 9: 151–70.

Kandlikar, M., Risbey, J., and Dessai, S. (2005) 'Representing and Communicating Deep Uncertainty in Climate Change Assessments', *Comptes Rendus—Geoscience*, 337: 443–55.

Kapur, Devesh (2004) 'Remittances: The New Development Mantra?' G-24 Discussion Papers 29, United Nations Conference on Trade and Development.

Kapur, Devesh (2011) 'The Shift to Cash Transfers: Running Better But on the Wrong Road?' *Economic & Political Weekly*, 46(21): 80–5.

Kay, J. (2013) 'Why Business Loves Capital Markets, Even if it Doesn't Need Capital'. Financial Times, 14 May.

Kebede, Emebet (2006) 'Moving from Emergency Food Aid to Predictable Cash Transfers: Recent Experience in Ethiopia', *Development Policy Review*, 24: 579–99.

Keynes, John Maynard (1930) 'Economic Possibilities for Our Grandchildren', in *Essays in Persuasion*, New York: W.W. Norton: 358–73.

Keynes, John M. (1936) *General Theory of Employment, Interest and Money*, London: Macmillan.

Keynes, John Maynard (2008) *The General Theory of Employment, Interest and Money*, London: Atlantic Publishers

Knight, Frank H. (1921) *Risk, Uncertainty and Profit*, Boston, MA: Houghton Mifflin.

Knight, Malcolm (2014) 'Reforming the Global Architecture of Financial Regulation—The G20, The IMFAnd The FSB', *CIGI Papers* 42, Ontario: Centre for International Governance Innovation.

Knight, Peter (2014) 'Plotting Future Directions in Conspiracy Theory Research', in M. Butter and M. Reinkowski (eds), *Conspiracy Theories in the United States and the Middle East*, Berlin: De Gruyter.

Koelble, Thomas and LiPuma, Edward (2006) 'The Effects of Circulatory Capitalism on Democratization: Observations from South Africa and Brazil', *Democratization*, 13(4): 605–31.

Kohlberg, Lawrence (1981) *Essays on Moral Development, Vol. I: The Philosophy of Moral Development*, San Francisco, CA: Harper & Row.

Koning, J. P. (2013) 'Would Bernanke accept a trillion dollar platinum coin?',The Blog of JP Koning: http://jpkoning.blogspot.com/2013/01/would-bernanke-accept-trillion-dollar.html [accessed August 2018].

Koning, J. P. (2014) 'To Recapitulate…', The Blog of JP Koning: http://jpkoning.blogspot.com/2014/07/to-recapitulate.html [accessed August 2018].

Krugman, Paul (2009) 'How did economists get it so wrong?', The New York Times, 2 September.

Krugman, Paul (2013) 'The Conscience of a Liberal', *The New York Times*, 16 November.

Kuper, Andrew (2002) 'More than Charity: Cosmopolitan Alternatives to the "Singer Solution"', *Ethics & International Affairs*, 16(1): 107–20.

Landes, David (1998) *The Wealth and Poverty of Nations*, London: Abacus.

Landis, Joshua (2011) 'Western Press Misled—Who Shot the Nine Soldiers in Banyas? Not Syrian Security Forces', Syria Comment, 13 April: https://www.joshualandis.com/blog/western-press-misled-who-shot-the-nine-soldiers-in-banyas-not-syrian-security-forces/ [accessed September 2018].

Larson, Adam (2014) 'Fail Caesar: Exposing the Anti-Syria Photo Propaganda, *Monitor on Massacre Marketing*, 8 November: http://libyancivilwar.blogspot.com/2014/11/fail-caesar-exposing-anti-syria-photo.html

Layard, Richard (2011) *Happiness: Lessons from a New Science*, 2nd edn, London: Penguin.

LeBor, Adam (2013) *Tower of Basel: The Shadowy History of the Secret Bank that Runs the World*, New York: PublicAffairs.

Leiter, Brian (2005) 'Oliver Kamm, Marko Attila Hoare, and the Importance of Being Able to Read', *Leiter Reports*, 25 November: https://leiterreports.typepad.com/blog/2005/11/oliver_kamm_mar_1.html [accessed August 2018].

Levinson, Sanford (ed.) (2006) *Torture: A Collection*, Oxford: Oxford University Press.

Levy, Stephanie (2013) 'Cash Transfers and Economic Growth: Uncovering the Myth', The *Guardian* 28 November: https://www.theguardian.com/global-development-professionals-network/2013/nov/28/cash-transfers-economic-growth-myth

LiPuma, Edward and Koelble, Thomas (2009) 'Currency Devaluations and Consolidating Democracy: the Example of the South African Rand', *Economy and Society*, 38, 203–29.

Liu, Henry (2002a) 'US Dollar Hegemony Has Got to Go', Asia Times, 11 April.

Liu, Henry (2002b) 'The BIS vs National Banks', Asia Times, 14 May.

Lohmann, Larry (2012) 'Financialization, Commodification and Carbon: The Contradictions of Neoliberal Climate Policy', *Socialist Register*, 48: 85–107.

Lucas, Scott and Morey, Alistair (2000) 'The Hidden "Alliance": The CIA and MI6 before and after Suez', *Intelligence and National Security*, 15(2): 95–120.

Lynch, M., Freedon, S., Aday, D. (2014) 'Syria's Socially Mediated Civil War: Blogs and BULLETS', Ron Paul Institute, ed. Washington, USA: United States Institute for Peace and Prosperity, 91:1–38.

Lyons, Richard K. (2001) *The Microstructure Approach to Exchange Rates*, Cambridge, MA: MIT Press.

Lysandrou, Photis and Nesvetailova, Anastasia (2014) 'The Role of Shadow Banking Entities in the Financial Crisis: A Disaggregated View', *Review of International Political Economy*, 22(2): 257–79.

MacAskill, William (2015) 'Doing Good Better: Effective Altruism and a Radical New Way to Make a Difference', *Guardian Faber*.

MacAuslan, Ian and Riemenschneider, Nils (2011) 'Richer But Resented: What Do Cash Transfers Do to Social Relations and Does it Matter?' International Conference: "Social Protection for Social Justice" Institute of Development Studies, UK 13–5 April: http://www.ids.ac.uk/files/dmfile/MacAuslanRiemenschneider2011Cashtransfersandsocialrelations CSPconferencedraft.pdf [accessed August 2018].

MacBride, Elizabeth (2016) 'How To Get Cash to the Next Billion: Women at the Frontier of FinTech', *Forbes*, 29 August: https://www.forbes.com/sites/elizabethmacbride/2016/08/29/what-fintech-in-emerging-markets-means-to-women/#825ed89ba04d [accessed August 2018].

Macfarquhar, Neil (2013) 'A Very Busy Man Behind the Syrian Civil War's Casualty Count', The New York Times, 9 April: https://www.nytimes.com/2013/04/10/world/middleeast/the-man-behind-the-casualty-figures-in-syria.html

MacKenzie, Donald (2016) 'Must Do Better' *London Review of Books*, 38(9) 5 May: 29.

MacKenzie, Donald, Beunza, Daniel, Millo, Yuval, and Pardo-Guerra, Juan Pablo (2012) 'Drilling Through the Allegheny Mountains', *Journal of Cultural Economy*, 5(3): 279–96.

Madsen, Wayne (2011) 'Libyan rebels using Western arms, looting Libyan Central Bank in Benghazi; Evidence of NATO war crimes', Free Press, 5 June: http://freepress.org/article/libyan-rebels-using-western-arms-looting-libyan-central-bank-benghazi-evidence-nato-war [accessed August 2018].

Magdoff, Fred and Foster, John Bellamy (2014) 'Stagnation and Financialization: The Nature of the Contradiction', *Monthly Review*, 66(1): 1–24.

Magdoff, Harry and Sweezy, Paul (1987) *Stagnation and the Financial Explosion*, New York: Monthly Review Press.

Mankiw, N. Gregory (1992) 'The Reincarnation of Keynesian Economics', *European Economic Review*, 36: 559–65.

Mansour Robaey, Sonia (2011) 'Tom MacMaster, Britta Froelicher, The Guardian, Academia, And the Much Wider Web of Deceit Behind Gay Girl in Damascus', *Les Politiques* Blog, 16 June: https://lespolitiques.blogspot.com/2011/06/tom-macmaster-britta-froelicher.html [accessed August 2018].

Martinez-Alier, Joan (2002) *Environmentalism of the Poor*, Cheltenham: Edward Elgar.

Mason, Seth (2015) 'The "Better Than Cash Alliance" Has An Orwellian Plan', ZeroHedge, 4 June: https://www.zerohedge.com/news/2015-06-04/better-cash-alliance-has-orwellian-plan [accessed August 2018].

Mawe, Timothy and Bufacchi, Vittorio (2015) 'The Global Luxuries Tax', in H. Gaisbauer, G. Schweiger, and C. Sedmak (eds), *Philosophical Explorations of Justice and Taxation*, Dordrecht: Springer: 203–17.

Mayhew, Anne (2011) 'Money as Electricity', *Journal of Cultural Economy*, 4: 245–53.

Mazzucato, Mariana (2013) 'Financing Innovation: Creative Destruction vs. Destructive Creation', Industrial and Corporate Change, 22(4): 851–67.

McGreal, Chris (2011) 'Libya rebels face last stand as Gaddafi Forces zero in on Benghazi', The *Guardian*, 15 March.

McKay, Claudia and Pillai, Rashmi (2016) 'Aggregators: The Secret Sauce to Digital Financial Expansion', *CGAP* (Consultative Group to Assist the Poor) Blog, 27 January, Washington, DC: http://www.cgap.org/blog/aggregators-secret-sauce-digital-financial-expansion [accessed August 2018].

McKeigue, Paul (2017) 'Using probability calculus to evaluate evidence for alternative hypotheses, including deception operations': https://timhayward.wordpress.com/2017/08/11/how-to-weigh-a-mountain-of-evidence-guest-blog-by-professor-paul-mckeigue-part-1/ [accessed August 2018].

McKeigue, P., Mason, J., Miller, D., and Robinson, P. (2018) 'Briefing note: the alleged chemical attack in Douma on 7 April 2018, and other alleged chlorine attacks in Syria since 2014', Academic Working Group on Syria, Propaganda and Media, 20 August: http://syriapropagandamedia.org/working-papers/briefing-note-the-alleged-chemical-attack-in-

douma-on-7-april-2018-and-other-alleged-chlorine-attacks-in-syria-since-2014 [accessed August 2018].
McKinney, Cynthia (ed.) (2012) *The Illegal War on Libya*, Atlanta, GA: Clarity Press.
Mehrling, Perry (2013) 'The Inherent Hierarchy of Money', in Lance Taylor, Armon Rezai, and Thomas Michl (eds), *Social Fairness and Economics: Economic Essays in the Spirit of Duncan Foley*, London: Routledge.
Miller, D. and Dinan, W. (2008) *A Century of Spin*, London: Pluto Press.
Minsky, Hyman P. (1982) *Can "it" happen again?: Essays on Instability and Finance*, New York: M.E. Sharpe.
Mitchell, Robert (2008) '"Beings that have existence only in ye minds of men": State Finance and the Origins of the Collective Imagination Robert Mitchell', *The Eighteenth Century*, 49(2): 117–39.
Moyo, Dambisa (2009a) 'Why Foreign Aid is Hurting Africa', *The Wall Street Journal*, 8 March: https://www.wsj.com/articles/SB123758895999200083.
Moyo, Dambisa (2009b) 'Aid Ironies: A Response to Jeffrey Sachs', *HuffPost Blog*, 26 May: https://www.huffingtonpost.com/dambisa-moyo/aid-ironies-a-response-to_b_207772.html.
MSF (2017) 'No Eyes on the Ground', Project Update 13 March: https://www.msf.org/syria-no-eyes-ground [accessed August 2018].
Mukunda, G. (2014) 'How the Financial Sector's Outsize Influence is Undermining Business', *Harvard Business Review*, June, 71–8.
Murphy, Dan (2014) 'Syria 'smoking gun' report warrants a careful read', Christian Science Monitor, 21 January: http://www.csmonitor.com/World/Security-Watch/Backchannels/2014/0121/Syria-smoking-gun-report-warrants-a-careful-read
Nagel, Thomas (1977) 'Poverty and Food: Why Charity Is Not Enough', in Peter G. Brown and Henry Shue (eds), *Food Policy: The Responsibility of the United States in Life and Death Choices*, New York: Free Press: 54–62.
Narayanan, Sudha (2011) 'A Case for Reframing the Cash Transfer Debate in India', *Economic and Political Weekly*, XLVI(21): 41–8.
Nazemroaya, Mahdi Darius (2012) 'The Big Lie and Libya: Using Human Rights NGOs and Humanitarianism to Launch Wars', in C. McKinney (ed.), *The Illegal War on Libya*, Atlanta, GA: Clarity Press.
Nesvetailova, Anastasia (2006) 'Fictitious Capital, Real Debts: Systemic Illiquidity in the Financial Crises of the late 1990s', *Review of Radical Political Economics*, 38: 45–70.
Nesvetailova, Anastasia (2007) *Fragile Finance: Debt, Speculation and Crisis in the Age of Global Credit*, Basingstoke: Palgrave Macmillan.
Nesvetailova, Anastasia (2014) 'The Evolution of Nowhere Banking', *Risk & Regulation*, 27: 6–7.
Nesvetailova, Anastasia (2015) 'A Crisis of the Overcrowded Future: Shadow Banking and the Political Economy of Financial Innovation', *New Political Economy*, 20: 431–53.
Nesvetailova, Anastasia and Palan, Ronen (2013) 'Sabotage in the Financial System: Lessons from Veblen', *Business Horizons, Special Issue: The Politics of International Banking & Finance*, 56, 723–32.
Newman, Alex (2011) '"Libyan Rebels" Create Central Bank, Oil Company', *New American*, 30 March.
Norton, Ben (2017) 'Meet Idrees Ahmad, an obsessive hawk who smears anti-war voices and lobbies for regime change in Syria', *Ben Norton's Blog*: https://bennorton.com/idrees-ahmad-syria-war-regime-change/ [accessed September 2018].

Nossel, Suzanne (2004) 'Smart Power', *Foreign Affairs*, 83(2): 131–42.

Nye, Joseph S. (2004) 'Soft Power and American Foreign Policy', *Political Science Quarterly*, 119(2): 255–27.

O'Brien, Denis (2014) Murder in the SunMorgue: A Critique of the Sarin Myth and a Cyber-Investigation of the Ghouta Massacre: https://www.scribd.com/document/230748990/Murder-in-the-SunMorgue [accessed September 2018].

O'Neill, John (2002) 'Value Pluralism, Incommensurability and Institutions', in J. Foster (ed.), *Valuing Nature? Economics, Ethics and Environment*, London: Routledge.

O'Neill, John (*forthcoming*) 'Financialization, Environment and Justice', *Contemporary Political Theory*.

O'Neill, John and Spash, Clive L. (2000) 'Conceptions of Value in Environmental Decision-Making', *Environmental Values*, 9: 521–36.

O'Neill, John and Uebel, Thomas (2018) 'Between Frankfurt and Vienna: Two Traditions of Political Ecology', in K. Forrester and S. Smith (eds), *Nature, Action and the Future: Political Thought and the Environment*, Cambridge: Cambridge University Press.

Oberman, Kieran (2015a) 'Poverty and Immigration Policy', *American Political Science Review*, 109: 239–51.

Oberman, Kieran (2015b) The Myth of the Optional War: Why States are Required to Wage the Wars they are Permitted to Wage', *Philosophy & Public Affairs*, 43(4): 255–86.

Olson, Kevin (2007) 'Paradoxes of Constitutional Democracy', *American Journal of Political Science*, 51(2): 330–43.

Orghangazi, Ozgur (2007) 'Financialization and Capital Accumulation in the Nonfinancial Corporate Sector: A Theoretical and Empirical Investigation on the US Economy, 1973–2004', *MPRA Paper* No. 7724, Munich Personal RePEc Archive.

Ostrom, Elinor (2008) 'Tragedy of the Commons', in Steven N. Durlauf and Lawrence E. Blume (eds), *The New Palgrave Dictionary of Economics*, 2nd edn, Basingstoke: Palgrave Macmillan.

Oweiss, Ibrahim M. (1974) 'Petrodollars: Problems and Prospects', Address before the Conference on The World Monetary Crisis, Columbia University: http://faculty.georgetown.edu/imo3/petrod/petro2.htm [accessed June 2018].

Oxfam (2017) 'An Economy For The 99%: It's time to build a human economy that benefits everyone, not just the privileged few', Oxfam Briefing Paper.

Pagliari, Stefano and Young, Keven (2014) 'Leveraged Interests: Financial Industry Power and the Role of Private Sector Coalitions', *Review of International Political Economy*, 21(3): 575–610.

Palan, Ronen (2013) 'The Financial Crisis and Intangible Value', *Capital & Class* 37: 65–77.

Palan, Ronen (2015) 'Futurity, Pro-cyclicality and Financial Crises', *New Political Economy*, 20, 367–85.

Palley, Thomas (2007) 'Financialization: What it is and Why it Matters', Working Paper 525, Washington, DC: The Levy Economics Institute.

Palley, Thomas (2012) *From Financial Crisis to Stagnation: The Destruction of Shared Prosperity and the Role of Economics*, Cambridge: Cambridge University Press.

Pan, Chengxin and Turner, Oliver (2016) 'Neoconservatism as Discourse: Virtue, Power and US Foreign Policy' *European Journal of International Relations*, 23(1): 74–96.

Pani, Narendar (2012) 'The Situational Dimension of Cash Transfers: The Inflationary and Differentiated Effects of the Proposed Changes in Food Subsidies in India', *Indian Journal of Human Development*, 6(1): 31–48.

Parmar, Inderjeet (2009) 'Foreign policy Fusion: Liberal Interventionists, Conservative Nationalists and Neoconservatives—the New Alliance Dominating the US Foreign Policy Establishment', *International Politics*, 46(2/3): 177–209.

Patomäki, Heikki (2008) *The Political Economy of Global Security: War, Future Crises and Changes in Global Governance*, Abingdon: Routledge.

Pattison, James (2011) 'The Ethics of Humanitarian Intervention in Libya', *Ethics & International Affairs*, 25(3): 271–7.

Perkins, John (2004) *Confessions of an Economic Hitman*, San Francisco, CA: Berrett Koehler Publishers Inc.

Pernin, Christopher G., Nichiporuk, B., Stahl, D., Beck, J., and Radaelli-Sanchez, R. (2008) *Unfolding the Future of the Long War Motivations, Prospects, and Implications for the U.S. Army*, Santa Monica, CA: Rand Corporation.

Peterson, David and Herman, Edward S. (2010) 'The Oliver Kamm School of Falsification: Imperial Truth-Enforcement, British Branch', *Monthly Review*, MR Online 22 January: https://mronline.org/2010/01/22/the-oliver-kamm-school-of-falsification-imperial-truth-enforcement-british-branch/

Philipsen, D. (2015) *The Little Big Number: How GDP Came to Rule the World and What to Do about It*, Princeton, NJ: Princeton University Press.

Pigden, Charles (2016) 'Are Conspiracy Theorists Epistemically Vicious?' in Kasper Lippert-Rasmussen, Kimberley Brownlee, and David Coady (eds), *A Companion to Applied Philosophy*, London: John Wiley & Sons, Ltd.

Piketty, Thomas (2014) *Capital in the Twenty-First Century* (trans A. Goldhammer), Cambridge, MA: Harvard University Press.

Pistor, Katharina (2013) 'A Legal Theory of Finance', *Journal of Comparative Economics*, 41: 315–30.

Pistor, Katharina (2017) 'Money's Legal Hierarchy' in Lisa Herzog (ed.), *Just Financial Markets?: Finance in a Just Society*, Oxford: Oxford University Press.

Poast, Paul (2014) 'Central Banks at War', *International Organization*, 69(1): 63–95.

Pogge, Thomas (2002) *World Poverty and Human Rights*, Cambridge: Polity Press.

Pogge, Thomas (2013) 'Q & ASAP—After the MDGs: Thomas Pogge Sees Some Promise, Many Potential Pitfalls in First Official Recommendations for Millennium Development Goals Replacement Effort', Academics Stand Against Poverty website: http://academicsstand.org/q-asap-after-the-mdgs-thomas-pogge-sees-some-promise-many-potential-pitfalls-in-first-official-recommendations-for-millennium-development-goals-replacement-effort/ [accessed August 2018].

Pogge, T. and Mehta, K. (2016) *Global Tax Fairness*, Oxford: Oxford University Press.

Pomeranz, Kenneth (2000) *The Great Divergence*, Princeton, NJ: Princeton University Press.

Pope Francis (2015) Encyclical letter laudato si'. On care for our common home, The Vatican: http://w2.vatican.va/content/francesco/en/encyclicals/documents/papa-francesco_20150524_enciclica-laudato-si.html [accessed July 2018].

PPNS (2006) *Forging a World of Liberty and Law: US National Security in the 21st Century*, Final report of the Princeton Project on National Security, The Woodrow Wilson School of Public and International Affairs, Princeton University.

Quiggin, John (2008) 'Stern and His Critics on Discounting and Climate Change: An Editorial Essay', *Climate Change*, 89: 195–205.

Quijones, Don (2015) '"First They Came for the Pennies..." in the War on Cash', in Wolf Street Blog, 7 November: https://wolfstreet.com/2015/11/07/first-they-came-for-the-pennies-in-the-war-on-cash/ [accessed June 2018].

Raghavan, Sudarsan and Grimaldi, James V. (2011) 'Libyans "robbed our own bank" to fund uprising', Washington Post, 24 May: https://www.washingtonpost.com/world/middle-east/libyans-robbed-our-own-bank-to-fund-uprising/2011/05/24/AFAPZhAH_story.html?utm_term=.edeacc7e5445 [accessed August 2018].

Rapp, Stephen J. (2015) 'Overcoming the Challenges to Achieving Justice for Syria', *Emory International Law Review*, 30: 155–67.

Rawls, John (1971) *A Theory of Justice*, Oxford: Oxford University Press.

Rawls, John (1999) *The Law of Peoples*, Cambridge, MA: Harvard University Press.

Risse, Mathias (2005) 'How Does the Global Order Harm the Poor?' *Philosophy and Public Affairs*, 33(4): 349–76.

Robeyns, Ingrid (2008) 'Ideal Theory in Theory and in Practice', *Social Theory and Practice*, 34(3): 341–62.

Robicheau, Daniel (2014) 'Syria, the MENA Region, and International Finance Capitalism', *International Critical Thought*, 4(2): 198–207.

Robinson, Piers (2017) 'Learning from the Chilcot Report: Propaganda, Deception and the "War on Terror"', *International Journal of Contemporary Iraqi Studies*, 11(1).

Rockström, Johan et al. (2009) 'A Safe Operating Space for Humanity', *Nature*, 461: 472–75.

Rogoff, Kenneth (2016) *The Curse of Cash*, Princeton, NJ: Princeton University Press.

Ronzoni, Miriam (2009) 'The Global Order: A Case of Background Injustice? A Practice-Dependent Account', *Philosophy & Public Affairs*, 37: 229–56.

Rothschild, Lord (2015) 'Chairman's Statement', in *RIT Partners Report for Year End 2015*, London: RIT Capital Partners PLC.

Ruggie, John Gerard (1982) 'International Regimes, Transactions, and Change: Embedded Liberalism in the Postwar Economic Order', *International Organization*, International Regimes (Spring), 36(2): 379–415.

Sabates-Wheeler, Rachel and Devereux, Stephen (2010) 'Cash Transfers and High Food Prices: Explaining Outcomes on Ethiopia's Productive Safety Net Programme', *Food Policy*, 35: 274–85.

Sacco, V. and Bossio, D. (2015) 'Using Social Media in the News Reportage of War and Conflict: Opportunities and Challenges', *Journal of Media Innovation*, 2: 59–76.

Sandefur, J., Birdsall, N., and Moyo, M. (2015) 'The Political Paradox of Cash Transfers', International Growth Centre: https://www.theigc.org/blog/the-political-paradox-of-cash-transfers/ [accessed August 2018].

Schubert, Bernd and Slater, Rachel (2006) 'Social Cash Transfers in Low-Income African Countries: Conditional or Unconditional?' *Development Policy Review*, 24: 571–8.

Schumacher, E. F. (1993) *Small Is Beautiful: A Study of Economics as if People Mattered*, London: Vintage Books.

Schumpeter, Joseph ([1954] 1994) *A History of Economic Analysis*, London: Routledge & Kegan.

Schweller, Randall L. and Pu, Xiaoyu (2011) 'After Unipolarity: China's Visions of International Order in an Era of U.S. Decline', *International Security*, 36(1): 41–72.

Scott, Brett (2016a) 'The War on Cash', *openDemocracyUK*, 30 August: https://www.opendemocracy.net/brett-scott/war-on-cash.

Scott, Brett (2016b) 'How Can Cryptocurrency and Blockchain Technology Play a Role in Building Social and Solidarity Finance?' United Nations Research Institute for Social Development, Working Paper 2016-1.

Scott, Brett (2017) 'In Praise of Cash', *Aeon*: https://aeon.co/essays/if-plastic-replaces-cash-much-that-is-good-will-be-lost [accessed August 2018].

Scott, Peter Dale (2007) *The Road to 9/11: Wealth, Empire, and the Future of America*, Berkeley and Los Angeles: University of California Press.

Seccareccia, Mario (2017) 'Which Vested Interests Do Central Banks Really Serve? Understanding Central Bank Policy Since the Global Financial Crisis', *Journal of Economic Issues*, 51(2): 341–50.

Sen, Amartya (2006) 'What Do We Want from a Theory of Justice', *Journal of Philosophy* 103(5): 215–38.

Sen, Amartya (2009) *The Idea of Justice*, London: Allen Lane / Penguin.

Sen, Kasturi, Hussain, Hamid, and Al-Faisal, Waleed (2016) 'Ethics in Times of Conflict: Some Reflections on Syria, in the backdrop of Iraq', *BMJ Global Health*, (1): 1–6.

Shah, Mihir (2008) 'Direct Cash Transfers: No Magic Bullet', *Economic and Political Weekly*, 43: 77–9.

Shaxson, Nicholas (2016) *Treasure Islands: Tax Havens and the Men who Stole the World*, London: Vintage.

Sherman, Sandra (1996) *Finance and Fictionality in the Early Eighteenth Century: Accounting for Defoe*, Cambridge: Cambridge University Press.

Shipley, Tyler (2007) 'Currency Wars: Oil, Iraq, and the Future of Us Hegemony', *Studies in Political Economy*, 79: 7–33.

Shue, Henry (1996) *Basic Rights: Subsistence, Affluence and U.S. Foreign Policy*, 2nd edn, Princeton, NJ: Princeton University Press.

Shue, Henry (2007) 'What Would a Justified Military Attack Look Like?' in H. Shue and D. Rodin (eds), *Preemption: Military Action and Moral Justification*, Oxford: Oxford University Press.

Shue, Henry (2009) 'Making Exceptions', *Journal of Applied Philosophy*, 26(3): 307–22.

Singer, Peter (1972) 'Famine, Affluence, and Morality', *Philosophy & Public Affairs*, 1(3): 229–43.

Singer, Peter (2006) 'What Should a Billionaire Give—and What Should You?' The New York Times.

Singer, Peter (2013) 'The Why and How of Effective Altruism', TED Talk. March: https://www.ted.com/talks/peter_singer_the_why_and_how_of_effective_altruism?language=en [accessed August 2018].

Snow, Keith Harmon (2012) 'Petroleum and Empire in North Africa: NATO propaganda and the betrayal of Muammar Qaddafi', in C. McKinney (ed.), The Illegal War on Libya, Atlanta, GA: Clarity Press.

Soddy, Frederick (1926) *Wealth, Virtual Wealth, and Debt*, London: George Allen & Unwin Ltd.

Sornarajah, M. (2017) *The International Law on Foreign Investment*, 4th edn, Cambridge: Cambridge University Press.

Soros, George (2003) *The Alchemy of Finance*, Hoboken, NJ: John Wiley & Sons, Inc.

Soros, George (2008) *The New Paradigm for Financial Markets: The Credit Crisis of 2008 and What It Means*, New York: Perseus Books Group.

Sottile, J. P. (2014) 'Hillary Clinton and the Weaponization of the State Department' *Common Dreams* 6 June: https://www.commondreams.org/views/2014/06/06/hillary-clinton-and-weaponization-state-department [accessed August 2018].

Spash, Clive (2007) 'The Economics of Climate Change Impacts à la Stern: Novel and Nuanced or Rhetorically Restricted?' *Ecological Economics*, 63: 706–13.

Spash, Clive (2010) 'The Brave New World of Carbon Trading', *New Political Economy*, 15(2): 169–95.

Spash, Clive (2013) 'The Shallow or the Deep Ecological Economics Movement?' *Ecological Economics*, 93: 351–62.

Steele, Jonathan (2008) *Defeat: Why They Lost Iraq*, London: Taurus.

Steiner, Hillel (1999) 'Just Taxation and International Redistribution', *Nomos*, XLI: 171–91.

Steiner, Hillel (2011) 'The Global Fund: A Reply to Casal' *Journal of Moral Philosophy*, 8: 328–34.

Sterling, Rick (2016) 'The Caesar Photo Fraud that Undermined Syrian Negotiations', Syria Solidarity Movement website: http://www.syriasolidaritymovement.org/2016/03/03/the-caesar-photo-fraud-that-undermined-syrian-negotiations/ [accessed August 2018].

Stern, Nicholas et al. (2006) *Stern Review: The Economics of Climate Change*, London: HM Treasury.

Stout, Lynn (2012) *The shareholder Value Myth: How Putting Shareholders First Harms Investors, Corporations, and the Public*, San Francisco, CA: Berrett-Koehler Publishers.

Strange, Susan (2016) *Casino Capitalism*, Manchester: Manchester University Press.

Streeck, Wolfgang (2017) 'Whose Side Are We On? Liberalism and Socialism are Not the Same', in David Coates (ed.), *Reflections on the Future of the Left*, Newcastle upon Tyne: Agenda Publishing.

Suliman, Aktham (2012) 'Vergiss, was du gesehen hast!', *Frankfurter Allgemeine*, 11 December: http://www.faz.net/aktuell/feuilleton/medien/ein-abschied-von-al-dschazira-vergiss-was-du-gesehen-hast-11988966-p2.html?printPagedArticle=true#pageIndex_1

Summers, Lawrence H. (2016) 'The Age of Secular Stagnation: What It Is and What to Do about It', *Foreign Affairs*, 95(2): 2–9.

Sunstein, Cass and Vermeule, Adrian (2009) 'Conspiracy Theories: Causes and Cures', *The Journal of Political Philosophy*, 17(2): 202–27.

Swan, Melanie (2015) *Blockchain: Blueprint for a New Economy*, Sebastopol CA: O'Reilly Media.

Sweezy, Paul (1982) 'Why Stagnation', *Monthly Review*, 34(2): 1–10.

Swift, Adam (2008) 'The Value of Philosophy in Nonideal Circumstances', *Social Theory and Practice*, 34(3): 363–87.

T-West (2012) 'America's Black Pharoah and Black Genocide in Libya', in C. McKinney (ed.), *The Illegal War on Libya*, Atlanta, GA: Clarity Press.

Teubner, Gunther (2011) 'Self-Constitutionalizing TNCs? On the Linkage of "Private" and "Public" Corporate Codes of Conduct', *Indiana Journal of Global Legal Studies*, 18(2): 17–38.

Thiemann, Matthias (2014) 'In the Shadow of Basel: How Competitive Politics Bred the Crisis', *Review of International Political Economy*, 21(6): 1203–39.

Thomson, Alex (2012) 'Set up to be shot in Syria's no man's land?', Channel 4 News 8 June: https://www.channel4.com/news/by/alex-thomson/blogs/hostile-territory

Tobin, James (1970) 'On Limiting the Domain of Inequality', *The Journal of Law & Economics*, 13(2): 263–77.

Tobin, James (1978) 'A Proposal for International Monetary Reform', *Eastern Economic Journal*, 4: 153–9.

Toll, Matthew (2010) 'Minsky and the Financial Crisis', Blog post 27 May: http://dostoevskiansmiles.blogspot.com/2010/05/minsky-and-financial-crisis.html [accessed August 2018].

UN General Assembly (2005) 'In larger freedom: towards development, security and human rights for all: report of the Secretary-General', 21 March: A/59/2005: http://www.refworld.org/docid/4a54bbfa0.html [accessed 25 August 2018].

US Treasury Department (2006) 'Semiannual report on international economics and exchange rate policies', Washington, DC: US Treasury.

Uscinski, Joseph E. and Parent, Joseph M. (2014) *American Conspiracy Theories*, Oxford: Oxford University Press.

Vaïsse, Justin (2010) 'Why Neoconservatism Still Matters', Brookings Institution Policy Paper 20.

Valentini, Laura (2012) 'Ideal vs. *Non-ideal Theory: A Conceptual Map', Philosophy Compass, 7, 654–64.*

van Es, Ana (2018) 'Nederland stopt steun aan Syrische oppositie wegens gebrekkig toezicht op hulpprojecten; Britse organisatie ontkent kritiek', *de Volkskrant*, 10 September. https://www.volkskrant.nl/nieuws-achtergrond/nederland-stopt-steun-aan-syrische-oppositie-wegens-gebrekkig-toezicht-op-hulpprojecten-britse-organisatie-ontkent-kritiek-~bda7b84e/

Van Parijs, Philippe (2004) 'Basic Income: A Simple and Powerful Idea for the Twenty-first Century', *Politics and Society*, 32(1): 7–39.

Van Parijs, Philippe and Vanderborght, Yannick (2017) *Basic Income: A Radical Proposal for a Free Society and a Sane Economy*, Cambridge, MA: Harvard University Press.

Vanderschraaff, Peter (2006) 'The Circumstances of Justice', *Politics, Philosophy & Economics*, 5: 321–51.

Veblen, Thorstein (1921) *The Engineers and the Price System*, New York: BW Huebsch Inc.

Vincent, Katharine and Cull, Tracy (2011) 'Cell Phones, Electronic Delivery Systems and Social Cash Transfers: Recent Evidence and Experiences from Africa', *International Social Security Review*, 64(1): 37–51.

Wachtel, Howard M. (2000) 'Tobin and Other Global Taxes', *Review of International Political Economy*, 7: 335–52.

Walzer, Michael (1983) *Spheres of Justice: A Defense of Pluralism and Equality*, New York: Basic Books.

Warburton, Peter (2003) *Debt and Delusion*, Harmondsworth: Penguin Books.

Ward, J. D., Sutton, P. C., Werner, A. D., Costanza, R., Mohr, S. H., and Simmons, C. T. (2016) 'Is Decoupling GDP Growth from Environmental Impact Possible?' *PloS One*, 11(10), e0164733.

Weidel, Timothy (2016) 'Philanthropy, Cosmopolitanism, and the Benefits of Giving Directly', *Journal of Global Ethics* 12(2): 170–86.

Weiss, Thomas G. (2014) 'Military Humanitarianism: Syria Hasn't Killed It', *The Washington Quarterly*, 37:1.

Wenar, Leif (2011) 'Poverty is no Pond: Challenges for the Affluent', in P. Illingworth, T. Pogge, and L. Wenar (eds), *Giving Well: The Ethics of Philanthropy*, Oxford: Oxford University Press.

Westra, Richard (2010) *Political Economy and Globalization*, Abingdon: Routledge.

Wiedenbrüg, A., Hayward, T. & O'Neill, J. (2020) 'Disenchanting Global Justice: Liberalism, Capitalism and Finance', *Contemporary Political Theory*: https://doi.org/10.1057/s41296-020-00440-2

Williams, John Fischer (1930) 'The Legal Character of the Bank for International Settlements', *The American Journal of International Law*, 24(4): 665–73.

Wisor, Scott (2011) 'Against Shallow Ponds: An Argument against Singer's Approach to Global Poverty', *Journal of Global Ethics*, 7(1): 19–32.

Wood, E. J. (2006) 'The Ethical Challenges of Research in Conflict Zone', *Qualitative Sociology*, 2: 373–86.

Wood, Michael J. and Douglas, Karen (2013) "What about building 7?" A Social Psychological Study of Online Discussion of 9/11 Conspiracy Theories', *Frontiers in Psychology*, 4: 1–9.

World Bank (2012) *Global Development Finance: External Debt of Developing Countries*, Washington, DC: World Bank Publications.

Yaffe, Helen (2009) 'Che Guevara's Enduring Legacy: Not the Foco but the Theory of Socialist Construction', *Latin American Perspectives*, 36(2): 49–65.

Yaffe, Helen (2012) 'Che Guevara and the Great Debate, Past and Present', *Science & Society*, 76(1): 11–40.

Yeung, Ying and Howes, Stephen (2015) 'Resources-to-Cash: A Cautionary Tale from Mongolia', *Development Policy Centre Discussion Paper*, 42: 1–40.

Yli-Huumo, J., Ko, D., Choi, S., Park, S., and Smolander, K. (2016) 'Where Is Current Research on Blockchain Technology?—A Systematic Review', *PLOS ONE* 11(10): e0163477. https://doi.org/10.1371/journal.pone.0163477

Yoon, Sangwon (2015) 'Ackman-Backed Harvard Grads Make Aiding the Poor a New Business', Bloomberg Business Week, 22 September: https://www.bloomberg.com/news/articles/2015-09-21/ackman-backed-harvard-grads-make-aiding-the-poor-a-new-business [accessed August 2018].

Ypi, Lea (2008) 'Statist Cosmopolitanism', *The Journal of Political Philosophy*, 16(1): 48–71.

Zhou, Jianping et al. (2012) 'From Bail-out to Bail-in: Mandatory Debt Restructuring of Systemic Financial Institutions', IMF Staff Discussion Note 24 April.

Zollmann, Florian (2017a) *Media, Propaganda and the Politics of Intervention*, Oxford: Peter Lang.

Zollmann, Florian (2017b) 'Bringing Propaganda Back into News Media Studies', *Critical Sociology*, OnlineFirst: https://doi.org/10.1177/0896920517731134

Index

Printed and bound by CPI Group (UK) Ltd, Croydon, CR0 4YY